THE NEW AGE OF GENOCIDE

Also by Martin Shaw and published by Agenda

Political Racism: Brexit and its Aftermath

The Campaign for Nuclear Disarmament

THE NEW AGE OF GENOCIDE

Intellectual and Political Challenges after Gaza

MARTIN SHAW

First published in 2025 by Agenda Publishing
Reprinted 2026

Agenda Publishing Limited
PO Box 185
Newcastle upon Tyne
NE20 2DH
www.agendapub.com

ISBN 978-1-78821-872-6 (hardcover)
ISBN 978-1-78851-873-3 (paperback)

British Library Cataloguing-in-Publication Data
A catalogue record for this book is available from the British Library

Typeset by JS Typesetting Ltd, Porthcawl, Mid Glamorgan
Printed and bound in the UK by 4edge Limited

EU GPSR authorised representative:
Logos Europe, 9 rue Nicolas Poussin, 17000 La Rochelle, France
contact@logoseurope.eu

CONTENTS

ACKNOWLEDGEMENTS

A book of this kind owes many intellectual debts and for the most part these are indicated by the works I cite. However, I wish to express particular thanks to Dirk Moses, whose work has both informed and challenged my approach, and who as editor of the *Journal of Genocide Research* (*JGR*) has curated an essential space in which I (like other scholars) have been able to develop my ideas – including the innovative forums on Ukraine and Gaza in which I published early versions of the arguments which are developed in this book. This debt is particularly important for me to acknowledge since Chapter 7 explains some significant disagreements with Dirk's work.

I am also grateful to other friends and fellow scholars for invitations during the period I was writing this book, which helped me focus its arguments: to Uğur Ümit Üngör for inviting me to deliver the 2024 lecture of the NIOD Institute for War, Holocaust, and Genocide Studies in Amsterdam, which I gave under the title, "In Defence of the Concept of Genocide"; to Sarah Danielsson for inviting me to contribute to a volume reconsidering "war and genocide" and a panel on this topic at the 2024 conference of the International Network of Genocide Scholars; and to Jeff Bachman and John Cox for inviting me to write on the same issue for the *Routledge Handbook of Genocide Studies*. Presentations in early 2025 at the Institut Barcelona d'Estudis Internacionals (IBEI), where I am a research professor, and Royal Holloway, University of London, were also helpful in testing parts of the argument. Chapter 8, the argument of which has been long in gestation, benefited from discussions in a *JGR* workshop at IBEI in 2013 and a British International Studies Association Historical Sociology group workshop at the University of Sussex in 2017.

Wider communities of genocide scholars and activists, especially on Twitter, have been important for me, sharing ideas, information and sources that have enriched my understanding. At a time when genocide analysis is marginalized and even regarded as subversive, and when universities in some Western countries are internalizing official censure and unwilling to host open discussions of it, the solidarity among concerned scholars has been especially important. In the

UK, where I am mainly based, I have not experienced strong hostile pressure; however, my ideas have been largely ignored by the mainstream British media, although I am frequently contacted by journalists from other countries. I therefore particularly appreciate the opportunity to publish in *Byline Times*, which carried my warning of Israeli genocide only six days after 7 October 2023.

Earlier versions of three chapters have appeared elsewhere: Chapter 4 as "Russia's genocidal war in Ukraine: radicalization and social destruction" in the *Journal of Genocide Research* 25:3/4 (2023), 352–70; Chapter 6 as "Palestine in an international historical perspective on genocide" in *Holy Land Studies* 9:1 (2010), 1–25; and Chapter 9 as "Britain and genocide: historical and contemporary parameters of national responsibility" in the *Review of International Studies* 37:5 (2011), 2417–38. I am grateful to these journals and their publishers for being able to reuse parts of these articles, although all are substantially revised.

I particularly wish to thank Dirk, Uğur and the publisher's reader for reading parts or all of the manuscript; each made suggestions that improved the final text, but I alone am responsible for the argument. I am grateful to my editor, Alison Howson, for her exemplary support on this book, my third with her at Agenda. My deepest thanks go to Annabel.

1 INTRODUCTION

This book addresses two significant developments of our times: the return of the *phenomenon* of genocide to a central place in world politics and of the *concept* of genocide as a key idea for understanding deliberate violence against civilians. At the same time, it aims to explore the intellectual and political challenges of the genocide perspective, which these developments bring to the fore.

The original catalyst for this work was Russia's full-scale invasion of Ukraine in 2022. This was a striking departure that obviously raised issues of genocide: a major state and permanent member of the UN Security Council was attempting to eliminate an entire state, national society and culture through force. However, I had barely begun writing when, in late 2023, Hamas' atrocities and Israel's huge assault on Gaza seemed to pose the question of genocide even more definitively. In Israel's case, the perpetrator was the state that claimed to represent the quintessential victims of genocide, and Gaza's civilians were almost as helpless as the Jews had been in Europe.

With these twin conflicts, it became clear that genocide, which of course had never gone away in some regions, was returning to the centre of a brutal new constellation of world politics. Over the previous decade, analysts had noted the "returns" of geopolitics (Mead 2014) and of the authoritarian far right in domestic politics (Mudde 2019), but now it seemed that these were combined with a return of genocide. In what was influentially called the "polycrisis" of the world system (Tooze 2022), the effect of each disruptive trend magnified the others.

Moreover, Israel's campaign directly implicated the dominant Western states, sharply challenging the complacent self-images of societies that believed themselves to be on the right side of history. Samantha Power famously argued in her 2003 study of "America in the age of genocide" that the Western failure to prevent genocide was structural: there was a "consistent policy of nonintervention in the face of genocide", which offered "sad testimony not to a broken American political system but to one that is ruthlessly effective" (2003: xxi). However, her argument was designed to usher in a new age in which the USA and other Western states paid not only lip-service to genocide prevention but seriously tried to implement it. She herself joined the Obama administration and in 2012 was appointed to head a new Atrocities Prevention Board, before becoming ambassador to the UN.

With Gaza, these hopes died. The new age proved to be one of Western *participation in*, not prevention of, genocide. Power herself, who returned to head the US Agency for International Development under Biden, fell victim to the structure she had identified and effectively denied the Gaza genocide, although she admitted the USA had failed to stop the carnage (Beaucar Vlahos 2024). Indeed, now *all* the permanent members of the Security Council were actively complicit in genocidal campaigns, with the USA, UK and France enabling Israel's as well as China facilitating Russia's.

As I was finishing this book in early 2025, the return of Donald Trump dramatically linked these crises, further concretizing the connections between genocide and the new world politics. His idea of expelling the Palestinians to create a tourist "Gaza riviera" envisaged a huge expansion of the US role in Israel's genocide, but his apparent willingness to facilitate Russian annexations in Ukraine was even more striking, since up to that point the USA had fundamentally opposed these.

With Trump alongside Vladimir Putin and Xi Jinping – whose Chinese regime had long worked to erase Uyghur society and culture in Xinjiang – the leaders of all three main military powers (and dominant members of the Security Council) possessed openly genocidal mentalities. Indeed, a veritable axis of genocide appeared to be emerging at the highest level of world politics: Trump and Xi were economic and geopolitical rivals, but they effectively agreed about allowing Putin to annex and Russify substantial parts of Ukraine; Xi and Putin nominally supported the Palestinians, but neither would seriously try to prevent Trump and Israel crushing them. Nor of course were these leaders alone: many lesser leaders had similar approaches, while even those who didn't were often prepared to condone one or other genocidal campaign – in the case of many European leaders, Israel's, and of many in the Global South, Russia's.

With the world changing rapidly, no one can forecast exactly where these trends will have led by the time you read this book, or which further threats will have arisen. While many world leaders have genocidal mentalities, often rooted in nationalist, racist and authoritarian ideologies, their policies are primarily driven by ambitions for power and wealth, and the extent to which they implement genocide will be conditioned by shifting political and economic realities. Other actors, including states and movements aligned with the victims, have the capacity to mobilize countervailing power.

In this turbulent world politics, the genocide idea can be part of a challenge to the shocking new tolerance for the deliberate destruction of civilian populations, which is one reason why it is so important to understand its meaning and scope. Another is to connect today's systematic atrocities to the deeper patterns of destructive violence in modern world history. This book aims to contribute to both of these tasks.

Recognizing today's genocides

Recognition of the genocidal shift in world politics has not come easily, since denial is genocide's inevitable concomitant, typically enveloping not only the practitioners of violence but also many who find it convenient to turn the other way. Even scholars who work on these realities have not been immune; some did not acknowledge at all the genocidal element in Putin's war, and many failed initially to recognize it in Israel's. There were many reasons why even some who eventually understood that Israel was committing genocide were slow to understand, including the idea that as paradigmatic victims of genocide, Jews could not really be perpetrators, and the insidious effects of the Israeli ideology that tars opponents with antisemitism (Klein 2025).

Against these trends, my approach, which emphasizes the socially as well as physically destructive meaning of genocide (as I explain later in the book), enabled me to diagnose it in both Ukraine and Gaza at an early stage – in the latter case, in an article published only days after 7 October 2023 (Shaw 2022b; 2023b). Among genocide scholars, Raz Segal (2023a) also publicly argued the genocide case against Israel at this very early stage, but it was only in the following year that many others, such as Amos Goldberg (2024), Omer Bartov (2024) and William Schabas (2024), as well as historians of Palestine such as Rashid Khalidi (2024) and Avi Shlaim (2024), also published analyses of the state's genocide.

By then, in contrast to the pattern over Ukraine (where genocide commentary faded as the war became stalemated), the argument was already spreading rapidly in the public sphere. It was especially catalysed by the case that South Africa brought against Israel in the International Court of Justice (ICJ) (2023); the three consecutive warnings of genocide (International Court of Justice 2024a; 2004b; 2024c) that the ICJ made in response in January, March and May 2024; and an authoritative report by the UN special rapporteur on the Occupied Palestinian Territories, Francesca Albanese (2024a). Indeed, after a year of Israel's campaign, the accusation of genocide had become the well-documented common sense of major human rights organizations, in substantial reports by Amnesty International (2024) and Human Rights Watch (2024b). However, it remained the subject of systematic denial by governments, media and even universities in the USA, UK, Germany and other Western countries, as well as in Israel itself.

Many pointed out that while Israel's genocide was a reaction to Hamas' atrocities, the conflict did not begin on 7 October 2023. However, they often failed to acknowledge that in Palestine not only the conflict, but also the genocide, had deeper roots. My approach had led me to explore these over a decade earlier, when I had analysed the "incipiently genocidal" mentality of early Zionism (Shaw 2007: 58–61) and discussed the 1948 Nakba within "an international historical perspective on genocide" (Shaw 2010). However, most genocide scholars failed to acknowledge these warning signs from Palestine's history. As the historian Esmat Elhalaby (2025) notes, even critics of Israel – including some who opposed the Gaza genocide – were embedded in "a theoretical and intellectual discourse – with its endowments and institutions – where Nakba denial has been the norm". Pro-Israelis predictably regarded my argument that Israel's destruction of historic Palestinian society amounted to genocide as indicative of antisemitism (Charny 2016; reply by Goldberg *et al.* 2016). Even Omer Bartov, who became a determined opponent of the Gaza genocide, concluded a debate about my 2010 article with the claim that "the argument of Israeli genocide of the Palestinians is clearly meant to delegitimize the state and to say that it was born in the blood of innocents and should therefore also go down in blood"; it meant telling Israelis that "they have no right to exist" (Shaw & Bartov 2010: 259).

Needless to say, this was never, and is not, my purpose. Neither the Nakba, nor the following seven decades of oppression, nor even the post-2006 blockade of Gaza justified Hamas's 2023 massacres, just as the latter gave Israel absolutely no licence to commit genocide in return: genocide is illegitimate regardless of by whom or for what reason it is committed. Yet the long history of genocidal ideology, expulsions and violence in Palestine does help to *explain* Hamas' and Israel's actions, as I show later in this book.

The marginalization of the genocide idea

There were also more fundamental reasons, to do with the understanding of genocide in general, which helped explain the failure to recognize it in Gaza as well as Ukraine. By the early 2020s, the idea had been part of global politics and intellectual life for almost 80 years. Raphael Lemkin, a lawyer of Polish-Jewish origin, had first presented it in his book on Nazi Germany's occupation of continental Europe (1944), and within four years the United Nations adopted the Convention on the Prevention and Punishment of the Crime of Genocide (United Nations 1948). But contemporary discussion of genocide, even in academic and legal circles, was not the culmination of a coherent discourse based on Lemkin and the convention that had been elaborated continuously since the 1940s. Although the reality of genocide had never gone away – as was demonstrated in the 2020s in countries such as Ethiopia, Sudan, Myanmar and

Azerbaijan – the idea had waxed and waned according to repeated changes in political circumstances and intellectual fashion as well as the actual pattern of genocidal events, while its meaning had become, if anything, more unclear and contested.

In law, the crime remained on the international statute book but was systematically marginalized, often being replaced when atrocities were brought to court – which mostly they were not – by other charges and interpreted unduly narrowly when they were. Even over Gaza in 2024, the prosecutor of the International Criminal Court (ICC) brought charges of war crimes and crimes against humanity against Israel's leaders, but not of genocide, although the ICJ had already recognized the risk of it some months earlier and legal opinion was increasingly recognizing it as a reality.

In global politics, "genocide" was largely avoided even when powerful states, the UN itself and civil society organizations responded to atrocities, which again they frequently failed to do: most preferred to euphemistically acknowledge "ethnic cleansing" or a "humanitarian crisis". The explicit recognitions of the Gaza genocide by Amnesty International and Human Rights Watch were almost unprecedented.

In academia, too, the genocide idea had a chequered career, as scholars, who were initially slow to explore its implications, often preferred to substitute other notions ("ethnic cleansing", again, but also a plethora of new "-cide" terms) and largely failed to realize its potential as a coherent framework for socio-historical understanding. Indeed, almost on the eve of the Ukraine and Gaza crises, the editor of the *Journal of Genocide Research*, Dirk Moses, published an influential study (2021a) that concluded that the "problems of genocide" were so great that the concept should be retired. Even after the Gaza conflict erupted, the prominent international lawyer Philippe Sands (2024) echoed this position.

In all these contexts, therefore, "real" genocide had to fight repeatedly to gain recognition through the genocide idea. In this sense, it was not the denial of the Gaza genocide by politicians, media and intellectuals which was surprising; it was rather the fact that "genocide" cut through, that in this case, at least, the idea began to return to the central place that it always ought to have in thinking about mass atrocities.

Approach of the book

This book therefore hails the return of the genocide idea "after Gaza" – this term only implies that its genocide has been recognized, not that it has ended, which at the time of writing is not the case – and addresses the issues that it raises. To fully understand and cogently criticize the ongoing genocides there and in other regions, there is a new urgency to clarify the many debates about and conflicted foundations of the concept itself, to which critics such as Moses and Sands have drawn attention. This work therefore aims to assist in laying the basis of a more secure understanding of what is certain to be a continuing problem in the new world politics.

The reason that I was able to recognize genocide early in the recent cases was not only that, in the case of Palestine, I had already developed a specific framework for understanding earlier developments; it was also that I had been working for a quarter of a century to make the concept of genocide more coherent. My *War and Genocide* (Shaw 2003) exposed the links between the two phenomena; *Genocide and International Relations* (Shaw 2013) developed a framework for analysing the shifting patterns of genocide in the political transformations of the modern world; and, last but not least, *What Is Genocide?* (Shaw 2007/2015) comprehensively elaborated the concept itself and proposed resolutions of the dilemmas it raises.

The present book argues that the new age of genocide requires us to extend all three types of argument.

First, legal, political and intellectual struggles over Gaza have created a new urgency for finding a satisfactory basis on which to understand the relationships between genocide and war, which need to be grasped in all their complexity and variety. The common form of denial, in which actors use the claim that they are fighting wars to obfuscate their genocides, must be countered with coherent analyses of the interconnections.

Second, the sharpening of armed conflict and the new strength of the far right pose new challenges in understanding the relationships between the changing forms of genocide and both international and domestic politics. The historical stereotype of the genocidal regime, largely based on Nazism, must be superseded by complex analyses of the variety of contemporary genocidal actors in the new world disorder.

And third, these challenges make it essential that we achieve a settled answer to the question, "What is genocide?" The many ways in which the concept has been misunderstood, misrepresented and marginalized must be overcome through a clear, theoretically viable explanation of its meaning that, while incorporating the founding insights of Lemkin and taking account of the Genocide Convention, is adequate to today's knowledge.

My approach to these questions is framed within a sociological understanding. Although Lemkin first defined genocide with a view to establishing a new crime in international law, and it was elaborated as such in the convention, the concept is fundamentally one that captures *social* phenomena in *history* – indeed he followed his initial work with an unfinished history of genocide (Lemkin 2012). The new attention to genocide in the 2020s has had a strongly legal cast, but this does not mean that the discussion should start from the law. Rather, the law of genocide is only a partially adequate expression of its underlying social reality, which we must first of all articulate through sociological categories. Indeed, we must study the law itself as a social phenomenon, forged in the context of social and political conflict.

When I say that my approach is basically sociological, I do not identify it narrowly with a particular discipline. Rather, I work from social theory – understanding this as the arena within which the conceptual and theoretical concerns of socio-historical knowledge as a whole (including interdisciplinary fields such as genocide research) are most fully developed – and from historical sociology, with some of my work involving the kind of theoretically informed macrohistorical analysis associated with this tradition, which is now established in International Relations as well as sociology. In this book, which re-examines fundamental questions in the light of the Gaza genocide, I combine these social theory and historical sociology approaches with a critical political perspective, addressing the challenges of the new age of genocide.

Like other historical sociologists, in my discussions of specific cases I combine a conceptual and analytical frame with a reading of the historical literatures and (when I am discussing recent events) contemporary reports and commentary. I am therefore a generalist approaching Palestine, Ukraine, etc., rather than a specialist in any one area, and I am largely dependent on the English-language literature. I hope that my general perspective, combined with the attention I pay to specialist writing, will make my analysis of value to readers who are primarily interested in the particular cases.

Structure of the book

In form, this book is an interlinked set of essays, combining analyses of Gaza/Palestine and Ukraine with examinations of key conceptual, analytical and historical issues, all addressed partly in a "Gaza" perspective, and returning in conclusion to address the key requirements for engaging with the question of genocide after this definitive new catastrophe.

The structure of the book follows from these aims. Part I discusses the context of genocide as the second quarter of the twenty-first century begins. Chapter 2 outlines more fully the idea of the "return of genocide" and the intellectual, legal and political challenges that it poses. Chapter 3 poses the analytical questions raised by the new age of genocide, discussing the structural contexts in which genocide is produced and the problem of "forgotten genocides" in other regions. Chapter 4 homes in on Russia's assault on Ukraine, in the context of which the return of the genocide was first mooted. I analyse how Vladimir Putin's initial partially genocidal aims were first radicalized and then checked by the dynamics of the war. I also examine their partial success in the occupied areas, which reminds us that military occupation and annexation, the context in which Lemkin first analysed genocide, remain prime means for carrying it out, as we see also in Palestine.

Part II develops an extended analysis of the Gaza war-genocide and the larger problem of genocide in Palestine. Chapter 5 argues that the Israeli "countergenocide", responding to Hamas' smaller genocidal massacres, has involved very distinctive relationships between war, forced removal and genocide, and between Israel itself and its international system of support and denial. The experience of Gaza challenges many prevailing assumptions, and not only those of the apologists. Following from this, Chapter 6 expands my argument that the Nakba involved genocide. As mentioned above, the first version provoked strong opposition, but it has been vindicated by the way that Gaza has pushed attention towards the deeper genocidal "structure" of the Palestine situation. This new version addresses this question more explicitly, while also picking up the distinctive genocidal elements of Israeli occupation, annexation and apartheid.

The third part of the book broadens out the discussion to address key problems of contemporary scholarship that are important for analysing the new age of genocide. Chapter 7 defends the fundamental importance of the concept of genocide, with a critique of Moses' proposal that "permanent security" should replace it as the master concept in the study of anti-civilian violence. I argue that not only has this idea been challenged by the necessary return of genocide thinking in the 2020s but also – in the light of a sociological understanding of concept formation – the two ideas should be understood as complementary rather than opposed. The value of permanent security is as an explanatory perspective in the analysis of genocide, rather than as a replacement.

Chapter 8 addresses the thorny question of genocide against "political groups", which is in danger of becoming more topical as Trump and other far-right authoritarians direct repression and violence against political opponents as well as ethnic and national enemies. This chapter explores the history of this phenomenon, arguing that what we would better call "class-political" genocide was historically a precursor of the "ethnic-national" version around which the concept was first formulated and with which it continues, mistakenly, to be identified. I argue that understanding these dynamics underline the need for a generic concept of the targets of genocide, as "civilian social groups" rather than any particular types of them.

Chapter 9 places Western complicity in Gaza in a longer historical perspective, exploring the relationships of empire and genocide through a focused analysis of the British state and society. This chapter expands another argument that I made earlier (Shaw 2011): that the UK has been widely involved in genocidal conflicts, directly and indirectly, as an imperial, colonial and postcolonial great power. Unlike my controversial case about Palestine, this seems to have flown under the radar. As a new generation examines US and Western complicity in Israel's genocide, I hope that in its revised form this will now prove a useful resource for readers in other countries as well as the UK, as an example of a national analysis of genocide responsibility.

In conclusion, I lay out key theses on how to engage with genocide after Gaza.

PART I

Twenty-first-century genocide

2
RETURN OF THE GENOCIDE IDEA

The idea of genocide has suffered many vicissitudes. Raphael Lemkin had to narrow his original idea considerably to get it embedded in the Genocide Convention, while simultaneously the UN turned a blind eye to the murderous mass expulsions that were occurring even as it was drafted: of Germans by the Soviet Union (USSR) and eastern European states; and of Hindus, Muslims and Palestinians by proto-Pakistani, Indian nationalist and Zionist forces respectively, under the aegis of the British Empire. Even Lemkin was prepared to see genocidal violence disregarded in such cases to secure the enshrinement of genocide in international law (Cooper 2008: 154, 157). The USSR had shown its real attitude two weeks before the convention's adoption, when its Supreme Soviet had voted to recognize "in perpetuity" Stalin's genocidal expulsions of national groups such as Chechens and Crimean Tartars (Werth 2007: 413). The United States Senate would soon show its own by refusing to ratify the convention that the USA had helped to draft.

The Genocide Convention fell further into abeyance as the Cold War unfolded in the late 1940s and 1950s. The UN had been set up by the major victors of the Second World War in order to consolidate their victory and proclaim a new world order in which they would prevail. However, the emergent American super-empire, the expanding Soviet empire and the old European empires – which were scrambling to restore their shattered dominance in the face of rising anticolonial movements – would not allow their own or their allies' new crimes to be brought to account as a result of the convention, or even to bring more than rhetorical charges against their rivals. The idea of an international criminal court to try genocide and war crimes soon disappeared, and there was a sense that the convention, like the other high-sounding international agreements of the late 1940s – the 1945 UN Charter itself, the Universal Declaration of Human Rights agreed the day before the convention and the 1949 Geneva Conventions on the laws of war – was what Mark Mazower (2009: 7) calls a "promissory note never intended to be cashed".

So it was that genocide became, almost from the outset, more of an ideological than a legal notion, as anti-Communists (including Lemkin) mobilized it against Soviet despotism in eastern Europe and Communists and others against racial oppression in the USA (Gurmendi Dunkelberg 2025: 8–12) and the European colonies. Although as I have shown elsewhere (Shaw 2013: 98–123), on a rigorous accounting there were many genocidal episodes in the subsequent decades of Cold War, wars of decolonization and conflicts within new postcolonial states, the main development was not a return to the law but the generalization of a political rhetoric of genocide: it was soon the standard charge where civilian harm was involved during the political struggles and hot wars of the period. While the convention remained an authoritative reference point, the lack of international prosecutions helped this expansion of the language of genocide beyond the legal framework.

Genocide also became a "keyword" in Raymond Williams' (1976) sense, part of our core vocabulary of culture and society; although he did not include it in his list, Dirk Moses (2008a) presents it in this light. By the 1980s, it was beginning to be elaborated within academia. Even here, however, political drivers were clear as the rapidly growing field of Holocaust studies, in which Jewish scholars were understandably prominent, helped stimulate the emergence of "comparative genocide studies" (Moses 2021a: 441–76). Scholars from Armenian backgrounds played a particularly important role, partly in order to secure, via "bridging" from the Holocaust (Alexander 2002), recognition of the 1915 Armenian genocide (Hovanissian 1987). This pathway would soon be followed by scholars from other backgrounds.

However, as academics tried to provide the genocide idea with more secure foundations, they came up against its intrinsic and necessary complexity, which neither Lemkin nor the convention's drafters had adequately captured. Almost all agreed that it meant the "destruction" of social "groups", but what did *these* terms mean: was destruction more than mass killing; what were groups and which of them counted? Almost all also agreed that genocidal destruction was necessarily "intentional", but what did *that* mean, and should not a purposive understanding of genocidal acts be related to the concerns of social scientists and historians with "structural" phenomena? How should we manage a concept that was applied both to total mass extermination and to extremely violent but proportionally less murderous cases of persecution and mass expulsion? Was genocide a matter of rare mega-episodes of destruction (Straus 2007), even of Holocaust "uniqueness", or an all-too-common tendency of modern states and armed organizations? How was it related to war, in the context of which most cases occurred?

Just as political demands led actors to pull the genocide idea in one direction or another, so these dilemmas, pursued in the context of broadening empirical studies, led to divergent new academic definitions. Some narrowed genocide almost exclusively to intentional mass killing (Chalk & Jonassohn 1990; Charny 1994), while for others, it was a structural tendency of the modern international system as a whole or at least of a regional imperial system (Levene 2005a; Bloxham 2005).

For those for whom killing wholly or largely defined genocide, episodes where the number killed was less than those expelled were often labelled "ethnic cleansing", a term that escaped from the Serbo-Croat language into international discourse during the post-Yugoslav wars of the 1990s (Bell-Fialkoff 1996; Naimark 2001; Mann 2005). For those for whom genocide was an exclusively ethnic or national phenomenon, the destruction of "political groups", which had been excluded from the Genocide Convention (partly, we shall see, for the political reasons of the UN powers), should be regarded as "politicide" (Harff & Gurr 1988). After genocide studies belatedly discovered gendered genocidal violence, this became "gendercide" (Jones 2000).

Amid this conceptual proliferation, much of it arguably unnecessary since Lemkin's and the convention's definitions were already capable of encompassing the phenomena referred to, there were always sceptics who questioned whether the term genocide was needed at all: when, for example, the language of counterinsurgency excess might describe what was being called genocidal (Gerlach 2010).

A key issue, not always explicitly discussed, was how far scholars should follow the legal definition, which by general consensus among non-lawyers was at least partially flawed. Sociologists generally opted for redefinition, albeit sometimes hewing close to the legal standard and even rationalizing what many saw as its defects, such as the exclusion of political groups (Fein 1990; Chalk & Jonassohn 1990); historians often operationalized the UN version so as to avoid definitional controversy.

The ending of the Cold War during 1989–91 was the signal for a partial return to the genocide idea. There was a huge increase in all kinds of attention to large-scale violence and atrocities, and the rapprochement between the West and the Soviet Union briefly enabled the UN system and international law to begin to work rather more in the ways that they had been designed. But the return to "genocide" was not straightforward: the 1993 initiative to establish the International Criminal Tribunal for Former Yugoslavia (ICTY), which became the most important forum for legal charges related to mass violence, did not lead to a coherent implementation of the Genocide Convention. Although there were genocide convictions, the conceptual confusion caused by a narrow interpretation of the crime as physical harm, together with the introduction of the idea of "ethnic cleansing" (although this was not legally codified), led to judgements that did not reflect the extent of the genocide committed in the wars of Yugoslav succession.

This problem was exacerbated in the case that Bosnia-Herzegovina began against federal Yugoslavia in the ICJ in 1993, which was finally decided with Serbia-Montenegro as Yugoslavia's successor state 14 years later. In its majority judgement, the ICJ (International Court of Justice 2007a) restricted its determination of genocide to the 1995 Srebrenica massacre, excluding the larger post-1992 pattern of killings, smaller massacres, rapes and expulsions – the grounds on which Bosnia had originally brought the case – from its scope. The rationale for this verdict was that the Serbians' intention to destroy the non-Serb population as such could not be more widely proved, since the court converted deliberate mass killing into a criterion of intent (I discuss this flawed key judgement more fully in Chapter 4).

The 1994 killing in Rwanda was a different question. Although during the early phase, when it might have been halted, almost all international actors denied that genocide was being committed (Barnett 2002), this turned in retrospect into the only undisputed genocide of the post-Cold War period. The International Criminal Tribunal for Rwanda, established the year after the Yugoslav one, duly recorded convictions for genocide, but in staggeringly small numbers (61 in total) given the number who had taken part in the killing, which was estimated at up to 200,000 (Straus 2006: 115–18). Even so, Rwanda's function now became to act as the legitimated exception, the contemporary Holocaust by comparison with which most other episodes could not be determined as genocide.

The confusion around the idea of genocide reflected the contradictory interests of all the main types of global actors when it was engaged. States that were signatories to the convention – most of them by the 1990s, even including the USA – were duty-bound to "prevent and punish" genocide, no matter by which state or other actor it was committed. Yet in almost every episode, perpetrators had wider state protection, and even states that were not affiliated to the perpetrators usually found that serious efforts to stop genocide were outside their perceptions of their own interests. In these circumstances, states almost always responded to new crises with efforts to avoid genocide determinations.

The UN was also affected by these contradictory interests of its member states and produced its own distinctive ways of avoiding "genocide" (Barnett 2002; LeBor 2006). So too were civil society organizations, even – indeed especially – those with humanitarian or human rights remits, which often depended on states for both funding and access to conflict zones. To secure what became known as "humanitarian intervention" (Wheeler 2002) – always an ambiguous idea, at best mixing aid and military prevention – or later, implementation of the "responsibility to protect" (Bellamy 2009), it was often more convenient to use the euphemistic terms "ethnic cleansing" and "humanitarian crisis" than genocide. At the peak of official humanitarianism in the 2000s and early 2010s, when "R2P" (as the responsibility to protect became known) was widely propagated and the Obama administration set up its Atrocities Prevention Board, genocide was still often the idea that dared not speak its name.

These new forms of ambiguity were also reflected in academia. The turn of the millennium saw new trends in genocide research, especially the investigation of colonial genocide that opened up more global and critical approaches, in which Western states were seen for the first time as a part of the problem as much as – or even more than – of the solution (Moses 2000; Wolfe 2006). The historic affinities of the original, North America-based professional grouping, the International Association of Genocide Scholars (IAGS), with the USA and Israel led some scholars from other regions to establish an alternative European – which quickly became International – Network of Genocide Scholars (INOGS). Whereas the IAGS adopted an openly activist stance, including a pro-Israeli resolution in 2006 after the Iranian president, Mahmoud Ahmadinejad, issued threats against the Jewish state, the INOGS eschewed collective political positions and, becoming the sponsor of the *Journal of Genocide Research* (*JGR*), instead promoted critical perspectives through academic rigour.

The end of the road for "genocide"?

For all that, there was no strong consensus in INOGS and *JGR*, any more than in the IAGS or the field as a whole, on the meaning or scope of the concept of genocide. On the contrary, the diversity of views remained as wide as ever, and when the *JGR*'s long-term editor, Dirk Moses, a pioneer of the interest in colonial genocide, produced his sustained critique of *The Problems of Genocide* (Moses 2021a), which I discuss in Chapter 7, it was more than a summation of his own concerns.

Moses brought to the table recent research on Lemkin – whose view of genocide as the imposition of one national "pattern" on another he had earlier cited as an inspiration for the colonial turn (Moses 2008a: 9) – and new work on the Second World War Allies' determination, in postwar legal cases, to separate "military necessity" from genocide. His findings were clear: there were fatal flaws in Lemkin's concept that were compounded by the Allies' insistence that genocide was necessarily driven by racial hatred. His conclusion was stark and potentially very disruptive: the "problems of genocide" were so severe that the very concept should be abandoned. Instead, he argued, we should recognize the dominant common motive in both "military" and "genocidal" violence against civilian populations: the pursuit of a paranoid, total form of "permanent security". This, rather than genocide, should be the master concept in the study of violence against civilians and should even be made a new overarching crime to replace genocide in international law. Genocide, Moses later doubled down, was "a category mistake in the legal regime ostensibly protecting civilians" (2023: 15).

In some respects, Moses' case was compelling. He not only interrogated the genocide idea's roots but with "permanent security" also provided a new basis for the long-standing view of critical genocide scholars that the practice of atrocity was not restricted to "illiberal" regimes, as assumed by some in the field, but had a "liberal" variant too. The idea of permanent security could help to close the conceptual gap, which the notion of racial ideology as the driver of genocide had done much to create, between military and genocidal activity. Since my own contribution to the field had focused on precisely this linkage, I found much to agree with. And yet his conclusion, abandoning "genocide", seemed inappropriate, and not only because it took insufficient account of my and others' attempts to address the weaknesses of Lemkin's and the convention's definitions and bridge the war–genocide gap.

It was also surprising, given that Moses (2008a) had drawn attention to "genocide's" role as a keyword – and to its political and cultural diffusion in the legally lean Cold War years (e.g. Moses & Heerten 2018) – that he should think it possible, even if desirable, to dispense with the term. I am far from believing that social scientists and historians should uncritically adopt everyday terminology: I myself have campaigned against adopting "ethnic cleansing", since this is a perpetrator euphemism and the forced removal of peoples can be considered a method of genocide (Shaw 2015: 66–83). And the field has accepted that "race" cannot be a scientific category, despite its inclusion in the Genocide Convention. But the attempt to abolish "genocide", the only comprehensive concept of deliberate destructive violence against civilians, seemed to me to ignore cultural needs as well as scientific imperatives and doomed to failure. If the strength of Moses' argument derived from his approaching the concept as a historical construct, this was also a source of its weakness. In critiquing the key nexus of Lemkin, the convention and international law, he allowed their contradictions a lock on the meaning of genocide.

Moses' framing of the dilemma was distinctive but it was also an expression of where thinking about genocide was in the first quarter of the twenty-first century. Despite a rapidly growing body of research and analytical innovation, the conceptual debate had not advanced much further since the 1990s and the divergence of approaches largely continued. Some were openly uninterested: the historian Donald Bloxham (2025) called the debate about whether Israel's policies include genocide "scholastic". And it was not only in genocide studies that doubts about the concept were rising. As already noted, Philippe Sands drew the same conclusion as Moses, out of his frustration with international law. Having failed in his attempt, as an advocate for Croatia in its case against Serbia, to get the ICJ to "lower the threshold" for genocide, Sands (2024) launched into a parallel critique. Despite his respect for Lemkin, he was "not sure if it was a socially useful thing to invent the concept of genocide"; indeed, he claimed its invention "may actually have given rise to more genocide", as the political use of the concept "inflamed passions" over situations such as Gaza.

It is important to examine the reasons for this situation. Changes in academic thought are not solely the consequence of cumulative improvements in knowledge and theoretical sophistication. Although the pioneering idea of "revolutions" in scientific "paradigms", advanced by Thomas Kuhn (1962), is no longer fully accepted, it is clear that there are rapid shifts of perspective; thinking in the social and historical sciences, especially, evolves partly in response to real-world changes. Thus Lemkin had been thinking about mass atrocities for over a decade when he formulated his idea, but it took the Nazis' destruction of European nations and especially Jewry for "genocide" to crystallize, and we know how extraordinarily it captured the imagination in the late 1940s.

What marked the 30 years after the Rwandan genocide, in contrast, was precisely the absence of any similar strong development. In the early 2000s, Darfur was the focus of an unprecedented popular movement for genocide recognition, chiefly in North America (Hamilton 2011), but in general the absence of defining events offered limited incentives for further innovation in genocide discourse. At the same time, this was the period in which the general conceptual certainties of the Cold War era – including the dominant critical paradigm, Marxism – collapsed, while replacements failed to arrive (Tooze 2024). In these senses, the conceptual blockage appeared overdetermined.

Even the increasing attention to Israel-Palestine early in the new century, which included the first application by Patrick Wolfe (2006) of the "settler-colonial genocide" paradigm, was marked by conceptual conservatism. Hardly anyone was prepared to argue directly that the Nakba involved genocide; even the critical Israeli scholar Ilan Pappé (2007) opted for "ethnic cleansing" as his frame.

Ukraine, Gaza and the new age of genocide

So what has changed? Less than a year after Moses' book appeared, Russia invaded Ukraine, and 19 months after that, Hamas' violence against Israeli civilians provoked Israel's destruction of Gaza. Both these developments rapidly stimulated genocide debates.

Critics soon charged Russia's new invasion as genocidal, citing Vladimir Putin's explicit intention to destroy a distinct Ukrainian state and society, and the revelations a few weeks later of atrocities at Bucha together with the destruction of Mariupol greatly magnified the accusation, which was even taken up by President Joe Biden, as I discuss in detail in Chapter 4. Among academic commentators, Moses (2022) was quick to note that "Russia's campaign against

Ukraine is precisely what Lemkin was trying to capture with his new word". Putin's genocidal war quickly exceeded his original plans, as I argued in my contribution to a *JGR* forum (Shaw 2023a), which is updated in this book: Ukrainian resistance radicalized Russian violence. Yet by mid-2023, it appeared that the two sides were increasingly locked into a grim attritional war whose victims were primarily soldiers rather than civilians. Absent further large-scale atrocities, the Ukraine genocide debate subsided, with too little attention to how Russia was consolidating its occupation in the southern and eastern areas, which raised issues very similar to those of the Nazi occupation that Lemkin had analysed in *Axis Rule*, and, indeed, the long Israeli occupation in Palestine.

However, when Israel assaulted Gaza, charges of genocide were quick to develop and before long overtook the initial repulsion at Hamas' slaughter of kibbutz-dwellers and festival-goers. International support for Gaza was enormous both at the level of states and in Western civil society, with pro-Palestinian demonstrations of a size and frequency that had not been seen for Ukraine except in central Europe. Gaza soon impacted domestic politics in many countries, especially on the centre-left: Biden became "Genocide Joe" as his support for Israel's atrocities was contrasted with his opposition to Russia's; Germany saw bitter political conflict as its institutions and media tarred pro-Palestinian sentiment as antisemitic (Streeck 2024); and the British Labour Party's return to power was partially threatened as pro-Palestinians were outraged by its initial refusal to call for a ceasefire.

Academia also saw sharp conflict, as pro-Israeli mobilizations of Holocaust scholars were countered by calls by many genocide scholars for Israel to stop destroying Gaza (Segal 2023b; Segal & Daniele 2024). Moses opened a new *JGR* forum, taking its cue from this polarization: my impression that there was an even greater level of genocide concern over Gaza than over Ukraine seemed to be confirmed when my short contribution to the new forum quickly reached four times the number of hits of my more substantial article on Ukraine, which had been thought to do well. The new genocide also broke the taboo on discussing the larger Palestinian situation in a genocide frame. Israel had gradually destroyed Palestinian society through its occupation for five decades, which surely should have set Lemkinian warning bells ringing, but only now did it widely do so.

Why was the idea of genocide supercharged in these new conflicts, and why much more over Gaza than Ukraine? Indeed, why in these cases, more than any since Darfur or indeed Rwanda? Why were so few connections made between the Ukraine and Palestine cases, and why didn't the common issue of occupation come to the fore?

On the surface, neither seemed a maximal case of genocide: no one believed that either Russia or Israel aimed to physically exterminate the entire civilian population to which it was hostile, as the Hutu Power regime had the Rwandan Tutsis and of course the Nazis had European Jews. Moreover, both campaigns were manifestly armed conflicts. Russia's onslaught was designed to conquer Ukraine and Israel's to destroy Hamas, so the central claims against both states concerned actions in war. There was much evidence of the specific targeting of cultural institutions, but each genocide case hinged primarily on the physical harm to which civilians were subjected in the course of ostensibly military action. This enabled both Russia and Israel to claim that civilian harm was a by-product, "collateral damage", but while Israel's claims – unlike Russia's – were taken seriously by Western governments and media, within a few months few still fully believed them and defences of Israel became remarkably less full-throated.

By 2024, therefore, the genocide idea was back, but its ability to transcend geopolitical dividing lines was less clear. It was not only Western politicians who were open to charges of hypocrisy in recognizing one genocide but not the other: few of the Global South states that supported South Africa – indeed, not even South Africa itself – acknowledged genocide in Ukraine and many supported Russia, at least implicitly. There were certainly states who supported both Palestine and Ukraine in UN General Assembly votes, but there was no strong international grouping organized around this position. The Hague Group, established in 2025 by nine states including South Africa to support international law, the ICC and ICJ, restricted itself to Israel-Palestine, demanding enforcement of the criminal indictment against Netanyahu but not that against Putin.

The greater magnification of genocide charges in the case of Gaza had multiple causes. First, identification with Ukraine's suffering was largely confined to Europe and (more weakly) North America; although Russia's invasion was manifestly a reassertion of empire, global anticolonial politics, structured around opposition to Western empires, mostly did not embrace Ukraine. Palestine, in contrast, had a strong, established anticolonial constituency within Western societies as well as large official and popular support in the Global South.

Second, although the new Russian aggression in Ukraine dated to 2014 and had antecedents in the Soviet era, Israel's against the Palestinians had been a central international issue continuously since 1948; serial episodes of war and violence had seared the conflict into global consciousness at large as well as into particular transnational constituencies. Indeed, wars in Gaza during 2008–9, 2012, 2014 and 2021 had already aroused similar concerns to those of 2023–5, even if the scale of the destruction was less. While the Ukraine war might be more important for global geopolitics (although the Middle East was hardly insignificant), the new conflict in Palestine stirred great emotions among far larger populations: above all Muslims, but also the liberal left.

Third, although the most destructive episode in Russia's invasion, in Mariupol, was comparable to what Israel did to Gaza, it involved a smaller population, resulted in fewer deaths (although possibly not in proportional terms) and the suffering was visibly displayed over a shorter period, not least because most survivors were able to escape. Crucially, Ukraine was able to resist, Gaza was not: with Hamas a local oppressor and a literally underground presence, its civilians appeared as stereotypical helpless victims of genocide, despite the attempts of Israel's propaganda to present them otherwise.

Finally, Gaza came *after* Ukraine: the new genocide consciousness was already stirred before it was presented with what, from the point of view of both politics and culture, was almost a perfect case for a major moral panic.

International courts and the return of genocide

The return of the genocide idea was demonstrated by the three hearings of the ICJ on Gaza in early 2024. The court had actually ruled on a case involving Ukraine (International Court of Justice 2022); it had rejected spurious Russian claims, used to justify its invasion, that the invaded state had itself committed genocide against Russian speakers in its eastern regions. Indeed, the ICJ had even ordered Russia to cease its intervention, but Putin's ignoring of this was so completely foreseen that it failed to become an international *cause célèbre*. And before that, in the case that provided the crucial legal precedent, the Gambia had brought the genocide of Rohingya Muslims in Myanmar to the court (International Court of Justice 2020).

Despite these previous cases, the impact of South Africa's case against Israel was striking. The post-apartheid state was the perfect nemesis for Israel – increasingly recognized as itself based on apartheid – and the perfect champion of Global South resentment at Western hypocrisy. To this Southern moral power, South Africa was able to harness some of the best resources of the global Anglophone legal establishment, including its own. Its case for preliminary orders to stop Israel's genocide was well designed to expose the pro-Israeli obfuscations of Western politicians and media. Yet the court's first ruling was, one international lawyer suggested, rhetorically strong but operationally weak (Krisch 2024); it failed to halt Israel's atrocities although it contributed strongly to their delegitimation.

Through this process, the significance of the international law of genocide began to change, even if we must await the ultimate determination of South Africa's case to see if the law itself has advanced. The situation that the Israeli onslaught produced was well calibrated to engage legal understandings of genocide, however problematic these may be from the point of intellectual coherence, as I explain in Chapter 4. Whereas, in some situations, a low ratio of numbers killed to those expelled has lent itself to an interpretation of "merely" ethnic cleansing (Bosnia is the paradigmatic case, but the Nakba has also been understood in this way), in Gaza the rapidly mounting toll of death, injury, starvation and cruelty soon made it difficult to deny that Israel had created conditions in which there was a deliberate threat to life, contravening especially clause II(c) of the convention.

Whether Israel "intended" this outcome, in the somewhat arcane sense which the court would use, was not at this stage the question in front of it; but evidently it saw that as sufficiently probable as to constitute a ground for preliminary orders. Through this underappreciated mechanism, the ICJ found itself exposing genocide law to a global audience in an unprecedented way. Regardless of the effectiveness of the court's orders, the case reinforced the way in which "genocide" was being thrust back in global politics and thought.

Gaza and the genocide field

Gaza therefore led to an explosion of genocide commentary by legal and other scholars interested in mass violence. The implications were evidently significant for the fields of Holocaust and genocide studies, in which, Raz Segal and Luigi Daniele (2024: 1) argued, it provoked a deep and unprecedented "crisis". The basis for their claim was the very different ways in which Holocaust scholars, on the one hand, and those working on genocide, on the other, had responded to the unfolding violence after 7 October 2023. They believed that the evidence for genocide in Israel's attack on Gaza had "exposed the exceptional status accorded to Israel as a foundational element in the field, that is, the idea that Israel, the state of Holocaust survivors, can never perpetrate genocide". For them, this was a moment of reckoning with "a foundational case of marginalization and disavowal – *and* justification – of mass violence", holding the "potential for the kind of systemic change that goes well beyond calls for balance in the way we study and teach about mass violence".

It was certainly true, as I had long argued, that the exceptional status of the Holocaust had fundamentally distorted genocide research, that Israel benefited from this status and that the understanding of Palestine in a genocide frame was largely blocked as a result. However, overt Israel-Holocaust exceptionalism was increasingly confined, as Segal and Daniele themselves highlighted, to the narrower field of Holocaust studies, even if fear of being castigated as antisemitic maintained an insidious hold on the wider field, which partly accounted for the slowness of many to recognize the Gaza genocide.

However, Palestine was just one – albeit overdetermined – case out of many entanglements of genocide discourse with political interests, and these were only one dimension of the "problems of genocide", which Dirk Moses was right to argue were fundamentally conceptual rather than political. If the return of the genocide idea was to be more than a passing intellectual fashion surfing yet another wave of horror, it required refounding on a more consistent conceptual basis.

At the heart of the challenge that Gaza presented was the fact that "genocide" was mostly identified in and through Israel's "military" campaign. This situation offered, above all, the opportunity to prise open the synthesis of military and genocidal objectives, which in its case was particularly tight. There were two principal keys to this enterprise. The first was the recognition that for Israel, *both* Hamas *and* the Palestinian population of Gaza were enemies to be destroyed: the military destruction of the one and the genocidal destruction of the other were intimately connected but analytically distinct elements of its campaign. The second was the understanding that while these twin objectives were pursued partly by distinctive anti-Hamas and anti-civilian acts, they were often entwined to the point of being combined in the same acts. At the beginning of Israel's campaign, drawing attention to these syntheses was a marginal opinion; a year later, the same arguments had become mainstream, even from a legal point of view (Amnesty International 2024; Haque 2024).

Despite the closeness of military and anti-population goals in this case (and in Ukraine), it is also important to recognize that these are not exceptions to usually distinct forms of the two phenomena but on the contrary particular instances of their "general hybridity" (Shaw 2006). This was recognized both in the origins of the genocide idea and in other attempts to grapple with the relationships between civilian destruction and modern war. Lemkin (1944: 80) originally formulated the idea of genocide by distinguishing it from the ideal type of modern "legitimate" war between states and armies, and in the light of the distinction between combatants and civilians in military thought. But equally, the idea of "total war", which emerged through the world wars of the twentieth century, recognized that modern war tends towards total social destruction. The critique of this tendency culminated in E. P. Thompson's outline of the "exterminist" logic of nuclear competition (1980), as well as in the idea of "degenerate war" (Shaw 2003: 43–61).

The challenge is, therefore, to understand both war and genocide in the context of *war and genocide.* War, an ancient type of social action, whose historic legitimacy is brought into question by its modern forms, and genocide, a newly recognized type defined by its fundamental illegitimacy, are simultaneously distinct but fundamentally related. Recognition of their mutual interdependence is necessary to see each for what it is: the ideas possess distinct but overlapping logics and they need to be grasped and applied through their relations. In limiting cases, there are wars that do not raise questions of genocide and genocides without a war context, but these are the extremes of a spectrum on which most cases are clustered in the messy middle that we can call genocidal war.

Challenges for international law

This conceptual matrix poses particular problems for international law, for which the contrasting (il)legitimacies of genocide and war appear foundational even if the ideas of "war crimes" and "crime against humanity" qualify the general legitimacy of military action. The Genocide Convention's definition entrenched the separation of genocide from military action even as it specified killing, the principal means of warfare, as the prime method of the new international crime. The ICJ, with its requirement that genocidal intention should be the "only possible inference" from the acts in question, appeared to erect a barrier between military and genocidal intentions, while in real-life genocidal wars these were rarely far apart. Yet commentary on Gaza increasingly emphasized that *certainty* about genocidal intentions does not preclude their *combination* with military intentions (Amnesty International 2024; Haque 2024).

Even where genocidal acts appear to be distinct from military ones, questions of their relationships cannot be avoided. Acts that appear to be specifically genocidal, such as the targeted killing of civilians of a particular group, may also have military purposes; those that appear to be specifically military, because they are targeted at an armed enemy, may serve genocidal purposes too. In the cases of Israel and Russia, where genocide appears to have been committed primarily *through* military action, the untenability of this separation is exposed. Although both states have engaged in conventional military action against their armed enemies and have committed atrocities against civilians that can be distinguished from this action, both have used methods of war as methods also of genocide. Aerial and artillery bombardments against urban areas, apparently major tools against Hamas and the Ukrainian state respectively, have been simultaneously used to destroy the two civilian populations and societies.

South Africa's case against Israel should force the ICJ to clarify these relationships, but whether it will do so remains to be seen at the time of writing. The preliminary orders which the court issued in 2024, while important markers, failed to challenge Israel's military rationale for its genocidal policies: they instructed Israel not to commit certain acts of genocide (which it did not recognize it was committing) but not to cease its military operations (which was all that Israel acknowledged undertaking), despite the fact that these were the context in which genocidal policies were being carried out.

The courts must interpret the existing corpus of international law, derived from international humanitarian law (IHL), the Genocide Convention, the Rome Statute of the ICC and its own and other courts' jurisprudence. Ukraine and Gaza underline that, in important respects, it is not just the ICJ's interpretations that are problematic: there are also major inadequacies in the underlying law, some of which pertain to the understanding of genocide. As I discuss more fully in Chapter 4, the convention left a fundamental ambiguity as to whether it refers only or primarily to the "physical" destruction of a population group, that is, causing the death of its members, or to a broader process. The ICJ appeared to have resolved this ambiguity in a narrow direction when it distinguished "ethnic cleansing" from genocide, for example distinguishing the intent to forcibly displace from "systematically destroying" a population, indeed as presenting the former as the *absence* of genocidal intent (International Court of Justice 2015: 126–7). Perhaps because of this confusion, Israel's forced removal of the vast majority of the Gazan population was not prominent in the ICJ's orders. It is not certain that it would consider its efforts to make removal from northern Gaza "permanent", or even the proposed expulsion of Palestinians to neighbouring countries, in themselves genocidal. But such a failure to recognize genocide would undermine the credibility of the court's approach.

The linkage between genocide and war in the Israeli and Russian cases also raises a more fundamental deficiency: the idea of war as a legitimate tool of state policy, a basic assumption of the modern international order that is embedded in the UN Charter. In theory, of course, the scope for legal war was greatly narrowed: the charter allows it only when a state acts in self-defence or on the UN's own authorization. Therefore, Russia's war, a blatant campaign of aggression, and Israel's, defending an illegal occupation – as the ICJ confirmed (International Court of Justice 2024d) – were both clearly outside the law; in each case, violations of IHL and the law of genocide compound a fundamental illegality. Yet both aggressors exploited, by misrepresenting, the narrow loophole for legal military action that the charter provides, claiming to act in "self-defence", and achieved wide international support for and tolerance of these claims. In principle, judges could well denounce these distortions, but the ICJ's failure to challenge Israel's military rationale in Gaza suggests that this will not necessarily be the case.

Such distortions are deeply embedded in the international consensus around the in-principle legitimacy of military force. The exception has become the rule and the loophole has become the foundation of state policy, not only in Russia and Israel but also in every state that maintains armed forces capable of aggression. Even Ukraine's legitimate war of defence against Russian aggression – the exception that *proves* the rule – underlines the kind of problem that war has become, since it has only been able to hold back Russia by inflicting hundreds of thousands of casualties in a campaign that has led Russia to threaten the use of nuclear weapons. It is difficult to think of another twenty-first-century war that has even been legal in principle, yet the world is saddled with a framework that is widely believed to allow states this crucial leeway.

Another example of this problem is military occupation, which is envisaged in international law as a temporary situation in which the victors are obliged to respect the rights and social arrangements of the population, and are barred from annexation, institutionalizing their rule and importing colonists. Yet we know that historically, occupation has often arisen from genocidal war and has often led to colonization and the consolidation of genocidal expulsions. The norms on occupation were incorporated in the Geneva Conventions shortly after the Soviet Union, with US and British connivance, had used its occupation of eastern Europe to expel unwanted nationalities and import Russians and other Soviet citizens in their place. Since then, the West has allowed Israel to exploit a half-century occupation to annex and colonize the West Bank; has ratified the genocidal Serbian conquest of large parts of Bosnia; and appears poised to help make permanent Russia's occupation of southeastern Ukraine.

Thus the return of genocide to the courts cannot solve the problem in reality, which is manifestly much more than a problem of a flawed, misinterpreted or misused legal framework. And it certainly cannot resolve the fundamental contradiction of an international order based on the general illegality of war and military occupation, but which is interpreted on many sides as a licence to pursue them. The return of genocide and its intimate relationships to war and occupation could in principle alert global society to the need to readdress these deeper problems, which have long been structurally fudged in the UN system, but it will require radical action to achieve this change.

3

GENOCIDE IN HISTORY AND IN OUR TIME

The Gaza genocide has been widely recognized, despite its denial, because of the pressure of active protest movements, global public opinion and states in the Global South, as well as the ICJ's judgements. Yet most other cases of genocide in today's world are largely unrecognized, not only because of the same Western denial or indifference but also because they are not causes for the Global South – from which indeed many perpetrator states and movements arise – or for large-scale protest movements, and they do not reach the ICJ. Most twenty-first-century cases therefore remain "forgotten" genocides, unable to attract even a fraction of the global political and media attention given to Gaza. The UN and its agencies, as well as various states, non-governmental organizations (NGOs) and academic institutions, continue to (unevenly) document atrocities and offer support to threatened populations, but lacking the exceptional political attention that Gaza has received, most cases remain marginal to world politics. Even when they are addressed, their genocidal dimensions are often submerged.

Given the way that mediated global politics works, the polarization that makes the Gaza genocide an active issue may even have reduced further the already inadequate attention to crises such as those in Myanmar, Ethiopia, Sudan and Azerbaijan. It is frequently stated that "genocide" is invoked carelessly, but there is usually a kernel of truth when those representing victims claim that it has been committed. Even if arguments are sometimes made simplistically, for example with superficial comparisons to the Holocaust, many political and armed campaigns do indeed involve framing populations as enemies and targeting them for destruction.

It is therefore a precondition of a genuine return of genocide understanding that we go beyond the headline cases and establish the parameters of targeted anti-civilian violence in today's world. The aim of this chapter is to outline some of the dimensions of this task, first by surveying the problem of forgotten genocides and its salience to our times, and second by exploring the structural factors that currently produce – and will continue to produce – genocide.

From "forgotten genocides" to structural patterns

The idea that genocides are "forgotten" has become a significant theme in the academic literature, usually meaning that they are neglected, ignored or overlooked in the public imagination about genocide in the Western world. Yet they are rarely truly forgotten by the survivors, the descendants of the victims or their communities; rather, their memories and representations of events have failed to make significant impacts on wider understanding. It is also inaccurate to say that marginalized recent events have been forgotten; rather, they were insufficiently known about or recognized as they occurred, and observers cannot be said to have forgotten what they hardly knew about in the first place.

Nevertheless, the idea that many genocides in all periods have failed to make the "canon" and are "hidden" or "forgotten" is now well established as a major theme in the academic field, and with the above reservations we can use the term. Recent genocidal events join a long series of twentieth-century and older cases that are increasingly being uncovered by scholars. "Human history is filled with genocide", say Douglas Irvin-Erickson, Thomas La Pointe and Alexander Laban Hinton in introducing one recent survey of this issue, but academic study has only recognized this in fragmentary and uneven ways. They demonstrate the scope of the problem by tabulating the field's hierarchy of cases: this descends from a "triad" of universally agreed cases (the Holocaust, the Armenians and Rwanda) via other widely considered "core cases" (such as Bosnia and Darfur) to the "second circle" and "periphery" of the field, and finally the true "forgotten genocides": a "multitude of more or less invisible/hidden/forgotten cases" (Irvin-Erickson, La Pointe & Hinton 2014: 5–6).

This is only one of three substantial collections that have now been devoted to identifying these cases and the manner in which they have been obscured (Lemarchand 2011; Hinton, La Pointe & Irvin-Erickson 2014; Bachman & Brito Ruiz 2024), although any perusal of genocide journals will reveal more. To illustrate the scope of the problem as it emerges from the three studies, Table 3.1 lists the cases that these volumes identify. However, it will be noted that they vary greatly in scope and duration and that other editors include as "forgotten" cases that figure in Irvin-Erickson *et al.*'s "periphery", so this table should not be taken as a comprehensive survey or analytical framework.

Indeed, it will be noted that only one case featured in these volumes is from the period of the Second World War, which is generally considered the nadir of modern genocide: few believe that the Nazis' is the only genocide of those years. Even in the colonial and postcolonial periods that are better represented in these collections, the cases listed are best seen as a sample; many more cases are still forgotten than those that have been uncovered. The key point is that there is indeed a "multitude" of cases: genocide is a widespread, recurring problem and

Table 3.1 Selected "forgotten" genocides

Victims	Location	Dates	Source
Indigenous peoples	USA	Seventeenth–nineteenth centuries	Hinton, La Pointe & Irvin Erickson (2014)
Aboriginal Tasmanians	British colony, Tasmania	1803–32	Lemarchand (2011)
Algerian Arabs	Algeria, French conquest	1830–47	Bachman & Brito Ruiz (2024)
Herero and Nama	German South West Africa	1904–8	Lemarchand (2011)
Circassians	Karbadia, Russian empire	1864	Hinton, La Pointe & Irvin Erickson (2014)
Ainu (indigenous people)	Hokkaido, Japan	1870s–1920s	Bachman & Brito Ruiz (2024)
Aboriginal and Torres Islander children	Australia	1909–1970s	Hinton, La Pointe & Irvin Erickson (2014)
Assyrians	Ottoman Empire	1914–16	Lemarchand (2011)
Ukrainians	USSR, famine	1932–3	Bachman & Brito Ruiz (2024)
Bengalis	British India, famine	1943–4	Bachman & Brito Ruiz (2024)
Tibetans	Tibet, Chinese occupation	1950–9	Lemarchand (2011)
Peasants	China, Great Leap Forward	1958–61	Hinton, La Pointe & Irvin Erickson (2014)

Table 3.1 *(continued)*

Victims	Location	Dates	Source
Communists	Indonesia	1965	Hinton, La Pointe & Irvin Erickson (2014)
Biafrans	Biafra, Nigeria	1966–70	Bachman & Brito Ruiz (2024)
Hutus	Burundi	1970–2	Lemarchand (2011)
Left-wing activists	Argentina	1974–83	Bachman & Brito Ruiz (2024)
Kurds	Northern Iraq	1988	Lemarchand (2011)
Nuba	Sudan	1989–mid-1990s	Bachman & Brito Ruiz (2024)
Rwandan Hutus	Eastern Democratic Republic of Congo	1996–7	Lemarchand (2011)
East Timorese	East Timor, Indonesian occupation	1999–2002	Hinton, La Pointe & Irvin Erickson (2014)
Yezidis	Iraq, Islamic State	2014–16	Bachman & Brito Ruiz (2024)
Yemenis	Yemen, Saudi invasion	2016–19	Bachman & Brito Ruiz (2024)

requires structural explanation. This idea is only surprising because it has been obscured by the restriction of genocide to a few supposedly exceptional cases.

The colonial and party-state types of genocide

The idea that genocide has been prevalent throughout human history has been present since the earliest days of the concept. We have seen that although Lemkin analysed genocide in largely legal terms in his work on Nazism (1944), he also saw it as a sociological concept with wide historical applicability. In addition to his political focus on achieving the Genocide Convention, he began to develop a history of genocide; although he failed to finish this before he died in 1959 and it long remained unpublished, it has now been brought to light (Lemkin 2012). A major focus of his writing was genocide's colonial expressions, which were overlooked in the early development of the academic field, although even *Axis Rule* contained the seeds of the idea that genocide is inherently colonial and that colonialism tends to produce genocide (Lemkin 1944: xi).

As colonial genocide became a major area in the twenty-first-century expansion of genocide studies, the juxtaposition of colonial with Nazi genocide was disruptive for the narrow conceptual type to which the Holocaust standard led, which militated against recognizing genocide as a complex historian phenomenon. The colonial destruction of indigenous peoples did not fit well with ideal type of "mega-genocide" (Levene 2005a: 163), that is, very large-scale, state-centric destruction, driven by an extreme political regime with a tight racial ideology. Rather, colonial genocide included many relatively discrete, smaller-scale episodes – Moses (2000) argued that Australia alone saw over 600 – often directed more by local settlers, administrators, military units and paramilitaries than by a central imperial state, and informed by racial ideologies that were not always fully specified in state policy.

In order to describe the patterns of colonial genocide, scholars therefore produced new descriptive and explanatory concepts. Leo Kuper (1981: 32) reconceptualized the local expression of genocide (destruction of a group "in part", as the convention puts it) as a "genocidal massacre"; Tony Barta (1987) examined colonial Australian society in structural terms, as constituted by "relations of genocide"; while Michael Mann (2005: 70–110) analysed successive "waves" of localized episodes in North America. In my own work, reflecting Lemkin's view that genocide includes many different kinds of brutality, I generalized Kuper's term by proposing the concept of "genocidal violence" to include genocidal expulsions, rapes, detentions and torture as well as massacres (Shaw 2013: 6).

The genocidal dimensions of colonialism and imperialism also concerned more than the "settler colonialism" on which both scholarly and popular discussion focused. They included the widespread destruction of indigenous societies to provide slaves; the continuing processes of social destruction within colonial slave societies; the destruction, at least in part, of indigenous societies during conquest even where settlement was not widespread, often because of a combination of intentional violence and unintended effects such as disease; and, last but not least, the violent, sometimes countergenocidal, suppression of colonial rebellions.

Moreover, colonial genocide, taken as a whole, was only one side of the role of empires and the interimperial system in genocide. If the world dominion of the European, and later US and Japanese, empires included systematic brutality against colonized peoples, it also culminated in large-scale genocides during the interimperial wars of the twentieth century. When the empires' rivalries erupted into the two world wars, turning in on Europe and Asia, they produced the classical party-state type of genocide.

The emergence of this type reflected the synergy between the new "total" war produced by industrialized weaponry and mass armies and the new forms of militarized, "totalitarian" mass politics that it in turn produced: the militarized party-state, in its archetypal fascist and Stalinist forms, was a product of the first pan-European experience of total war from 1914 to 1918. The new warfare generally involved a strategic tendency to destroy civilian populations, including by "democratic" states. However, the party-state type of genocide was a particular form of this warfare, in which particular racialized populations were attacked as enemies in themselves, even if it was often combined with other forms.

From postcolonial to post-Cold War genocide

While one effect of placing colonial genocide alongside the Nazi case is to suggest that genocide is a much more differentiated phenomenon than often assumed, another is to point to the need for a larger macrohistorical perspective, which can explain the links between the principal types. And while we can posit "colonial" and "party-state" as the major types of genocide in the first half of the twentieth century, linked through the interimperial system, they partially lose their purchase when we grapple with the late twentieth-century period of Cold War and decolonization, let alone the period from the end of the Cold War to the present day.

Certainly, Communist regimes in China, Cambodia and North Korea carried the party-state model of genocide into the third quarter of the century and beyond, while colonial genocide took new forms in the wars of decolonization in Vietnam, Algeria and elsewhere. However, different patterns also emerged as nationalist movements, often drawing on ethnic and religious identities, fought for control over the postcolonial state or to break it up. Wars of secession, of which Pakistan's from India and Israel's from Palestine in the late 1940s were early new cases, provided a frame for genocidal violence in places such as Nigeria, East Pakistan, Sudan and Ethiopia. Overall, there was a shift in the locus of genocide: after three-quarters of a century of European genocide culminating in the massive episodes of the Second World War, the problem more or less disappeared from the continent in the late 1940s, only to become a major issue across the postcolonial Third World.

The postcolonial genocides partly echoed their colonial predecessors. They were often less state-centric and more demotic than party-state cases, and they often saw genocidal violence from more than one side. Because they were different from the European stereotype in these ways, few made the grade in most versions of the genocide canon. Yet death tolls of hundreds of thousands were almost commonplace, from the Indian Partition to the killing of Indonesia's Communists in 1965, Biafra in 1966 and Bengal in 1971, to Cambodia from 1975 to 1979. Indeed, if we count the terror-famine of Mao Zedong's Great Leap Forward – as we should, because the destruction of peasant communities was an original intention and the resulting starvation became policy – at their highest they reached the tens of millions, dwarfing even the Holocaust (Dikötter 2010). Alongside these partly overlooked peaks of mass killing there were large genocidal expulsions, destroying historic communities, and many episodes with killings on a lesser scale.

The end of the Cold War brought further shifts in the pattern. Some were obviously related to this major geopolitical change: the implosions of the multinational Communist states, like the earlier disintegrations of the Ottoman and Tsarist empires, led to wars that widely involved genocidal expulsions both in former Yugoslavia and in the former Soviet Union.

Other cases were indirectly related to the end of the Cold War, such as a series of genocidal episodes in Iraq: the Saddam regime's terrorizing of Iraq's Kurdish population in 1991; US-promoted UN sanctions that caused mass death in the late 1990s; and the low-level, genocidal civil war between Sunni- and Shia-based militias – each of which murdered civilians from the other group and expelled them from the areas of Baghdad that they controlled – after the US invasion of 2003.

However, the new pattern of genocide, including these cases, involved more than geopolitical shifts. The end of the Cold War was also a moment of widespread democratization, as authoritarian systems crumbled not only in Communist but also in Western client states. Mann (2005) argued that democracy was the larger context of modern violence against civilian populations: democratizing societies were more genocide-prone than stable authoritarian regimes, even if states became less democratic as their genocides escalated. Geopolitical change, war and conflict provoked violence, but democratization created instability and gave populations a larger role: since the "demos" was often identified with the dominant group, ethnic and religious minorities were targeted. Democratization was a key factor in the post-Yugoslav and post-Soviet genocides, as it was in Rwanda.

In the era of democratization, elections were often focal points for genocidal violence. This was by no means new: the rise of fascism in Italy and Germany had combined electoral campaigning and paramilitary violence, as had the competition between Congress and the Muslim League that culminated in the murderous expulsions of the Indian Partition. But with the end of the Cold War, authoritarian regimes increasingly felt the need to legitimize themselves through electoral processes; elections were often rigged or stolen, leading to protest, repression, expulsions and killing. Parties often represented competing ethnic or religious groups, so that contested electoral outcomes represented as "sectarian" or "intercommunal" were initiated by political activists and militias. The distinction between "ethnic" and "political" groups, which the Genocide Convention's drafters had assumed capable of objective definition, often made little sense where the effective boundaries of ethnicity were established through the formation of rival, pan-ethnic electoral coalitions, as in Kenya during the violence following the stolen election of 2007, in which a thousand died and half a million were forced from their homes (International Crisis Group 2008).

Another increasingly important context was conflict centred on religion. Although both geopolitical and democratizing trends played their part, the extreme violence of first al-Qaida and then Daesh (ISIS) targeted nonbelievers as well as other Muslims, leading to the genocidal Islamic State (IS), which controlled territory across Iraq and Syria after 2014. Their violence was most often categorized as "terrorist", but it had a clear genocidal component, from al-Qaida's mass targeting of American civilians in its 9/11 attacks in 2001 to IS's massacres and enslavement of Yezidis in 2014. Yet IS's brutalities were committed in the context of a civil war in which the Syria regime, targeting opposition-supporting populations and especially the Sunni majority, was responsible for most deaths. Islamism was far from being the sole context of genocidal violence, as some Western ideologues believed.

Genocide in the 2020s

On the surface, genocide continued in the early 2020s in the pattern of the post-Cold War period: most cases arose from civil wars in postcolonial states, and the involvement of greater powers constituted at most secondary interventions. The case that was most fully recognized was that of the Rohingya, hundreds of thousands of whom were murderously expelled from their homes by Myanmar's military regime during 2016–17 (Ibrahim 2018). This group had long been denied citizenship, despite a population having existed since pre-colonial times, but now the majority were forced into displaced person camps and then to refugee camps in neighbouring states, principally Bangladesh, where most still languished a decade later. The regime, together with some local Buddhists in Rakhine state, thus carried out a comprehensive "erasure" of Rohingya society (MacLean 2019), with the complicity of much of the Buddhist-nationalist democratic opposition, notoriously including the Nobel Peace Prize winner Aun San Syu Ki. Even after the regime reneged on promises of democratization and a wider insurgency developed, an opposition armed group, the Arakan Army, joined in targeting the remaining Rohingya in 2024.

The Rohingya genocide gained greater traction in the international legal system than other recent cases, since it was recognized through the Gambia's pathbreaking genocide case. The small West African state was able to secure provisional measures instructing Myanmar to refrain from acts of genocide (International Court of Justice 2020). The Gambia's intervention did not lead to a radical improvement of the situation of the remaining Rohingya within Myanmar, but it increased the profile and credibility of the genocide arguments and attention to the plight of the refugees. It also showed that even in international law, violent mass expulsion could be considered a means of genocide.

While targeted violence against civilian population groups in other wars did not receive the same legal recognition as genocide, several also represented plausible cases. The Syrian regime of Bashar al-Assad responded to a pro-democracy uprising in 2011 with extensive bombardments of opposition-supporting civilian populations, primarily Sunnis, culminating in massacres perpetrated with chemical weapons in 2013. In Yemen, a Saudi-led coalition, intervening to defeat an insurgency, systematically targeted civilian populations in what Bachman (2019) also argues constitutes a case of genocide.

Similarly, wars in Ethiopia and Sudan, both reviving earlier conflicts, involved widespread genocidal violence. In the 2020–22 war over control of Ethiopia's Tigray province, Ethiopian and Eritrean state forces, their Amhara militia allies and the opposing Tigrayan nationalists all targeted atrocities at enemy civilian populations, including massacres, extrajudicial killings, rape and expulsions (Ibreck & de Waal 2021: 85–8; New Lines Institute 2024). In Sudan, genocidal massacres and mass expulsions were committed in the new civil war that began in 2023, six months before the Gaza war-genocide, between the Sudanese Armed Forces and the Rapid Support Forces (RSF). Many atrocities, especially in Darfur, were directed at the non-Arab Masalit people by the RSF and its allies the Janjaweed, which had been responsible for much of the genocide in the region 20 years earlier (the Sudanese government brought a case against the United Arab Emirates, for supporting the RSF, to the ICJ in 2025). War rape appeared to have been widely committed by both sides, and both used starvation as a tactic, leading to famine as in Gaza. In its dying days, the Biden administration – even as it supplied new weapons for Israel's genocide – recognized RSF genocide in Sudan.

In these conflicts, the combination of genocidal targeting with often wanton military destruction and the restriction of food and other supplies caused famine and huge forced movements of population: up to ten million were reported to have been displaced in Sudan by late 2024. Although war crimes were widely recognized (the ICC was investigating both cases), the allegations of genocide were often lost in the perception that these were complex and messy conflicts with diverse actors, easily hidden within the familiar narrative of "humanitarian disaster".

The new conflict during 2022–3 over Nagorno-Karabakh (Gavin 2025), the Armenian-majority enclave within Azerbaijan, differed from these others because it was openly fought between the two recognized states. This was a violent resurgence of a conflict that had earlier included a violent pogrom of Armenians in Sumgait, a city in Azerbaijan proper, in 1988, and a massacre of Azeri civilians by Armenian troops in Khojali, another Azerbaijani city, in 1992. In 2020, an Azerbaijani attack regained all the Armenian-occupied territories and occupied one-third of Nagorno-Karabakh, and during 2022–3, Azerbaijan used a blockade to prevent food, fuel and medicines entering the rump Armenian enclave (the Republic of Artsakh), before launching a new offensive that destroyed the statelet and led to the flight of almost all the Armenian population.

Thus, in a matter of months, Azerbaijan succeeded in destroying the remaining Armenian society in Nagorno-Karabakh and integrating the territory, minus most of its population, into its own state. This Armenian disaster in 2023, easily pigeonholed as "ethnic cleansing" since the death toll of hundreds was small in comparison to the 100,000 expelled – even Armenia' lawyers in the ICJ characterized it as such – occupies a distinctive position in the spectrum of contemporary genocide. Like the Russian assault on Ukraine, it was intended to eliminate a culturally distinct society; but unlike the former campaign, it was completely successful.

Unfortunately for the Armenians, their state's marginality and the strategic importance of Azerbaijan meant that – especially as Ukraine consumed international attention to the post-Soviet region – this case gained little recognition, and Azerbaijan hardly paid a political price for the destruction it caused. Yet it stood as a reminder that the classic mid-twentieth-century paradigm of statist genocide during interstate war had not lost its relevance, and that Ukraine and Gaza were not simple outliers.

Genocide in the new era of great power rivalry and authoritarianism

The real paradigm shift in the 2020s was that genocide was being perpetrated not only in divided entities and by second-order states but also by a great power, Russia, and a key US ally, Israel: genocide had returned to strategically central global conflicts. Just as Azerbaijan openly sought the elimination of Nagorno-Karabakh, Russia and Israel were by their own admissions seeking the destruction of Ukraine and Gaza, supported by China and the USA respectively. Meanwhile China continued to systematically suppress the Uyghurs and eliminate their distinct identity, in a case also widely considered genocidal (Smith Finley 2020). Although in most genocidal conflicts in the present century, regional powers have been involved directly and global powers indirectly, in Ukraine and Gaza, the major world powers played key roles.

These developments underlined how far genocide had returned to the centre of the international system as the second quarter of the century began. The hopes of the 1990s, when the UN established criminal tribunals for the former Yugoslavia and Rwanda and "humanitarian intervention" was in vogue, and the 2000s, the era of R2P, had now largely disappeared. On a clear-headed assessment, of course, the roots of the return were already present in the earlier period. The USA, Russia and China were never fully committed to a world order based on law, even in the limited sense that it was proclaimed, and none of them signed up to the ICC.

New students of genocide tend to ask, when confronted with the inadequacies of the Genocide Convention, "Couldn't it be revised?" Even at the turn of the century that seemed a very unlikely prospect, but it is now a complete fantasy. Great powers that are directly or indirectly responsible for some of the major ongoing episodes of genocide are hardly going to improve the legal framework that could bring them to account, let alone replace it with something that would catch even more of their anti-civilian violence, as Dirk Moses' proposal for an international crime of "permanent security" is intended to do.

The hardening geopolitics of the great powers has gone hand in hand with repression and genocidal tendencies. In the case of Putin's Russian Federation, the brutal internal repression of Chechnya was followed by more aggressive and genocidal international policies: first in its Georgian invasion of 2008 and then in its hybrid war and annexations in Ukraine in 2014. The Tiananmen Square massacre of 1989, arguably an episode of political genocide, meant that China's modernization also had a stubbornly authoritarian cast, and after 2012 Xi Jinping's more dictatorial regime sharpened the repression of the Uyghurs and suppressed the democratic forces in Hong Kong. Moreover, the new Sino-Russian axis also helped rehabilitate the totalitarian North Korean regime, responsible for a genocidal famine in the 1990s.

Yet it was not only in the East that more extreme politics was arising. Across the West, the democratic promise of the early post-Cold War era increasingly gave way to a new political environment in which right-wing authoritarianism flourished, with more extreme policies against migrants, refugees and minorities. The first decade of new far-right governments, in Trump's USA, Brexit Britain, Hungary and Italy, did not widely produce genocide; the Bolsonaro regime's extension of historic settler genocide in Brazil was an exception. However, genocidal rhetoric flourished in the online "alt-right" scene and was increasingly normalized by political leaders.

By the mid-2020s, the revival of the historic link between right-wing authoritarianism and genocide was no longer mainly discursive. First, Israel's far-right government, in which genocidal ideologues were prominent, committed the first genocide by a Western state in the twenty-first century and succeeded in involving Biden's USA and the major European democracies in supporting it. Second, Trump's new administration immediately produced a new genocidal threat to the Palestinians with his proposal that the USA should take over the Gaza genocide, permanently expel the entire population and establish the beachfront realm of "Trump Gaza". Trump followed this up by proposing to abandon the Ukrainians to Putin. Genocide was further normalized in world politics.

4
DYNAMICS OF WAR AND GENOCIDE IN UKRAINE

As we have seen, the return of the genocide idea really began after Russia launched its new invasion of Ukraine on 24 February 2022. At first, Ukrainian and international actors mostly charged Russia with war crimes and crimes against humanity, and these were soon under investigation (United Nations 2022; Office of the Prosecutor General, Ukraine 2022; Marchuk 2022). There was also concern about the overall character the war, which focused on the case that since Russia's invasion was an act of aggression, President Vladimir Putin and other senior leaders should be charged before a special international tribunal (Woolfson 2022; Green, Henderson & Ruys 2022; Kreß 2022; Heller 2022).

However, as the severity of Russia's assault became clear, a genocide case also emerged: as early as 9 March 2022, President Volodymyr Zelensky called the bombings of a children's hospital and maternity ward in Mariupol "proof the genocide of Ukrainians is taking place". Yet it was when atrocities at Bucha and elsewhere were revealed in early April 2022 that such charges became widespread (Kursani 2022: 4–5). Zelensky now referred to Russia's new campaign in general as "genocide" involving "the elimination of a whole nation of people"; in May he alleged that it was carrying out "a genocide" through deportations and mass killings in the Donbas (Saul 2022; Kursani 2022: 5–7). His terminology was echoed by President Biden, and investigations into Russian atrocities led Clint Williamson, an adviser to the Atrocity Crimes Advisory Group for Ukraine established by the USA, EU and UK, to say that there were "very compelling indications that we are seeing a genocide" (Kumar Sen 2022).

These allegations had deep historical resonance; Ukraine's foreign ministry soon linked Russia's policies to historic Stalinist genocide in the country: "On the 90th anniversary of the ... Holodomor in Ukraine, Russia's genocidal war of aggression pursues the same goal as during the 1932–1933 genocide: the elimination of the Ukrainian nation and its statehood" (Ukrainska Pravda 2022). Yet although these claims generally referenced the crime as it was understood in international law, Ukraine did not bring a case alleging Russian genocide to the ICJ, even as it successfully challenged Russia's own use of genocide as a pretext for its invasion (International Court of Justice 2022; Marchuk & Wanigasuriya 2022). Russia's specious claim was the original focus of debate about "genocide" in the war, which was then superseded by the debate about Russia's actions (Kursani 2022).

While the new charges of genocide were largely prompted by the character of the Russian atrocities, they called in evidence Putin's (2021) denials of the existence and the right to exist of a Ukrainian nation and state in a lengthy essay on his website, which were widely elaborated by Russian propagandists and on social media (Harding 2022: 23–39; Garner 2022). The historian Timothy Snyder (2022) argued that Putin's language was "openly" and "clearly" genocidal, concluding from a survey based on multiple criteria that "the evidence for intent here is very clear by historical standards. It's very clear, unusually clear. The danger is that because there's so much evidence of intent, we start expecting even more, even clearer proof." Indeed, this genocidal thinking did not come out of the blue: previously marginal nationalist intellectuals had developed it over several decades before it was mainstreamed by Putin and his propaganda machine (Lewis 2025: 19–50).

Some legal authorities broadly agreed with Snyder. The Ukrainian scholars Denis Azarov, Dmytro Koval, Gaiane Nuridzhanian and Volodymyr Venher (2022) argued that Putin's language demonstrated genocidal intent and was reflected in Russia's aims of destroying the country's cultural heritage, the forcible transfer and Russification of Ukrainian children, and the deliberate infliction of "conditions of life aimed at the physical destruction of the Ukrainian nation," which together contravened several clauses of the Genocide Convention. Irwin Cotler (2023), a former attorney general of Canada, argued that Russia's "direct and public incitement to genocide" was a standing breach of the convention, "whether or not acts of genocide follow"; that genocidal intent could be "inferred from Russia's planning and execution of mass atrocity crimes"; and that "the crime of aggression, the direct and public incitement to genocide, and the condition of mass atrocity crimes" had created "a risk of genocide", which state parties were under an obligation to prevent without waiting for the commission of genocide itself.

Yet the case against Russia also met with reasoned objections from legal scholars who believed that its actions failed to meet the formal threshold for genocide. Noëlle Quénivet (2022: 153) concluded that "[i]t seems difficult to argue that a genocide is being committed as, so far, no *dolus specialis*, i.e., the intent to destroy Ukrainians as a national or ethnical group as such, can be identified". William Schabas (2022: 15), author of a text on genocide in international law (Schabas 2000), argued that "neither side makes out a compelling case for genocide committed by its opponent"; while his equation of Ukraine's allegations with the propaganda of the aggressor was inappropriate, his substantive argument echoed Quénivet's. Schabas added that those who "use the term 'genocide' without precise reference to a legal provision" were adopting a "Humpty Dumpty" approach, because without this reference "there can be no certainty as to what they mean" (2022: 14, 15). Yet he seemed blind to both the powerful common understanding of genocide and the possibility of intellectually coherent alternatives to the dominant legal conceptions.

Even in spring 2022, there was dissatisfaction with these terms of debate. The international lawyer Philippe Sands (2022) remarked that Lemkin "would be horrified ... by the parsing of words, the distracting fights over the labelling of such abject cruelty and the placing of his term on a perch so high that the legal meaning of 'genocide' is held apart from its ordinary conception". Dirk Moses (2022) noted that Lemkin's definition of genocide, which included the "crippling" as well as the extermination of nations, "reflects the lived experience of mixed population of Ukrainians, Poles and Jews living serially under Russian, Polish, German and Soviet rule on the territory of modern Ukraine during the 20th century, enduring multiple phases of genocide and ethnic cleansing"; he concluded that "Russia's campaign against Ukraine is precisely what Lemkin was trying to capture with his new word".

However, Moses (2022) also underlined that states had not followed Lemkin's definition in agreeing the convention, and argued that the uncertainty about whether Russia's violence counted as "genocide" revealed not only the limits of international law but also the problematic role of the concept itself: "It is time to rethink the obsession with linking that reaction solely to genocide, and to reimagine a threshold of shocking criminality that does not require analogies with Nazi Germany and the Holocaust." Thus, even as Moses linked the return of the genocide idea to its origins in Lemkin's 1944 writing, he repeated his challenge to the genocide canon.

"Genocide" in an analytical framework of Russia's war in Ukraine

Although academic debate on genocide and Ukraine would continue during 2023–4, the political and media debates died down after their April 2022 peak. This might appear paradoxical, since the remainder of 2022 saw the most dramatic phase of the war, culminating in Ukraine's liberation in November of the southern city of Kherson, the most important that Russia had captured. Yet this successful military resistance partially superseded the images of victimization that Mariupol and Bucha had conveyed, providing fertile ground for the genocide case. Although Ukraine did not maintain its advances through 2023 – and during 2024–5 was under severe pressure from the larger Russian forces – the offensives of mid and late 2022 substantially shifted the general terms of the debate. As the conflict appeared to settle into a grim war of attrition, Ukrainian advocates seemed to resort less to the genocide case and the state still did not bring a case to the ICJ.

In this situation, does the analytical genocide case advanced in my article on "Russia's genocidal war" (Shaw 2023a) stand up? At the beginning of 2023, it was only possible to take account of the first year's events. It is now necessary to update the analysis in the light of subsequent developments and research. Therefore, this chapter first resumes the original analysis, and then extends it and modifies the early conclusions. The original aim was to develop a critical approach to the debate on Russian "genocide" in Ukraine in three ways.

First, to critique the misplaced precision contained in the dominant legal understandings of genocidal "intent" invoked by the sceptical writers, through an examination of the Bosnian case in the ICJ that was central to their arguments.

Second, to treat Putin's genocidal mentality not as a definitive framework for establishing the character of Russia's campaign but only as a starting point for analysing its genocidal elements: the relationship between this ideology and its concrete plans, beginning with the original scheme for the invasion, were examined.

Third, to emphasize the significance of the Ukrainian resistance, which turned the conflict into a major war, for the question of genocide; it was proposed that the genocidal character of Russia's war had grown as it escalated, with its violence radicalizing into a more comprehensive assault on the foundations of social life across much of Ukraine.

The article therefore addressed the genocidal elements of the conflict as dynamic and closely related to its military logic, rather than in an abstract manner that treated Russia's intentions as fixed, and assumed that genocidal and military intentions were distinct. It argued that the genocidal elements of Russia's campaign had quickly changed from the elite destruction and brutal Russification envisaged in the original plans towards the more comprehensive social destruction pursued as the war developed during its first year. The article therefore proposed that the relevant analytical framework was that of a "genocidal war" rather than the freestanding campaign of destruction implied by talking of "a genocide".

Genocidal intent and the lessons of Bosnia

Pushback against the idea that Russia was committing genocide was predictable in the light of how legal authorities had understood the intention required to prove it. Defined as committed when certain "acts" (not only killing but also other types of violence and coercion) are carried out with the intent to destroy a protected population group ("as such" and "in whole or in part"), the crime, as originally specified by the Genocide Convention, had been incorporated in the statutes of international courts and elaborated in case law in recent decades.

There was little dispute that many of the acts that Russia committed corresponded to those that may constitute genocide; differences as to the extent of potentially genocidal acts were not central to the 2022 debate. The commentators who argued that genocide charges probably could not be brought successfully did not generally dispute the factual bases of the genocide case, or that Ukrainians could be legally protected as a "national group". Rather, they contended that the atrocities committed in 2022 did not demonstrate the intention to destroy Ukrainians "as such" to the exclusion of other possible interpretations.

This argument rested heavily on an interpretation of the judgement of the ICJ (International Court of Justice 2007a) in the case brought by Bosnia-Herzegovina against Yugoslavia and eventually defended by Serbia as the successor state, although this drew on earlier jurisprudence from the ICTY. "The problem", Noëlle Quénivet (2022: 151–2) summarized, was that in this case the ICJ offered "a very narrow interpretation of the level and type of evidence necessary to demonstrate genocidal intent". They explained (she quoted) that "[i]t is not enough that the members of the group are targeted because they belong to that group, that is because the perpetrator has a discriminatory intent. Something more is required. The acts listed in Article ii must be done with intent to destroy the group as such in whole or in part." The majority of judges in the ICJ only accepted, she noted,

> that the later part of the siege of Srebrenica and especially the ensuing events [the 1995 massacre] qualified as genocide as the aim was to eliminate the Bosnian Muslim communities living there and the Bosnian Serb forces "not only knew that the combination of the killings of the men with the forcible transfer of the women, children and elderly, would inevitably result in the physical disappearance of the Bosnian Muslim population of Srebrenica, but clearly intended through these acts to physically destroy this group."

The application of such standards to the siege of Mariupol, Quénivet concluded, was "unlikely" to lead to a verdict that genocide had been carried out. Hers was a plausible conclusion from the judgement, but the ICJ's understanding of Bosnia was not just "narrow"; from a historical point of view its conclusion bordered on the perverse, explaining away as non-genocidal the extensive pattern in which Serbian nationalists deliberately destroyed Bosnian Muslim and Croat communities during the three years *before* the 1995 massacre. The Serbian campaign in Bosnia had begun in 1992, following a similar campaign in Croatia from 1991, and was the basis on which Bosnia-Herzegovina originally brought the case to the ICJ in 1993, when the Srebrenica massacre had not yet occurred. As the court's vice-president, Judge Awn Shawkat Al-Khasawneh, argued in a dissenting judgement, the majority, in refusing to infer genocide from the Serbians' "consistent pattern of conduct", was "disregarding in this respect a rich and relevant jurisprudence of other courts" (International Court of Justice 2007b).

From the beginning of the war, Serbian forces – which initially comprised elements of the Yugoslav National Army together with paramilitary groups under the control of Belgrade – had demonstrated their intention of destroying the non-Serb element of the population. When they assembled for their Bosnian campaign in 1992, Gerard Toal and Carl Dahlman (2011: 113) show, "their task was to militarily seize territory proclaimed as Serb land and systematically round up non-Serbs for execution, internment, and expulsion"; from the start, "Muslim and Croat residents were murdered, imprisoned, or expelled", and most of the non-Serb population was quickly removed from Serbian-controlled territory. Throughout the war and afterwards, Bosnian-Serbian forces, which later became more autonomous from Serbia, attempted to consolidate and extend these successes from 1992 to 1993.

The court argued (International Court of Justice 2007a: 123) that "deportation or displacement of the members of a group, even if effected by force, is not necessarily equivalent to destruction of that group", but the Serbians' wholesale removal of the non-Serb population groups resulted from a deliberate policy of destroying the Muslim and Croat elements in society within the territory they controlled. Although they were not fully victorious in the war, this policy was largely successful: the 1996 Dayton agreement confirmed their control of Republika Srpska, the Bosnian entity they established through "ethnic cleansing". Non-Serb survivors were mostly unable to return despite complex international policies promoting this; indeed, displaced people were generally unable to return to areas where "their" ethnic group was a minority in the local postwar administration, including in Bosniak- and Croatian-controlled municipalities (Toal & Dahlman 2011: 293–320). Lemkin (1944: 81) had argued that "genocide is a new technique of occupation aimed at winning the peace even though the war itself is lost", and the permanence of ethnic removal in Bosnia, largely evident by 2007, confirmed this insight.

The ICJ's was not the only possible conclusion in the light of the Genocide Convention, but it was constructed around a critical incoherence in that document, where the "destruction" of a group appears to be defined in "physical" terms but this requirement is not clearly explained. The crucial preamble to Article II refers to "acts committed with intent to destroy, in whole or in part, a national, ethnical, racial or religious group, as such". It does not say that "destroying" a group means the "physical" destruction of the members of the group, and the lists of acts which complete the article include non-physical means of group destruction as well as killing and other physical harm. However, paragraph II(c) – ironically that which gives the broadest indication of the role of these non-physical means – refers to "deliberately inflicting on the group conditions of life calculated to bring about its physical destruction in whole or in part".

This clause therefore confusingly not only allows the role of non-physical means in producing group destruction but also specifies that destruction itself in physical terms. In this logic, destroying the social, economic, cultural and political life of a collectivity is not genocidal in itself but only when it is intended to lead to "physical destruction". The latter is understood to include not only direct killing but also death which is produced indirectly (e.g. by starvation) and the "biological" elimination of groups, for example through the transfer of children to another group.

It is important to emphasize that this understanding, now embedded in international law, is sociologically unsound. As social collectivities, national, ethnic and similar groups are not biologically constituted and are more than the sum of their individual members; they are, as Benedict Anderson (1983) famously described nations, "imagined communities". Collectivities of this type *cannot* be destroyed purely through the physical destruction of their members' bodies; killing members may undoubtedly assist group destruction, but full destruction is ultimately unrealizable through this means alone. Even where most putative members of a target group are exterminated, a collectivity is likely to survive, since mass killing generally serves to strengthen the determination of survivors and others to maintain its culture and traditions, as Jews showed after the Holocaust. Total physical destruction is a genocidal fantasy.

This dominant legal understanding inverts the typical historical relationship: as Benjamin Valentino (2005: 3) argues, perpetrators "seldom view killing as an end in itself"; it "is most accurately viewed as an instrumental policy" in a strategic perspective which usually involves a range of methods. Indeed, Lemkin (1944: xi–xii) had originally elaborated no fewer than eight main techniques of the Nazi genocide, including political, social, cultural, economic, biological, physical, religious and moral as well as "physical" destruction. In a more sociologically coherent view, the destruction of a group's culture, institutions, social networks, ways of life and territorial presence is considered genocidal in itself, rather than simply as means to physical destruction (Shaw 2015: 19–22, 50–52).

In the Bosnia case, the ICJ (International Court of Justice 2007a: 5) upheld in principle the dual understanding expressed in the Genocide Convention's paragraph II(c). It allowed that the wider pattern of violence across the country before the 1995 massacre – in its words, both "massive killings" and "massive mistreatment, beatings, rape and torture", as well as population removal – could have been held to constitute genocide, if proved to be driven by the intention to "physically" destroy the group. However, the court compounded the incoherence at the heart of the convention by deciding to rule out such a finding, through a claim that the required intent could not be proved in any other specific instances or the wider pattern as a whole, as it could in the case of Srebrenica.

The device that enabled this argument was a further exaggeration of the significance of "physical" destruction, in which it became not only the defining feature of genocide but also the prime criterion of the "special" intent required to prove the crime: an idea that was not only criticized by social scientists but also becoming increasingly controversial among legal scholars (Ambos 2010). This translated the quantitative difference between Srebrenica and previous massacres into a qualitative difference.

By the time of the Ukraine invasion, William Schabas (2022: 8) regarded this circular move as a legal norm, arguing that, "[a]lthough 'killing members of the group' is only one of the five punishable acts of genocide, it has a particular importance in proving genocidal intent given that international case law has insisted that the intended destruction be physical in nature". Moreover, he argued that:

> The greatest challenge in establishing whether genocide has been committed by Russian forces during the attack on Ukraine. ... is not a question of demonstrating the plausibility or even the likelihood of genocidal intent but rather of eliminating other explanations. Given what is known of the facts, it would seem difficult to conclude that the intent to destroy physically the people of Ukraine is the only reasonable explanation for Russia's military activities.

This also reflected the approach of the ICTY in criminal cases concerning Bosnia, including most recently against the Serbian leader Radovan Karadzic, in which inferences of genocidal intention were required to be the "only reasonable inference" (Ambos 2016), a standard that Sands (2022) argued was "impossibly high".

In principle, the ICJ was not mistaken in believing that perpetrators' intentions might change. The expectation that, in a lengthy historical episode, a singular intention must lie behind all the actions of a collective actor such as a state or an army is ahistorical. It is normal for the intentions of such actors (and of individuals within them) to be complex, varied and conflicting, and if genocidal intentions exist in the context of a war, it is inevitable that they are combined with more conventional military intentions. Genocidal plans often also develop in more radical and murderous directions over time: Valentino (2005: 3) argues that mass killing is often a "final solution" because "it is usually the last of a series of efforts to solve [the perpetrators'] problems by other means"; similarly, Mann (2005: 7) argues that intentions tend to radicalize as situations become more extreme, so that the most murderous violence "is rarely the initial intent of perpetrators" but "typically emerges as a kind of 'Plan C'" after other plans fail.

In Bosnia-Herzegovina, the Srebrenica massacre, involving larger-scale murder than previous atrocities, exemplified this pattern. However, the ICJ was mistaken in concluding that the possibility of non-genocidal inferences for earlier Serbian actions meant that genocidal intentions could not be proved. Even for the Srebrenica massacre, other inferences – for example, the military advantage of eliminating potential anti-Serbian fighters – were possible, but the court did not consider that they invalidated the assumption that genocide was intended. On these bases, the court arrived at an interpretation of genocide in Bosnia that was implausible in the light of the historical record, since the 1995 massacre was clearly an escalation of the previous pattern rather than a departure from it.

Yet what the judgement lacked in intellectual coherence it compensated for in political relevance, and it is difficult to resist the conclusion that it was at least partly for political reasons that the ICJ found it necessary to deny a tight connection between Srebrenica and the earlier pattern. This judgement gave something to both sides: Bosnia-Herzegovina welcomed the recognition that genocide had been committed at Srebrenica, while the Serbian state escaped with an attribution of merely indirect responsibility for its failure to prevent the Bosnian-Serbian army from committing the massacre, which could not have been argued of earlier atrocities committed by forces more closely controlled by Belgrade. A broader genocide finding would necessarily have recognized deeper complicity on the part of Serbia, which in 2007 under a post-Milošević government was being drawn into the Western orbit, and so would have been unwelcome to the Western powers whose support was essential to international courts as well as to Russia, which had backed Serbia in the war.

The lesson from this discussion is not that there are no legal routes to establishing Russian genocide in Ukraine. However, this jurisprudence clearly provides judges with means to avoid, possibly for political reasons, genocide determinations that might be justified in a coherent understanding of the crime. It is therefore necessary to step back from questions of the applicability of the law and address the question of Russian intentions unconstrained by legal technicality.

Russia's intentions in February 2022

Although Alexander Etkind (2022: 1) has argued that the genocidal aspects of Russia's war – which included "mass murders and deportations combined with intentional destruction of their cultural sites (monuments, museums, theatres, and so on), educational facilities, and history textbooks" – were "preplanned and intentional" since 2014, its specific aims in 2022 represented a radical shift.

Indeed, Russia's intentions towards Ukraine had demonstrably changed during the long period of Putin's rule. "Uncertainty about Russian objectives and military designs" was, Dominique Arel and Jesse Driscoll (2022: 38) argue, a defining feature in the conflict during 2014–22. For example, Russia's move to send troops into Crimea in February 2014, hours after the sudden removal of Ukraine's pro-Russian president, Viktor Yanukovych, suggested "a decision that was not fully premeditated", while its subsequent intervention in the Donbas provoked a coalition of local elites to challenge Ukrainian rule. "Contra Crimea", Arel and Driscoll (2022: 100, 150) conclude, "no evidence has emerged indicating a coherent plan for military intervention" in the Donbas at this stage, although Russian deployment of personnel and heavy weapons then helped escalate the conflict.

Therefore, Russia's 2022 invasion manifested *new* intentions towards Ukraine – after six further years of stalemated war – but these were shrouded in deliberate ambiguity. Despite Putin's genocidal mentality, his declared aims, which included "denazification", "demilitarization", ending the "genocide" in the Donbas and protecting Russia from NATO "aggression", were characterized by what Luke Harding (2022: 307) calls "fuzziness". To evaluate their genocidal character, we therefore need to examine how these general ideas were expressed in *concrete* plans and decisions, both at the beginning of the campaign and in the subsequent war. Although Nataliya Bugayova (2022) claims that "the Kremlin's intent regarding Ukraine is maximalist, inflexible, and will not change in the foreseeable future", what we need to address is precisely the apparent radicalization of Russia's policies towards Ukrainian society during 2022.

In his survey of genocidal radicalization, Mann (2005: 7) argues that "we must analyze the unintended consequences of a series of interactions yielding escalation". In the Russian case, this implies examining the consequences of the unexpectedly strong Ukrainian resistance, which led them to escalate their intended rapid invasion into a large-scale destructive war. It was not only Russia's leaders who underestimated Ukraine: Western experts also generally believed that Russia would easily prevail (Cohen & O'Brien 2024). As in Bosnia, while genocidal intentions were evident from the beginning of the invasion, Russian actions radicalized beyond their initial plans in a way that transformed their scope.

Russia's tangible goals in February 2022 were not explicit, but analysis by Mykhaylo Zabrodskyi *et al.* (2022: 10), based partly on captured Russian papers, shows that Russia aimed to swiftly establish full control over most of Ukraine, with the installation of a puppet regime in Kyiv together with "the coerced cooperation of regional governors and local authorities" in the occupied areas. In the light of Russia's expectation that it would quickly conquer much of the country, it envisaged violence to destroy the Ukrainian elite and force the bulk of the population into submission.

To support the first aim, the FSB, Russia's federal security service, was tasked with "kill-or-capture missions" against national and local officials, who were categorized as (1) those to be physically liquidated; (2) those in need of suppression and intimidation; (3) "neutrals" who could be induced to collaborate; and (4) those already prepared to collaborate. The capture of individuals in the first category included, the plans indicated, both "the murder of Ukraine's executive branch" and putting "on trial to be executed" many of those involved in the 2014 Revolution of Dignity (Euromaidan), which had specially offended Putin. The plan to murder Ukrainian leaders was taken seriously by international leaders, and Putin found it necessary to inform the then Israeli prime minister, Naftali Bennett, in October 2022: "I won't kill Zelensky" (McKernan 2023). The second category would be broadened from the occupiers' initial lists though registration operations and "filtration" camps, "to intimidate people, to determine whether they needed to be displaced into Russia, and to lay the groundwork for records to monitor and disrupt resistance networks" (Zabrodskyi *et al.* 2022: 10–11).

Even in this original scenario, the euphemistically named "special military operation" would never have been conducted with respect for civilian life. The drive to capture Kyiv quickly included both missile attacks on civilian residential areas and the atrocities at Bucha and elsewhere, both of which must have been within the scope of the formal or informal guidelines for the operation. But since Russia hoped to capture the Ukrainian state largely intact, it initially "eschewed", Dara Massicot (2023) notes, direct attacks on the general conditions of life of Ukrainian society like the mass strikes against Ukraine's civilian infrastructure that became a major feature of its campaign later in 2022.

Putin's genocidal mentality was therefore reflected in specific ways in this attempted "blitzkrieg". Key elements of the Ukrainian national elite were targeted for physical elimination, some civilians would be victims of invasion atrocities that would terrorize the rest, and the general population would have been affected by brutal coercion together with the suppression of national institutions, language and culture. In this approach, Russia would have followed well-established methods of conquest, colonization and imperial rule that had been practised in Ukraine and elsewhere – together with more extreme violence – by the Soviet regime in the 1920s and 1930s (Applebaum 2017) as well as Nazi Germany during the Second World War.

Lemkin, who analysed the latter case, regarded both elite elimination and cultural suppression as techniques of genocide, since they were designed to destroy national groups, but as we have seen the Genocide Convention departed from this understanding by identifying genocide more with "physical" destruction and excluding "cultural genocide" as a specific dimension. As we have seen, some scholars have taken this tendency further, identifying genocide exclusively with the total mass murder of the target group – which would exclude its application to many widely recognized cases – and proposing the category of "politicide" to describe the elimination of political elites (Harff & Gurr 1988). However, this idea would fragment our understanding of what Russia aimed to achieve in February 2022: it targeted the political class not as a group in itself but as the elite of the Ukrainian state and nation, the structural elimination of which was its overriding goal.

This approach also dictated Russia's attitude to the population. As Arel and Driscoll (2022: 37) argue, "the identity markers distinguishing Ukrainians from Russians" were now "more political than cultural", having been reconfigured during the conflict of the previous decade. Therefore Russia did not attack Ukrainians based on a purely ethnic classification; indeed, although it aimed to suppress the Ukrainian language, it denied there was a distinct Ukrainian ethnicity. Rather, it attacked all those, including self-identified ethnic Russians and Russian speakers, who subscribed to the "Ukrainian political identity" that had come into its own in a new "supermajority" after the first phase of war during 2014–15 (Arel & Driscoll 2022: 19).

Just as Russian strategy towards local elites was based on their political loyalties and their degree of acquiescence in the occupation, so its policy towards the population was based on political and security criteria. How far actual violence would go was not fully specified in the invasion plans but would depend on how the Russification of Ukraine progressed. The Ukrainian people needed to be de-Ukrainianized, since Ukrainianism was, in the regime's eyes, a militaristic, Nazi ideology. If they did not submit it was a question, as prominent television propagandist Pavel Gubarev put it, of "exterminating as many Ukrainians as had to be exterminated" (Snyder 2022). "This is the logic", Snyder summarized: "We exterminate all the ones who think they're Ukrainians until we get to the point where the remaining people understand: they are Russians."

Genocidal radicalization in the escalating war, 2022–3

If Russia's original plan was genocidal in the terms outlined, it was not successful. Putin had grossly underestimated the determination and capacity of Ukraine's elites, military and population to resist the conquest, as well as of Western states to support them. Any discussion of Russia's genocide must therefore recognize that its actual violence in the first year after the invasion did not simply reflect its original plans or ideology but resulted from how its campaign escalated in response to resistance.

If the original scenario for the invasion had been realized, the character and extent of Russian violence would have probably have been much more limited than they actually became during 2022. The war quickly developed into the largest in Europe since 1945, with fundamentals "much the same", the military historian Lawrence Freedman (2022) argued, as those of the Second World War. Indeed, the industrial killing of soldiers, with each side claiming to have killed tens of thousands of the other's in a matter of months, echoed the First World War as much as the Second. While independent figures are lacking, there seems little doubt that a very high rate of military deaths occurred from the beginning of the war, with the Russian campaign "waged regardless of losses" and the Kremlin appearing "entirely indifferent to the deaths of its servicemen"; casualties were reported to have been buried in mass graves and even rubbish tips (Harding 2022: 217; Borger 2022).

Although civilians were targeted from the start, the Russian campaign radicalized its violence against them in the first year after the invasion. Analysis must certainly address how far civilians were "collateral damage" from the pursuit of military objectives and recognize that some may have died from military indifference, the use of inaccurate weapons and how "the circumstances of war made life dangerous" (Harding 2022: 294, 223). Even the destruction of Mariupol, the most murderous case, was an exercise in conquest: military in purpose despite its large-scale brutality. Yet Freedman (2022) makes the case that even from a military standpoint, anti-civilian violence was intentional: what was different from the Second World War, he argues, was "the precision of modern weapons"; but while "the Russians had a number of precision-guided weapons", instead of using them against military targets, they often "used them against civilian targets. ... [W]e are seeing a coercive Russian strategy against Ukrainian society", even the "terrorizing" of the population, as a means of winning the war.

As Russia escalated after it realized that its initial plans could not be achieved, the war's genocidal dimensions deepened and expanded. It transitioned from the initial project of decapitating and brutally subordinating Ukrainian society towards a partial attempt to destroy that society, so as to control its territory, if necessary as an almost empty shell within which a layer of imported officials would manage a diminished, cowed and partially imported population: "Ukraine without Ukrainians", as Kyiv mayor Vitali Klitschko put it (Dettmer 2022).

Some features of this process were escalations of elements envisaged in Russia's original plans:

1. The original physical brutality of the expanding occupation increased, including many instances of torture, rape and execution of civilians (Human Rights Watch 2022b). The occupied territories became "a space of exception, a lawless zone where there was almost complete immunity

for Russian soldiers to act as they saw fit", as David Lewis (2025: 133) puts it. In particular, although Ukraine's successful defence of Kyiv and other major cities meant that Russia captured few of the national leaders and high-profile political figures that it was targeting, well over a hundred mayors and other government officials were taken, of whom four were killed. More than half were in the region of Kherson, the one large city that was occupied and where civilian resistance was strongest (Lewis 2025: 133–4).

2. Detention and "filtration" of people deemed potentially hostile to the occupation became a general process. This included the forcible transfer of civilians to the Russian Federation, which amounted to "a war crime and a potential crime against humanity", as Human Rights Watch (2022a) described it. These included thousands of children, many of whom were held in a network of facilities where they were often subject to "re-education" as Russians. This raised issues under paragraph II(e) of the Genocide Convention, which lists "forcibly transferring children of the group to another group" as an act of genocide.
3. The planned suppression of the national culture was now expressed as violent cultural destruction, as Russian forces extensively "targeted Ukrainian museums, historical monuments, and places of worship that are of special significance for the self-image of the Ukrainian nation" (Azarov *et al.* 2022: 30).

However, other features may not have been originally intended, at least in the forms and extents that they occurred:

4. The invasion rapidly led to a massive depopulation of the conquered and threatened eastern and southern areas, and to a lesser extent of other regions, draining normal life out of communities of all sizes. Huge numbers, especially of women and children (under martial law, Ukraine prohibited most men aged 18–60 from leaving the country), fled to safer western areas (6.5 million were estimated to be internally displaced in late October 2022, an increase of over five million from the pre-February level) and neighbouring states and elsewhere in Europe (where almost eight million, around a fifth of the population, had registered as refugees by the end of 2022) and the rest of the world.
5. The Russian conquest of large parts of the east and south involved extensive destruction of social as well as physical infrastructure. When Russia razed Mariupol, it: extensively destroyed housing, workplaces and health and social facilities while killing a significant minority; drove out the majority of its 300,000 population; detained, "filtered" and "transferred" to Russia many of the remaining inhabitants; suppressed Ukrainian culture

and institutions; and rendered much of the city uninhabitable. This largely complete destruction of local society was repeated to a greater or lesser extent in other conquered cities and towns, hollowing out many centres much more completely than the initial depopulation prompted by fear. These experiences also demonstrated to Ukrainians in the rest of the country and the diaspora the near-impossibility of living under Russian occupation. Therefore, this escalation converted a conflict, which at the outset appeared still partly about how and under whose rule people would live in Ukraine, into an existential struggle over whether most Ukrainians could live in their country at all.

6. These stakes were confirmed when, in the wake of Ukraine's military successes in late 2022 – including its liberation of almost all of Kharkiv oblast and of the city of Kherson – Russia launched many successive waves of missile and drone attacks in order to disable or destroy the electricity, water and heating systems of Ukraine's cities just as winter became more extreme. Many victims were the remaining older people, who were more affected by disability and poverty, less able or willing to flee, had attempted to stay behind in damaged homes and had already suffered disproportionate deaths and injuries (Amnesty International 2022). These attacks were strategic measures designed to destroy individuals' and communities' physical capacities to survive the winter of 2022–3, as well as to undermine Ukraine's military capacity. Taken together with the other policies, they also amounted to an attempted large-scale destruction of the economic basis of Ukrainian society.

As we have seen, Azarov *et al.* (2022: 38–42) argue that these policies demonstrated Russia's "deliberately inflicting conditions of life aimed at the physical destruction of the Ukrainian nation". They certainly caused a large number of civilian deaths; although Ukraine did not release figures, the UN recorded 6,300 up to October 2022 (United Nations High Commissioner for Human Rights 2022), with larger numbers of injuries, and acknowledged that these figures could be substantial underestimates. Other credible estimates suggested that at least 8,000 and possibly up to 25,000 civilians died in the siege of Mariupol alone (Hinnant *et al.* 2022; Lewis 2025: 72). These included hundreds who died in the Russian attack on the Mariupol Drama Theatre, the worst single massacre of the war.

It therefore seems possible that overall civilian casualties in the first year were in the tens of thousands, with the killing in Mariupol proportionately comparable to the toll in Gaza 18 months later, which was widely regarded as an indicator of genocide. Yet Russia was killing civilians in pursuit of its goal of destroying a distinct Ukrainian society, rather to physically destroy Ukrainians en masse, so that in legal terms, interpreting the situation in terms of the Genocide Convention's paragraph II(c) only returns us to the dilemmas discussed above. Rather than attempting to prove that the Kremlin's prime aim was the physical destruction of the Ukrainian nation, a more coherent account recognizes instead the centrality to its policies of social and cultural destruction, which should be considered as genocidal in themselves.

A genocidal occupation: southern and eastern Ukraine

Since Lemkin first analysed genocide as a phenomenon of military occupation, it is important for a genocide analysis to examine the occupation regime in southern and eastern Ukraine. By spring 2025, this had lasted for three years in most places that Russia had newly captured and since 2014–15 in both Crimea and the Luhansk and Donetsk "people's republics". Russia controlled around one-fifth of Ukraine's territory and over one-tenth of its total population (Gumanyuk 2025). However, the occupation was changing in the circumstances of the new phase of war, most importantly because of the resistance of the Ukrainian army and population (Malyarenko & Kormych 2023: 499).

Crimea can be seen as a special case because of its historic priority for Russian nationalists, its high (if still minority) pro-Russian sentiment before annexation and its conquest without fighting. Major economic investment and importation of Russians, using migration as a weapon, took place after annexation, and Russian institutions were imported (Malyarenko & Kormych 2023: 502–5).

In contrast, the "people's republics" were only indirectly ruled; support for Russian rule was less, resulting in higher level of a repression. Forcible displacement during 2014–15 had substantially emptied the cities, towns and villages, and 1.4 out of the 1.8 million who originally left had remained displaced in 2019. Despite Russian subsidies, "rapid and severe deindustrialization" had occurred, with tens of thousands of enterprises closed, looted or dismantled to Russia for scrap; countless homes and other buildings were permanently destroyed; coalmines were flooded; and farmland was littered with unexploded ordinance and landmines. As a result, gross domestic product was more than 60 per cent lower after four years (Mykhnenko 2020).

In 2023, Russia formally annexed Donetsk and Luhansk as well as the newly invaded oblasts of Kherson and Zaporitzhzhia, although it did not fully occupy any of them. It speedily consolidated its control over the newly occupied areas, improvising new power structures. Through legal, ideological and economic manipulation, Russia managed to institutionalize its control and compel the remaining population to comply. Rigged referendums – complete with foreign observers such as one from the youth league of South Africa's ruling party (Lewis

2025: 93) – helped make the annexations of the occupied regions appear "constitutional", although, like Israel's in the West Bank, they were internationally illegal.

David Lewis (2025: 284) argues that by mid-2024, Russia had established "a highly effective occupation regime", combining what Michael Mann (1993: 58–9) classically distinguished as "infrastructural power" – the state's penetration of society through bureaucracy, institutions and laws – with "despotic power" or coercion. Yet occupation institutions showed a "toxic mix of collaboration, violence, corruption and careerism", and were significantly dominated by imported Russians, while local officials were often people "who had long been marginal in their communities and had little respect". The remaining residents mostly took Russian passports, driving licences, etc., which were conditions of being able to function in the new order, but this did imply real support for the occupation. Indeed, Russia's goal was "not to win over the hearts and minds of Ukrainians under Russian rule, but to erase any remnants of their legal Ukrainian identity" (Lewis 2025: 103–7).

Despite the legal veneer, Russian rule was heavily reliant on "shocking levels of violence and repression", including torture, sexual violence and large-scale detentions; the UN recorded 77 extrajudicial killings in the first 15 months. This was not the semi-random violence of Bucha: there was "more method" in the occupation violence. Aimed at potential opponents, it used lists drawn up before 2022 supplemented by information from seized Ukrainian files, together with the names of the organizers of the significant protests that developed in places such as Kherson. "Filtration", which involved an extensive system of camps, was also highly abusive, involved extensive and proven cases of torture and violence and lacked any accountability mechanisms to protect individual rights (Lewis 2025: 5–6, 129–54).

Yet the occupation in early 2025 was a shadow of the regime that Putin envisaged three years earlier, which would have covered northern Ukraine as well as a larger area of the south, including the principal cities of Kyiv, Kharkov and Odesa. Russia had lost Kherson, the only large city that it had taken apart from Mariupol, and its "incorporation" of four eastern oblasts remained partly notional in 2025 since it was far from fully controlling them. In fact, Putin's annexation implied a drastic shrinking of his original goals, limiting them to the elimination of the Ukrainian nation "in part", in the Genocide Convention's terms.

In his analysis of German occupation policies, Lemkin had argued that "genocide has two phases: one, destruction of the national pattern of the oppressed group; the other, the imposition of the national pattern of the oppressor", and that this imposition "may be made upon the oppressed population which is allowed to remain or upon the territory alone, after removal of the population and the colonization by the oppressor's own nationals" (1944: xi). In February 2022, Russian leaders appear to have envisaged Lemkin's first option, assuming that they would quickly establish their rule and that the majority of the population could be coerced into accepting it. In the areas in which they consolidated their control, they implemented total Russification of all social institutions; whereas international law demanded that an occupying power change as little as possible, "Russia, by contrast, was intent on changing everything" (Lewis 2025: 114–16).

Yet Russia had ended up partially implementing Lemkin's second option. The occupied territories were hollowed out: the new phase of the war produced more extreme local destruction than the first, and some smaller occupied towns remained almost completely depopulated. Even where significant populations remained, they were substantially diminished: hundreds of thousands of civilians fled in advance of the Russian arrival in their areas while more departed as and after they were conquered. Around 120,000 people, a quarter of the city's population, were estimated to have escaped from Mariupol in just six weeks during March–April 2022 (Lewis 2025: 73). Russia's expulsions of discontented inhabitants only diminished the population further, and it was estimated that only 3 million remained in 2024, compared to 4.5 million claimed by Russia (Lewis 2025: 111).

Russian investments in new infrastructure were directed to the territories on the strategic land corridor to Crimea, not to the old industrial cities of the Donbass (Malyarenko & Kormych 2023: 508). Mariupol was a showcase of reconstruction, with parts of the central area rebuilt after two years and (mirroring the Israeli extreme right's plans for Gaza) seafront apartments available for sale. But the population – despite being boosted by Russian officials and other subsidized incomers – was barely half its original size.

Even with total coercion, Russification was acceptable to only a minority of the original population, leaving colonization as the principal means by which Russia could consolidate its rule. It had successfully pursued this option in Crimea, an attractive destination for Russian retirees. The occupation might be able to find enough colonizers for the showcase developments in Mariupol – although the remaining original inhabitants could not afford them – but colonization did not appear to be a viable option in the rest of occupied Ukraine.

Genocide and the war after 2022

During 2023–4, the war itself mostly became a classic war of territorial control with slowly changing front lines. In this context, its genocidal elements were largely confined to the occupied and contested areas, as the decline of intellectual focus on genocide reflected. As we have seen, Lemkin had considered genocide as a way in which the occupier could win even if it failed militarily. Even before Trump's involvement in 2025, the inability of Ukraine to further overcome the occupation pointed towards an outcome in which – in an echo of the result of the Bosnian war – Russia would more or less achieve its reduced goal of consolidating its genocidal annexations in eastern Ukraine, which were likely to become more deeply Russified over time. Yet this success was likely to prove hollow, given the depressed, depopulated and indeed "demodernized" condition of the territory (Malyarenko & Kormych 2023).

However, the war and occupation also had a impact on the remainder of Ukraine. As Natalia Gumanyuk (2025) argued, Moscow "used its control of significant numbers of Ukrainians to undermine the stability of the whole country, even without taking more territory". Three years of Russian aggression had weakened Ukrainian society, pushing a substantial section of the population into precarious living conditions, and much of the initial depopulation had not been reversed. Yet, compared to Putin's original aim of Russifying Ukraine as a whole, the war had weakened Russian language and culture in the large Ukrainian-controlled majority of the country, which was now much more unequivocally Ukrainian. This too was unlikely to change.

PART II

Gaza and the structure of genocide in Palestine

5
THE GAZA GENOCIDE

Genocide could be quickly recognized after Israel launched its assault on Gaza in October 2023. All reports indicated that this was a spectacularly destructive campaign, but even among those who acknowledged this, there was some hesitation in recognizing genocide. Over a month into Israel's campaign, Omer Bartov (2023) wrote that although its leaders' statements showed that there was "genocidal intent, which can easily tip into genocidal action", there was still "no proof that genocide is currently taking place in Gaza". Indeed, it was only after Israel attacked Rafah in May 2024 that he finally became convinced that

> the ultimate goal of this entire undertaking from the very beginning had been to make the entire Gaza Strip uninhabitable, and to debilitate its population to such a degree that it would either die out or seek all possible options to flee the territory. In other words ... Israel was acting 'with intent to destroy, in whole or in part' the Palestinian population in Gaza. (Bartov 2024)

Yet the rhetoric had actually been translated into action from the start. Mass killing and the destruction of civilian infrastructure – including the health system, on which survivors of the violence would depend – were both front-loaded. According to Israel's own claims, in two months it carried out over 10,000 airstrikes on the tiny, densely populated strip, dropping hundreds of 2,000-pound (900 kg) bombs with a wide destructive radius (Amnesty 2024: 207). In an intensive analysis of the first 25 days, Airwars (2024) showed that Israel killed at least 5,139 civilians, nearly four times more than those reported killed during any single month in any conflict the organization had documented over the previous decade. Benjamin Netanyahu acknowledged that he had, in a sense, implemented the nuclear option: Joe Biden (Times of Israel 2025) recounted that he told the Israeli prime minister, "you can't be carpet bombing these communities. And he said to me, 'well you did it, you carpet bombed'. Not his exact words, but 'you carpet bombed Berlin. You dropped a nuclear weapon.'" It was later revealed that Netanyahu himself had insisted, in the war cabinet, on targeting that was much greater than the Israel Defence Forces (IDF) chief of staff proposed (Morgan 2025).

The case was sufficiently clear that by late December 2023, South Africa had submitted an extensively documented case against Israel to the ICJ, and by late January the court (International Court of Justice 2024a) had found a plausible risk of "irreparable prejudice" to the rights of Gazan Palestinians under the Genocide Convention. The court enjoined Israel, using the latter's words, not to "deliberately inflict on the group conditions of life calculated to bring about its physical destruction in whole or in part", and ordered the state to "take all measures within its power" to prevent genocidal acts, prevent and punish incitement to genocide and ensure that urgent humanitarian aid reached the population. These instructions would be so little obeyed that the ICJ was twice compelled to enlarge on them, in March and May the same year (International Court of Justice 2024b; 2024c).

Also in March, Francesca Albanese (2024a), the UN's special rapporteur on the situation of human rights in the Palestinian territory occupied since 1967, published the first full "anatomy" of the genocide. Although the ICJ would probably not judge the substantive case against Israel for some years, Albanese presented an authoritative, richly documented argument that confirmed South Africa's case. Later, Amnesty International (2024) produced an even more comprehensive survey of Israel's actions up to June (also taking into account of events in the rest of 2024), in the light of the law of genocide. It also concluded in no uncertain terms that genocide was being committed and that this imposed widespread duties, not only on Israeli leaders, but also on the leaders of other states and UN organs, including the Security Council.

However, despite these interventions and the overwhelming evidence on which they were based, not only did Israel intensify its campaign against the population but the most powerful Western governments – while noticeably less vocal in Israel's support by late 2024 than they had been in 2023 – also continued to give it moral, political, financial and military aid, almost universally ignored the implications of the ICJ case and often repressed those who protested against the genocide. In these ways, the Gaza genocide became a pan-Western as well as an Israeli crime, long before Trump returned in 2025 and proposed that the USA itself should implement a final solution of the Gaza question by entirely expelling the population.

In this chapter, I take for granted much of the detail outlined by South Africa, Albanese, Amnesty International and others and instead explore Israel's genocide in Gaza in a broader socio-historical analysis. The discussion covers the period from October 2023 to mid-2025. It needs to be read together with Chapter 6, which situates this genocide in the context of the longer history of what I call the genocidal "structure" that developed from the project of a Jewish state in Palestine.

Anti-antisemitism, denial and humanitarian camouflage

The official, journalistic and even academic avoidance – or to use the technical term, denial – of "genocide" in describing Israel's assault on Gaza's civilian population drew heavily on the doctrine of anti-antisemitism, using the International Holocaust Remembrance Alliance's (2016) definition of antisemitism. Although supporters claimed that this allowed criticism of Israel (Stögner 2025), it was designed to equate anti-Zionism with antisemitism, and allegations of genocide were interpreted as comparing Israel to the Nazis, which the examples accompanying the definition dictated was antisemitic. In Germany, this anti-antisemitism was formalized as the explicit foundation of state policy, the *Staatsräson*; it functioned in a similar way in the USA and to a large extent in other Western states. This anti-antisemitism reflected the centrality of Holocaust memorialization to transnational Western political identity after the end of the Cold War, and especially after 9/11 (Renton 2025).

Anti-antisemitic denialism produced a narrative that since Jews had been victims of the paradigmatic genocide, they could not be perpetrators, and that those who alleged this must be supporters of Hamas. Logically, of course, this was nonsensical and historical knowledge suggested the contrary: those claiming to represent victims of genocide often commit it themselves, claiming indeed to avenge their own victims. In regions such as the Balkans and the African Great Lakes, such cycles of ideological, and all too often real, "countergenocide" are well established (Shaw 2013: 164–71).

However, the denial of genocide in Gaza also rested on a fundamental misunderstanding (or misrepresentation) of the relationships of war and genocide. It was assumed that these are exclusive categories, so that if Israel was fighting a war, it could not be committing genocide. The state claimed that its war was only against Hamas and that if civilians were harmed, this was a result of the Islamist organization's choice to embed itself in the population and use them as "human shields". Yet the idea that it was possible to "destroy" Hamas with a massive, largely indiscriminate bombardment without extensively destroying Gazan society was manifestly incoherent: the movement was, as Avi Shlaim (2024: 323) pointed out, "part of the fabric of Palestinian society" in the territory.

The idea that the prosecution of a "war" excluded genocide was also wholly mistaken from a legal point of view, even if Israel had been fighting a legitimate war of self-defence, which it was not, since the right of self-defence applies only to attacks from other states, while Israel was defending its internationally illegal occupation. As Amnesty International's thorough report made clear (2024: 17–18, 278): genocide is a crime that can be committed within war and through actions that combine genocidal with military intent. The idea that war excludes genocide is also entirely ahistorical: most genocides have been carried out not only during but also *as part of* the prosecution of a war, from the Ottomans' against the Armenians in the First World War, to the Nazis' of the Jews in the Second, to the Rwandan regime's of the Tutsis during the country's civil war.

Therefore, the claim to be fighting war rather than committing genocide is a standard denialist trope. However, Israel gave this a distinctive twist by repeatedly claiming to abide by international law in its choice of methods, using it as "humanitarian camouflage" as Albanese (2024a: 14–15) explained. Israel was "distorting the laws of war to conceal genocidal intent", she argued, in two ways: by subverting the balance between civilian protection and military necessity; and by deploying IHL concepts, such human shields, collateral damage, safe zones, evacuations and medical protection, "in such a permissive manner so as to gut these concepts of their normative content, subverting their protective purpose and ultimately eroding the distinction between civilians and combatants, as well as the customary rules of distinction, proportionality and precaution". This distortion, Albanese argued, obscured IHL's cardinal tenet, that "indiscriminate attacks, which do not distinguish military targets from protected persons and objects, cannot be proportionate and are always unlawful".

The key issue, Albanese continued, was the purpose this pattern of distortion served. On the ground, the policy "transformed an entire national group and its inhabited space into a destroyable target, revealing an eliminationist conduct of hostilities"; from Israel's pattern of conduct, therefore, "the requisite genocidal intent is the only reasonable inference to be drawn". Therefore, while Israel's distortion of IHL did the work of "transforming" Palestinians in Gaza into a legitimate target in its military ideology, the only credible sociological hypothesis was the opposite: Israel *began* with an intention to destroy Gazan society and *used* the distortion of IHL to enable this.

Israel's IHL distortion was not new. Its choice of disproportionate violence had been seen in previous attacks on Gaza and was codified in the "Dahiya doctrine" (Pearlman 2023), named after a Beirut suburb that Israel attacked in 2006 (it attacked it again in 2024). Indeed, the main purpose of the decades-old International Law Department of the IDF, Mayaan Geva (2016) showed, was not to constrain but to enable violence. While the sociologist Yagil Levy (2019) had demonstrated that it was partially possible to attribute Palestinian civilian casualties in Israel's earlier Gaza wars to the kind of "risk transfer" that Western militaries generally practice (Shaw 2005), there was always an additional element in its campaigns: its entrenched hostility towards Palestinians as such, which deepened after 7 October 2023.

Far from being a consequence of the state's distortion of international law, this hostility was the premise of its approach. Israel's supporters argued that US-led campaigns in Afghanistan and Iraq had also caused disproportionate civilian casualties (Foer 2024), but in a new analysis Levy (2024) showed that even on Israel's distorted – indeed, genocidal – assumption that all men of fighting age should be counted as combatants, the ratio of civilians to Israeli soldiers killed in Gaza exceeded the worst in recent US campaigns. The USA may have been indifferent to civilian harm in Iraq and Afghanistan, and its troops may have displayed racist attitudes, but it was never driven by the same overriding policy animus that Israel showed against the Palestinians.

The intimate relationship between war and genocide

Therefore the dramatic expansion of *tactical* brutality in Israel's campaign, producing carnage and destruction of a new order of magnitude, can only have represented the implementation of a *strategic* policy agreed by political and military leaders. Its military goals, Amnesty International found (2024: 205), were "insufficient to explain the scale and scope of Israel's ongoing unlawful actions. Only an intent to destroy the Palestinians in Gaza does so." There was "a pattern of direct attacks on civilians with no apparent military objective present, indiscriminate attacks and intentional destruction of cultural and religious sites with no apparent imperative military necessity". The cultural destruction was extensive and systematic (Palestinian Centre for Human Rights 2024a).

This Israeli policy may have been improvised after 7 October 2023, resulting from a spontaneous consensus among leaders (in the light of taken-for-granted hostility towards Palestinians), rather than from careful deliberation. Yet it was unmistakably clear in the IDF's actions within the first few days, while many statements by high-ranking members of Israel's government expressed its fundamental hostility to the very existence of Palestinian society within Gaza and its determination to destroy this as well as Hamas. These statements quickly became well known and were cited in the ICJ's January judgement (International Court of Justice 2024a); they continued to be amplified, as Amnesty International later showed (2024: 202–81).

There can be no real doubt that what Israel's leaders intended was that the "destroyable target", previously to be destroyed only in part, was now to be comprehensively destroyed. The centrality of the hostility evidenced by its leaders' statements could be seen in the absence of meaningful distinctions between its military and population-oriented tactics. The counterattack on Hamas was also from the start an attack on the civilian population, and the means used to destroy the armed organization – primarily, aerial bombardment – was also calibrated to be a method of attack against civilian society. Even the IDF's close-up methods on the ground, which might be thought to have offered the means of discriminating between the armed enemy and civilians, were instead often deliberately deployed against civilians. Males of fighting age were indiscriminately rounded up, humiliated, incarcerated and brutalized, while aid workers and journalists were deliberately killed, and even young children were targeted by snipers.

In Israel's campaign, therefore, we can identify an *unusually intimate* relationship between war and genocide. While most genocides occur within wars, perpetrators typically operate bespoke anti-civilian policies in parallel with their military operations: the two are entwined but distinct, for example in the way that Nazi anti-Jewish policy was carried out in conjunction with the German army's campaign against opposing armies during the invasions of Poland and the Soviet Union, or how Russia's efforts to destroy Ukrainian society in the occupied zones were combined with its conventional war against the Ukrainian army.

In such cases, genocidal armies still fought on military "fronts" more or less distinct from their targeting of civilian groups, much of which happened after the occupation of the territory. In Israel's case, however, the front simply encompassed civilian society. The entire battlespace in which it combated Hamas was also the space in which it destroyed this society ever more completely with each new phase of its aggression. Society *was* the battlespace, and there was no attempt to create a stable occupation regime. There was an almost seamless unification of Israel's campaigns against its armed and civilian enemies, who were simultaneously destroyed with the same methods.

In this context, the faux "humanitarian" mitigations that Albanese analyses were largely performances for the benefit of Western opinion. Yet rather than constituting departures from the genocide, they provided cruel additional means by which it was carried out, for example deceitfully offering civilians an illusion of safety in areas that Israel would then resume bombing. Similarly, Israel's "war" included the often arbitrary mass detention of civilians, mainly men, who effectively became "hostages", as much as the Israelis held by Hamas and in much greater numbers, with extensive brutalization and torture in the detention camps (Addameer Prisoner Support and Human Rights Association 2024).

The only real element of discrimination in Israel's campaign became clear as the restriction – and at times complete prevention – of the entry or distribution of goods, including foodstuffs and medicines, became a prominent feature. Together with its campaign, culminating in a complete ban, against the United Nations Relief and Works Agency (UNRWA), which had long been central to aid operations, this policy was directed almost entirely at the civilians rather than Hamas.

It was therefore unsurprising that the war crime of starvation headed both the ICC prosecutor's list of charges against Netanyahu and his former defence minister Yoav Gallant (International Criminal Court 2024a) and the subsequent summary of the warrants that judges issued against them (International Criminal Court 2024b), and that instructions to prevent starvation were the most specific that the ICJ directed at the state (ICJ 2024a; 2024b; 2024c). In its deliberate production of starvation, Israel's genocidal intent could be seen as separate from the "military" rationale of the bombardment, although the latter was the primary means through which civilians were killed and wounded and their environment destroyed.

The pattern of harm showed, therefore, that Israel was waging a specific type of genocidal war. This term most obviously describes a distinctly military enterprise with overall genocidal as well as military goals, combined with the means for destroying the enemy group or population that are distinct from those used against the armed enemy. In Israel's case, the military and genocidal goals were not only intertwined but also appeared to be of combined and equal significance. Military aims informed the genocide, in the sense that the destruction of Palestinian society was partially designed to aid the destruction of Hamas. However, the reverse was also true: the destruction of Hamas was used to destroy Palestinian society in Gaza.

A "crippling" genocide, or a genocide of starvation

In most wars, it is possible to formulate some idea of what victory would mean for the protagonists. In Gaza, however, not only did Hamas launch a spectacular demonstrative act that could never achieve permanent military gains but Israel also initially answered with a war that was very unlikely to achieve its stated aim of eliminating Hamas as a military and political force. Israel appeared to enter Gaza with only the flimsiest idea of a political and military solution, such as that of Arab states sponsoring a technical administration under its own military control.

In contrast, Israel's aim of wrecking and brutalizing Gazan society was clear and largely achieved within the first months, even if the destruction continued to deepen afterwards. That this was the state's goal was surely confirmed by the fact that with each new sign of the horrific consequences of its campaign, it doubled down on its onslaught, taking little notice of the orders of the ICJ or the pleas of the Biden administration.

Genocides are individual, historical events: "there's no Auschwitz in Gaza, but it's still genocide", as two Israeli historians, Amos Goldberg and Daniel Blatman (2025), put it. Israel's campaign was distinctive not only in its intimate combination of military and genocidal action but also in what appeared to be its specific aims:

1. To directly kill and maim a substantial number of civilians, making the population pay a huge physical price for its presumed complicity in Hamas' actions.
2. To pulverize the built environment, obliterating most of the housing stock and urban landscape, rendering the territory largely uninhabitable and forcing as much of the population as possible to recognize the necessity of leaving.
3. To destroy the social framework and institutions, including the healthcare system, making it almost impossible for normal life to be carried on.
4. To prevent sufficient food, medical supplies and other basic necessities from reaching the population, making it more and more difficult for survivors of Israel's direct violence to continue to live.

Therefore, Israel killed and wounded widely and largely indiscriminately, but neither in order to physically eliminate the population as a whole (which, in any case, is rarely the initial aim of genocide perpetrators), nor simply to terrorize them into flight (a much more common goal, for example in the Nakba and the Bosnian genocide), even if that was desired by many of Israel's leaders. Rather, it aimed primarily to *cripple* society towards the point of collapse, at which point expulsion – which was not an early option because of the opposition of neighbouring states to accepting refugees, as well as the reluctance of Biden to endorse it – might become possible.

Therefore, the character of Israel's genocide – neither totally murderous nor fully expulsionary – brought to mind from the outset (Shaw 2023a; 2023b) Raphael Lemkin's idea that genocide may involve the "crippling" as well as the total destruction of a society. Genocide was "the criminal intent to destroy *or cripple permanently* a human group", he wrote in 1947 (147, emphasis added). In *Axis Rule* (1944), Lemkin emphasized that the Nazi occupations of European countries not only destroyed the autonomous existence of nations but also led in many cases to the extreme weakening of the conditions of life, so that "a daily fight literally for bread and for physical survival" would "handicap thinking in both general and national terms" by the surviving population (Lemkin 1944: 85).

This appeared to be the pattern in Gaza. Within a few short months, Israel reduced the traumatized, injured and bereaved survivors to a threadbare society with a minimal economy, living amid the ruins of their former lives and homes. Something like this situation had been seen, over shorter periods, in the smaller populations of Mariupol and some other Ukrainian towns that Russia destroyed, but here it was deliberately inflicted on a population of more than two million who appeared permanently trapped in a tiny territory, helpless victims of each new wave of Israel's assault.

A pattern of round after round of bombardment and temporary flight, with each expulsion leading to even more precarious refuge and living conditions, gave the Gaza genocide its peculiar awfulness. People were forcibly removed from their homes and neighbourhoods – a large proportion of which were destroyed or badly damaged in the first weeks – in serial mass expulsions within the territory: from Gaza City to Khan Younis, Khan Younis to Rafah, Rafah to al-Masawi, back to Gaza City, and so on. Evacuation orders and "safe zones" actually helped to make the displaced targets (Al-Haq 2025). In this context, the relentless Israeli killing, wounding, physical terror and restriction of food and medical supplies reduced the population to ever greater helplessness. Meanwhile, the deliberate destruction of every kind of collective institution – above all, the hospitals and local administration, but also schools, mosques, universities, etc. – flattened Gazan society as well as its built infrastructure, debilitating attempts to restore social cohesion.

The International Relations scholar Nicola Perugini (2024) wrote of a "genocide of attrition" – echoing an idea of Helen Fein (1997) – but the centre of what Israel inflicted increasingly became a genocide of starvation. As with its bombing of civilian neighbourhoods, this was not a new tactic for Israel but one that it had honed long before 2023, as it used the control of foodstuffs into Gaza to create what famine expert Alex de Waal (2025a) calls "a unique kind of food insecurity". As he summarizes:

> The Ministry of Defence had carefully examined food availability and consumption in Gaza and came up with a diet devised on the basis of a calorie count per head that would satisfy the bare minimum nutritional requirements, and this was used to determine what food – along with other essentials – would be allowed into Gaza ... assessments before the war found that Gazan children were rarely underweight but had a restricted diet and, most important, that most families depended on food aid provided by UNRWA.

In this "fastidious" system of control, it had been Israeli policy "to put the Palestinians on a diet, but not to make them die of hunger", in the 2006 words of Dov Weissglas, an adviser to Ehud Olmert, the then Israeli prime minister.

After 7 October 2023, de Waal argues, the government "settled implicitly on a new red line: Palestinians might die in all kinds of ways, but not of famine, at least not according to the arcane formulas of the IPC", the internationally recognized Integrated Food Security Phase Classification system. Already by late November 2023, over half the population had been reduced to the IPC's "catastrophe" or "emergency" levels (most of the rest were in "crisis"), numbers that de Waal says were "extraordinary" in historical perspective, especially since Gaza was a compact territory that was easy to supply. After strong US pressure during April–May 2024, Israel temporarily eased its restrictions, effectively reverting to its former approach, de Waal notes: by "adjusting the aid flow just enough to satisfy Washington and controlling the humanitarian data to ensure a no-famine decision [by the IPC's Famine Review Committee] ... the US played a key role both in drawing the line and in deciding that Israel hadn't crossed it". Later, the situation deteriorated again, and when in March 2025 Israel decided to sabotage the ceasefire agreed that January, its blocking of food supplies was the first sign, preceding large new bombardments. As a result, food insecurity soon plumbed new depths (de Waal 2025b). Desperate people scavenged for food; looting, theft and violence were rife. By May 2025, growing starvation finally precipitated a serious crisis in Israel's international support.

Concentration camps: external or internal?

After the crippling of Gazan society had been achieved in the first year, Israel had largely created the conditions in which return would be impossible; displacement was intended to be permanent, as Human Rights Watch (2024a) argued. It had destroyed agriculture and food systems (Palestinian Centre for Human Rights 2025) and environmental infrastructure (Al-Mezan 2024). The destruction of healthcare meant that people with life-threatening diseases, such as cancer, could not receive treatment, while pregnant women, babies and their mothers lost almost all services (Al-Mezan 2025). During 2024–5, Israel extended what was called "non-operational" destruction, that is, the systematic demolition of buildings without even the pretence of an anti-Hamas justification (Rapoport & Ziv 2025).

After destroying this social and physical infrastructure, Israel's policy options for the population revolved, effectively, around different modes of concentration in camps: either externally, by expelling the survivors to refugee camps in other countries supervised by the UN and humanitarian NGOs, or internally, in a system of concentration camps under Israeli military control. Politicians and military leaders grappled with these options. At first, it appeared that they were moving towards a new plan for indefinite military occupation, involving permanent expulsion of the population from northern Gaza. In what was already largely a wasteland, new rounds of destruction made the prospects of those who had dared to return and survive within the ruins ever more tenuous, with renewed violence against the remaining hospitals, shelters and refugee camps, particularly Jabalia.

In autumn 2024, new proposals emerged, which envisaged dividing the territory into a purely military zone in northern Gaza, militarized sections along the strip's eastern and southern borders and an area for Palestinian survivors in the south. This "cartography of genocide" (Forensic Architecture 2024) pointed to a new model of control: the entire surviving population might be concentrated in a new camp complex, guarded by the IDF, occupying part of the southwest of the territory. In what some Israelis mockingly labelled "gated communities", Palestinians might even be serviced – since international relief bodies would be increasingly excluded – by Israeli commercial organizations.

However, plans for expulsion from Gaza, always a probable end game from the point of view of the far-right Israeli government, also continued to surface. Extremist ministers and settler groups renewed their campaign for Jewish recolonization, and real estate firms produced new prospectuses for beachfront properties. The installation of Trump in January 2025 increased support for this goal, since he repeatedly floated the removal of the Palestinians from Gaza to Egypt and Jordan, with the USA itself taking over the strip. It was reported that the USA and Israel were in discussions with the governments of Sudan, Somalia and Libya for the possible "relocation" of Palestinians to their territories. These ideas even exceeded Hitler's scheme to remove European Jews to Madagascar during the Second World War, since they apparently envisaged depositing the survivors in chronically war-ravaged countries, in one of which (Sudan) extensive genocide and starvation were actually ongoing.

While many criticized these ideas as "ethnic cleansing", they clearly amounted to additional means of genocide, since any version of them would be a way of completing the destruction of Gazan society that Israel had carried out over the previous year: Trump was aware of this, remarking in February 2025: "A civilization has been wiped out in Gaza." On 30 March 2025, Netanyahu announced what he called the "final stage": "Hamas will lay down its weapons. Its leaders will be allowed to leave. We will see to the general security in the Gaza Strip and will allow the realization of the Trump plan for voluntary migration." Of the latter, he tweeted: "This is the plan. We are not hiding this"; and although no detail was revealed, it was clear that the label "voluntary" was entirely euphemistic.

Yet it was not clear whether external removal was really in Israel's interests, since outside Gaza Palestinians would no longer be subject to its control, or how this would be carried out, since Egypt, Jordan and other Arab states remained opposed. It appeared at least as likely that Israel would return to the idea of a giant concentration camp complex in southern Gaza; in May 2025, Trump backed a plan for Israel to expel all international aid agencies and for a US-based agency take over the supply of minimal subsistence to inmates. What this could mean was shown when Israeli troops repeatedly shot desperate Palestinians seeking aid. There was be a grim irony in this denouement. During the territory's long blockade, Israel's critics were often rebuked for comparing Gaza to the Warsaw Ghetto, in which the Nazis concentrated the Jews during the first years of their occupation of Poland. Now, however, as life during the blockade appeared to the survivors as a kind of lost "normality", Israel seemed to be moving towards something very close to the ghetto model.

In any case, neither expulsion nor internal concentration would necessarily constitute a final stage of the genocide – let alone end it in a full sense, since it would traumatize survivors for decades. As starvation grew in Gaza, global tensions around the situation were sharpening. "Genocide" was increasingly recognized, even in media where the word had previously been banned. However, Western leaders persisted in what Cohen had called "implicatory" denial, urging Israel to change course but still refusing to break their alliances with it. The outcome of these tensions in the genocidal bloc was unclear in mid-2025.

A countergenocidal coproduction

From the point of view of many of Gaza's civilians – as intermittent protests as well as opinion polling suggested – the genocide was something that was done to them not only by Israel but also by Hamas, which provoked its assault. Leaving out Hamas' role and responsibility is neither an appropriate form of solidarity with Gaza's civilians nor an anticolonial stance; rather, it is a refusal to take Palestinian agency seriously because in this instance, it was deeply flawed from a social, political and legal point of view. To recognize Hamas' complicity is not to accept the Israeli notion that its policies, such as its embedding of fighters and arms in the urban area, made that organization solely or mainly responsible for the violence that Israel was committing. It is, however, to acknowledge the large impact of the violence that Hamas instigated, which fundamentally conditioned the initial Israeli and Western responses, and to locate this within a long pattern of similar "countergenocidal" conflicts in modern colonial history.

Of course, genocide in Palestine and Gaza did not begin on 7 October 2023; an examination of its longer history is obligatory and I turn to it in Chapter 6. Yet in historical perspective, the spectacular attack that Hamas launched against southern Israel played a very distinctive role: this was the first Gaza war not to be initiated by Israel (Shlaim 2024: 286), and this is where the worst genocide in Palestine's history commenced. It appears that the armed action went further than the organization envisaged, partly because of Israel's failure to respond quickly, and killed more Israeli civilians than originally expected, even if it did not involve all of the atrocities depicted in Israeli propaganda and obediently referenced by Western leaders and media.

However, there is no doubt that Hamas' leaders in Gaza, despite their later attempts to present the killing of civilians as accidental, deliberately planned to attack civilian settlements as well as military positions. Beverley Milton-Edwards and Stephen Farrell (2024) argue that the operation's primary aim was to take hostages, but clearly killing civilians was also an intended feature: more than 800, including scores of non-Israelis, were slaughtered. Hamas and the other armed organizations that took part may not have known in advance of the Nova music festival, but their militants regarded the young Israelis who were taking part as a bonus for their intended hostage-taking and killing spree. In the insurgents' eyes, all Israeli residents were "settlers" and therefore legitimate targets: the mirror image of the Israeli view that all Palestinians in Gaza were Hamas and there were "no innocent civilians". In the language of genocide scholarship – although, disappointingly, other scholars have failed to use it in this case – Hamas committed a large "genocidal massacre" or series of massacres, since it deliberately set out to kill civilians identified loosely as Israelis if not Jews.

Even if the operation was expected to be smaller, Hamas can only have known that any success would be received by Israel as a dramatic escalation and a huge blow to the prestige of its government and army. Many cases of the humiliation of political leaders – Argentina's of Margaret Thatcher over the Falklands, al-Qaeda's of George W. Bush on 9/11, Ukrainians' of Putin in 2014 – had shown that the greater this was, the greater their overreactions. Hamas inflicted a huge humiliation not only on the Netanyahu government but on Israel's entire political and military elite, and indeed on its society. Since Gaza had been on the receiving end of repeated murderous Israeli campaigns over the previous 15 years, Hamas can have been under no illusion that civilians would pay a large price and was clearly prepared to expose them to this.

In this sense, therefore, the Israeli genocide was a coproduction. Given their local knowledge, Hamas' leaders hardly needed to read the history of colonial genocide, but if they had, they would also have known that for hundreds of years, massacres of colonizers – especially when they included their "women and children" – had regularly produced vastly larger murderous responses. Consider the countergenocidal repression after the slave revolt in Haiti in 1801 (Girard 2007), the Great Rebellion or Mutiny in India in 1857 (Dalrymple 2006), the Herero and Nama revolts in German South West Africa in 1904 (Zimmerer & Zeller 2008) and the "Mau Mau" rebellion in British colonial Kenya in the early 1950s (Elkins 2005), among many others. Hamas might have hoped that in twenty-first-century conditions, Western humanitarian pushback would ultimately restrain Israel, but it could not have doubted that civilians would suffer hugely before that point would be reached.

The genocidal massacre of Israeli civilians was also a coproduction. Israel, by consistently prioritizing war over an agreement with Hamas, colluded in the deaths and suffering of its hostages – some of whom, indeed, were killed by the IDF – thus helping to extend the original massacre rather than end it. Israeli hostages' families faced a constant battle with a government that was prepared to sacrifice their loved-ones' lives in order to continue its genocidal war.

It is also significant that Israel was slow to charge Hamas with genocide: only when South Africa brought "genocide" to the ICJ did the state's representatives widely claim that if anyone had committed it, it was their enemy. The most plausible reason for this is that they realized that if it came to a discussion about genocide, the much larger scale of their own killing and destruction would see the issue quickly turned against them. Similarly, Israel later blocked the UN from investigating Hamas' sexual crimes, for fear of exposing its own to scrutiny (Rozovsky 2025).

We saw in the case of Ukraine that resistance extended and radicalized the genocidal side of Russia's war. In Gaza, too, Hamas' continuing resistance played a part in provoking Israel to even greater destruction and violence, but without offering the protection to the civilian population that the Ukrainian military was able to provide. However, at many points it was clear that Hamas was prepared to stop fighting, but that Netanyahu was determined to continue destroying and killing. This dynamic confirmed that for Israel, the anti-Hamas war had been overtaken by the pursuit of the genocide, which had become what the "war" was mainly about.

Israel's perpetrator bloc, international network and denial

The centrality of the military to Israel's genocide might lead us to see this as one of the more statist recent cases, but this would be mistaken: rather, this has shown us what a "democratic" genocide looks like. Many in Israel's citizen army enthusiastically embraced vengeance against Gazan civilians for Hamas' crimes and inflicted their own humiliations on them, for example through a "lingerie genre" of social media posting (Matthews 2025). Right-wing activists took the initiative to block and even physically destroy aid for the starving in Gaza. In the West Bank, settler bands – whose military protection was a major part of Israel's failure to defend its communities on 7 October, since almost all its military units were based there, with few in the south – drove a new wave of violence and expropriation with many more civilian victims.

A "genocidal imagination", previously confined mainly to ultra-orthodox, extreme-right and settler milieux, was mainstreamed by commentators as well as politicians, and a "wave of genocidal rhetoric" long circulated in the Israeli public sphere; observers noted a "genocidal fever" and "a chorus for annihilation" (Sorek 2025: 1; Shlaim 2024: 289–90). Polling showed that a large majority of the civilian population supported the destructiveness of the military campaign, and many would have supported even more extreme action. Certainly, huge demonstrations applied pressure on the regime for a ceasefire in order to return the Israeli hostages, but only a small minority showed solidarity with the victims in Gaza. The number who refused military service in Gaza was tiny for a long time, although it eventually increased.

This was therefore a genocide with a large activist base and wide popular support. This might once have appeared paradoxical, since genocide is often thought of as a centralized state enterprise, typically carried out by a totalitarian or authoritarian state. However, recent research has emphasized the normality of popular involvement. Mann (2005) even sees genocide as a phenomenon of the age of democracy, even if he emphasizes that states that perpetrate it become less democratic, as Israel manifestly did, as the persecution of critical individuals and groups escalated. For him, the classical trinity of perpetration comprises a radical party-state, paramilitaries and key social constituencies; Israel's far-right government, armed settlers and media-mobilized population map fairly closely on to this model, constituting what Andrei Gomez-Suarez (2007) calls the "perpetrator bloc". As Tamir Sorek (2025) shows, "the cultural toolkit of biblical imagination" provided by religious Zionists was a key legitimating device.

Yet while social support is a widespread feature of genocides, it is often largely passive by the time mass killing is underway. For example, the Nazi persecution of the Jews enjoyed a large measure of support in Germany, but the Holocaust was carried out without publicity by specialist agencies such as the army, the Schutzstaffel (SS) and the extermination camp administrations. Before Gaza, the 1994 Rwandan genocide appeared as a maximum case of popular participation: the Hutu Power regime mobilized large numbers of civilians to participate alongside the military and Interahamwe paramilitaries in killing Tutsis, many of them through the communal labour system (Straus 2006). The Israeli pattern of citizen-soldiers and armed settlers was different, but it could be argued that overall it matched this.

Moreover, "democracy" meant that Israel's domestic politics was deeply implicated in the Gaza genocide. I argued in *The New Western Way of War* (Shaw 2005) that Western wars are calibrated with the political and electoral fortunes of the leaders that carry them out, and Gaza proved that this is also true of Western genocide. Netanyahu used the 2023 crisis to rescue his failing far-right government, and subsequently opted for a "forever" war-genocide, rather than a peace agreement in which Hamas would release the Israeli hostages, in order to keep himself in power.

The implication of democracy was deepened by the fact that the group of major Western states that claim to represent democratic world leadership participated both directly and indirectly in Israel's campaign, using Israel's "democracy" as a justificatory trope. It is not unusual for regimes that commit genocide to depend partly on international allies: Russia mobilized military, political and economic support from China, North Korea and Iran for its attempt to destroy Ukraine. Yet Israel was exceptionally dependent on international support, without which it would have been unable to carry out its campaign in anything like the way that it did. If the direct perpetrator bloc linked the Israeli state and sections of its society, an international network of genocide sustained them.

The USA had long been the centre of Israel's international support system and it was also at the centre of this wider genocidal bloc that formed in late 2023. Under Biden, it continued to provide Israel with essential military, political and economic support; without its supplies of weaponry, Israel simply could not have continued bombing. The administration attempted to moderate Israel's actions from time to time, but given what Avi Shlaim calls Biden's "dogmatic and rigid rejection of conditionality" (2024: 339), it used hardly any of its huge leverage, repeatedly retreating from its proposals despite Israel's flagrant continuation of its atrocities. Netanyahu easily crossed Biden's one apparent red line by going into Rafah in May 2024 (Shlaim 2024: 229). When Trump returned, the USA pivoted towards becoming a direct perpetrator, even bidding to take over or share the direction of the genocide.

From the outset, US civil society as well as state integration into Israel's campaign was deep and extensive. In Congress, the majority of Democrats and almost all Republicans gave uncritical support, and under Biden's successor as Democratic candidate for the presidency in 2024, Kamala Harris, pro-Palestinians were even prevented from speaking at the party's convention. Many mainstream US media whitewashed Israel's atrocities and many university presidents, some of whom were browbeaten by extreme Republican lawmakers in late 2023, actively promoted anti-antisemitic repression on their campuses. Zionist networks, often harnessing Jewish community organizations, operated at all these levels, helping police the enforcement of anti-Palestinian sentiment. When Trump returned, he exploited this situation, turning anti-Palestinianism into the cutting edge of his wider repression of opposition. At the same time, transnational arms and technology industries centred in the USA, into which the IDF and Israel's military industry were extensively integrated, fuelled Israel's campaign.

Other Western states and civil societies played major supporting roles in this international network of genocide. Germany, which provided 30 per cent of Israel's military imports, was unwavering in its diplomatic support and its institutions pursued an unrelenting campaign against pro-Palestinians. The UK, although proportionately a small provider of weaponry, continued to supply key parts for Israel's F-35 bombers even after the government's lawyers had determined that Israel was violating IHL; it was also reported as providing almost half of the aerial surveillance of Gaza, intelligence from which was shared with the Israeli military. In both the German and UK cases, close links with Israel forged over decades largely cemented civil society as well as the state into the war-genocide. Only less geopolitically central states such as Spain, Ireland and Norway made significant, but not decisive, pro-Palestinian gestures in the first 18 months. In this internationalized Western genocide, the domestic politics of the major participating states also played important roles, with governments in the USA, Germany and the UK all seeing political advantage in their support of Israel, at least in the early stages of the genocide.

Together, Western states and institutions erected an effective panoply of denial over Israel's genocide. Denial begins with direct acts of genocide, for example Israel's systematic killing of Palestinian journalists, eliminating those witnesses who most authoritatively recorded its atrocities (Palestinian Centre for Human Rights 2024b), at the same time as it banned international journalists from Gaza. However, Western governments and media erected a wider ideological screen around Israel's actions. This system of denial exhibited all three "elementary forms" of denial that Stanley Cohen – a sociologist of Jewish origin, who wrote partly in the light of a period spent at the Hebrew University of Jerusalem in the late twentieth century – classically identified in responses to atrocities and genocide (2001: 1–20).

First, there was "literal" denial. The facts of Israel's crimes and Palestinian suffering were systematically suppressed or marginalized, with politicians and media failing both to consistently present the evidence and images of civilian harm and to acknowledge that what was presented was the result of deliberate Israeli actions.

Second, there was "interpretative" denial. Politicians and media largely reproduced the core themes of Israel's own denialist ideology: that this was a war of self-defence; that if civilians were harmed, this was a consequence of Hamas' actions; and that opposition to the war represented antisemitism and support for Hamas. Mass media generally prioritized pro-Israeli and marginalized pro-Palestinian voices.

Third, there was "implicatory" denial. Even when civilian harm and Israel's responsibility for it were recognized, this was not accompanied by the acknowledgement that radical action was necessary to halt it. Central to this third strand was the denial of the unprecedented international legal interventions in the Gaza genocide. No leaders of major Western states and few mainstream media outlets actively responded, by openly re-evaluating their policies, to either the ICJ's January 2024 finding of "plausible risks" of genocide or the ICC prosecutor's extensive charges of crimes against humanity and war crimes, or even the arrest warrants. Biden and the majority of US Democrats dismissed these, while far-right Republicans even sought to criminalize the ICC itself, as Trump did by executive order in 2025. The far-right-leaning British Conservative government (in office until July 2024) led a movement to block the ICC judges from responding to the prosecutor's charges; and even when centrist leaders defended international law in the abstract, as Britain's new Labour prime minister did, this was accompanied by disavowals of the relevance of "genocide" that disingenuously ignored the ICJ's judgements. Several EU governments indicated that they would not arrest Netanyahu, and the centre-left Polish government, which refused to invite the ICC indictee Putin to the 80th anniversary of the liberation of Auschwitz by Soviet troops, nevertheless extended a welcome to the ICC indictee Netanyahu to attend the event.

Therefore, broad Western interests participated extensively in Israel's genocide, both directly in maintaining its military and political capacity to pursue its violence, and indirectly in helping to construct and sustain the web of denial that insulated it from effective criticism and opposition. Yet it was not only the West that supported Israel: Arab states such as Jordan, Egypt, Saudi Arabia and the United Arab Emirates were keen for it to destroy Hamas, even if they held back from open support because of popular sympathy for the Palestinians. Egypt failed to open its border to the suffering civilians of Gaza, and in 2025, when Arab states proposed an "alternative" to Trump's plan for Gaza, they incorporated the buffer zones and military corridors that Israel had created, so that Israel could continue to militarily dominate the territory (Forensic Architecture 2025). Even states that condemned Israel did little to stop it. This was a radically internationalized genocide in which complicity was widely spread.

Effects of the Gaza war-genocide

Statistical measures confirm the physical harm that Israel caused. By spring 2025, the Gaza health ministry estimated well over 50,000 direct killings, but research suggested that it may have underreported by over 40 per cent; the true figure could already have exceeded 70,000, with an all-cause death toll of over 180,000, in mid-2024 (Jamaluddine *et al.* 2025: 475). As to hunger, Alex de Waal (2025a) concluded, "[t]he level of urban starvation in Gaza has not been seen since the Dutch Hunger Winter and the siege of Leningrad during the Second World War". The long-term death toll and health consequences were likely to greatly exceed figures estimated at the time, since average life expectancy was estimated to have plummeted from 75 to 40 during the first year (Guillot *et al.* 2025).

In particular, Israel had perpetrated a mass infanticide: children made up 44 per cent of verified casualties (United Nations 2024) and 5–9-year-olds were the largest category of deaths by age; many children were bereaved and the survivors included an unprecedentedly large cohort of child amputees. After a year of violence, a survey showed that 96 per cent of children felt that death was imminent, 79 per cent suffered from nightmares and 73 per cent exhibited symptoms of aggression (War Child UK 2024).

These outcomes underlined that Israel had substantially achieved its aim of wrecking the lives, livelihoods and well-being of the Gaza population. Although it had not defeated Hamas, it *had* achieved its aim of crippling Gazan society; as Lemkin argued, genocide is a way of winning even if military victory is not achieved.

From the start, the Gaza genocide also saw deeper dispossession of the Palestinians in the West Bank and East Jerusalem, where both settler violence and "legal" expropriations accelerated sharply from late 2023. By the end of 2024, Israeli authorities had wiped over 50 more rural communities off the map (Ziv 2024), carried out over twice as many "enforcement" operations against "illegal" Palestinian construction than in the previous year, demolished over 1,000 structures (Breaking the Silence 2024) and confiscated more land than ever. Meanwhile, far-right Israeli ministers increased their demands for full annexation, which were further renewed when Trump resumed office.

In early 2025, after a partial ceasefire in Gaza, Israel sent tanks in to destroy refugee camps in Jenin and elsewhere in the West Bank, proclaiming the permanent displacement of tens of thousands, in an effective extension of the genocide to this part of the occupied territories; it also occupied parts of southern Syria. "Targeting childhood" also escalated in these West Bank attacks (Defense for Children International – Palestine 2024). This wider pattern supported Albanese's argument (2024b) that seeing the Gaza genocide as a whole requires seeing it in "the broader political project of Israel in the region", which I discuss further in Chapter 6.

Meanwhile, Israel's campaign in Gaza had provoked new armed exchanges with the Houthis in Yemen, Hezbollah in Lebanon, and Iran. As Israel achieved short-term successes in these conflicts, it was emboldened into greater attacks across Lebanon, where the character of its destruction was also locally similar to Gaza. In an admission that the civilian harm that Israel caused was fully intended, Netanyahu threatened Lebanon with "destruction and suffering like we see in Gaza" (Gritten & Macintosh 2024). In June 2025, Israel and the USA were emboldened to make extensive aerial attacks on Iran, terrorizing millions into fleeing their homes.

Despite Israel's military successes, it was clear that its genocide would forever stain its international reputation, stubbornly inform the future status of the state and probably weaken its society as younger, more educated Israelis recognized this situation and left. One thing we know from the history of genocide is how long it lingers in the body politic, as memories of atrocity and suffering are perpetuated over generations, which Israelis and their international supporters should understand better than anyone. Although they have long dismissed Palestinian narratives of the Nakba, the new ones to which Gaza gives rise will be even more difficult to suppress and are likely to reverberate through the coming decades.

Globally, the genocide fed the growing division within the West and weakened its dominance in the eyes of the rest of the world. Governments, media and establishment intellectuals in the West were so focused on Israeli and Jewish victimization that they failed to realize Palestine's centrality for all those – from states in the Global South to liberals and Muslims in their own societies – who questioned these orientations. Likewise, with their preoccupation with antisemitism and equation of anti-Zionism with it, they not only delegitimized pro-Palestinian protest but also legitimized the anti-Palestinian racism that was at the heart of the Israeli genocide.

If these instinctive positions served Western leaders well during the early revulsion at Hamas' atrocities, they turned into liabilities as it became clear how monstrous Israel's own response was. In particular, support for Israel exposed its centre-left allies to great political risks. By opting to maintain this even as the genocide became evident – their own historic commitments reinforced by fear of how Trump would take advantage of any criticism – Biden and Harris helped collapse the Democrats' fragile electoral coalition and opened the way to his victory, with all this meant for the world. Contrary to Trump's propaganda, he won by only a small margin both nationally and in the swing states, and although there were certainly other factors, the Democrats' alienation of left-wing and Muslim voters contributed significantly to their losing the election and could even have been decisive.

The genocide only continued to divide the West further after Trump came to power. The new regime's open rejection of the Palestinian victims showed a genocidal consistency, on a par with its indifference to the suffering of Ukrainians, but the principal European leaders' abandonment of them was inconsistent with their support for Ukraine and compromised the latter, since it revealed how incomplete their commitment to international law was. As Ukraine became the focus of differences between the USA and Europe, Gaza also underlined them, as few endorsed Trump's blatant plan for total mass expulsion. By mid-2025, prominent European leaders finally began to indicate opposition to Israel's actions.

Thus the Gaza genocide signalled, reflected and stimulated major shifts in global power relations. The united Atlantic West, which had persisted through previous divisions (e.g. over Iraq in 2003), was now under greater strain than ever, and genocide was at the heart of this crisis. In one sense, it was remarkable that Gaza's tiny territory and its two million people – or even Israel-Palestine as a whole, which contains only an additional 12 million – should have such effects in world politics. Viewed objectively, the conflict shared many characteristics with others (McDoom 2023). Yet its geopolitical and symbolic registers had been so globally primed over such a long period that genocide here produced impacts that it failed to make in less pivotal locales such as Rakhine, Tigray and Darfur.

International courts and the recognition of genocide

As Western leaders' claims to uphold international order and justice became increasingly tattered, attention focused instead on the two principal international courts. As we have seen, South Africa's case forced the ICJ to recognize the risks of genocide to Palestinians in Gaza and issue provisional orders to Israel, with the fact that Israel was deliberately causing substantial physical harm making it easy for the court to fully recognize the risk of genocide in the terms of the Genocide Convention, obviating (at least at this stage) the problem that a narrowly physical interpretation caused in the Bosnian case.

The ICJ's January judgement (2024a) asserted the authority of international law over Israel's ongoing violence, but its actual instructions were marked by an "unbearable lightness", as Michael Becker (2024) put it. By failing to demand, as South Africa requested, the cessation of Israel's military operation – the necessary prerequisite for its compliance with the convention and the only way of directly contradicting the state's rationale for its genocide – the court left too much to interpretation, which inevitably helped Israel and its Western protectors to avoid the order's implications. South Africa's later return to request additional measures led to the court specifying its humanitarian requirements more tightly (International Court of Justice 2024b; 2024c), but it still failed to make demands that were full enough to directly oppose the ongoing genocide. A full year after the court's first order, a study concluded that "no meaningful actions to address Gaza's dire humanitarian conditions were observed, allowing the crisis to spiral further in blatant violation of the provisional measures" (Oxfam International 2025: 1).

Following the three hearings of the ICJ, in November 2024 the judges of the ICC finally issued the warrants against Netanyahu and Gallant that its prosecutor had requested six months earlier. The warrants seemed unlikely to produce arrests, and since there was no provision for trials *in absentia*, would be unlikely to lead to convictions. By the time the warrants were issued, Israel had killed all three of the Hamas leaders proposed for indictment, no doubt in part to avoid the slightest possibility that Hamas leaders were tried while its own were not. The warrants against Israel's leaders nevertheless delegitimized its whole campaign, challenged Western leaders and vindicated the protestors on the streets and campuses, deepening the mark that the genocide made on world politics.

The ICC prosecutor had not included genocide among his charges, but the judges noted, when issuing the warrants against Netanyahu and Gallant, that the alleged crimes against humanity "were part of a widespread and systematic attack against the civilian population of Gaza" (International Criminal Court 2024). Shortly afterwards, Amnesty International (2024: 279) argued a very similar case to support the argument that the entire campaign was genocidal:

> Viewed individually, the acts analysed in this report constitute serious violations of international humanitarian law and/or gross violations of human rights. Viewed holistically, a more disturbing picture emerges: the commission of prohibited acts under the Genocide Convention, including killing and causing serious bodily or mental harm to members of a protected group and deliberately inflicting on the group conditions of life calculated to bring about its physical destruction in whole or in part.

These comments echoed Lemkin's original (1933) proposal for the international crime which became genocide, which he then called "barbarity". "Taken separately", he argued, "acts of extermination directed against the ethnic, religious or social collectivities whatever the motive (political, religious, etc.); for example massacres, pogroms, actions undertaken to ruin the economic existence of the members of a collectivity, etc.", and also "all sorts of brutalities", were acts "punishable in the respective codes". However, "[t]aken as a whole", he continued, "all the acts of this character constitute an offence against the law of nations which we will call by the name 'barbarity'; considered together ... they should constitute offences against the law of nations by reason of their common feature which is to endanger both the existence of the collectivity concerned and the entire social order".

The judges' argument implicitly and Amnesty's explicitly represented openings for the ICC prosecutor to also take Israel's campaign "as a whole" and extend his charges to include genocide. Yet he had received enormous negative feedback from Western states, on which ultimately the system of international justice largely depends, for his charges of war crimes and crimes against humanity. It was not clear that he would risk the nuclear option of charging Israeli leaders with genocide, especially after Trump sanctioned the ICC and European states' attitudes to the initial charges showed ambivalence. By mid-2025, it was reported that US sanctions were badly affecting the court's ability to prosecute not only the Israeli case but others too.

Similar political pressures undoubtedly contributed to the indirectness of the ICJ's instructions and will bear on its deliberations when it finally judges South Africa's substantive case. In this context, the court's baggage from its previous decisions will also come into play: Israel could well argue, based on the ICJ's Bosnia judgement, that – absent a Srebrenica-like massacre – the intention to physically destroy the Palestinians as a group cannot be proved. It could also claim that the ICJ's requirement that genocide be "the only possible inference" means that it must be the sole aim of the perpetrator. Amnesty International argues that this would be to read the ICJ's rulings "extremely narrowly": "Specific intent does not mean single intent ... a state's actions can serve the dual goal of achieving a military result and destroying a group as such" (2024: 97, 105). Yet in an international context that is far more polarized than in 2007, precisely this "overly cramped interpretation of international jurisprudence" could come into play even if it "would effectively preclude a finding of genocide in the context of an armed conflict" (Amnesty International 2024: 101–2).

Moreover, even if the ICJ determined that genocide has been committed and the ICC issued genocide warrants, Israel and the USA would clearly defy both courts. Ultimately, while the Genocide Convention binds signatory states, the UN and international courts to "prevent and punish" genocide, law cannot – in the actually existing international system – be a sufficient means of achieving these goals. The convention and the ICC statute assume a genuine "rules-based international order" in which states mostly respect international law and the UN itself enforces it through its Security Council, but this does not exist. As is obvious from the irony that often surrounds the use of the "rules-based" phrase today, the UN is largely incapable of performing its assigned role, chiefly because the great powers use their vetoes to stop it doing so.

If the UN system were working, the Security Council would seek to enforce the ICJ's rulings; in reality, the USA will prevent it from acting against Israel, as Russia has protected itself, with China's backing, over Ukraine. Since none of these powers are even members of the ICC, they will continue to oppose it whenever their interests are at stake. In a world in which the dominant states are led by leaders with genocidal mentalities, opposition to genocide will not come from the top. International law can play a part in defending human freedom, but it will take broad coalitions of state, civil society and political actors to reverse the global crisis that Gaza has exposed.

6

THE STRUCTURE OF GENOCIDE IN PALESTINE

Israel's destruction of Gaza broke the taboo on using "genocide" to describe the situation in Palestine, which had largely been maintained ever since the word was coined. Although the Nakba occurred in the very months during which the Genocide Convention was finalized in 1948, and saw the intentional "destruction", "in part" of a national "group" which it defined as the essence of the crime, it was rarely considered under this rubric. The exclusion began – as denial normally does – even as the destruction of Palestinian society was underway, when the attempts of Arab states to raise it during the convention process were given short shrift. It continued through the decades in which the Holocaust standard increasingly superseded the formal definition of genocide, and remained almost absolute in the early years of the academic genocide field, where a combination of maximal definitions and taken-for-granted pro-Israeli politics marginalized Palestine (Elhalaby 2025). As an indication of the strength of the exclusion, consider its acceptance even by serious, critical historians to whom we have already referred: Ilan Pappé, with his avoidance of "genocide" in his pathbreaking analysis of the Nakba, and Omer Bartov, when he debated with the present writer in the *JGR*.

Bartov's target was the original version of this chapter (Shaw 2010), but this was not the first academic connection of Palestine and genocide. That was, so far as I know, in Patrick Wolfe's seminal article discussing Israel alongside settler-colonial societies in Australia and North America (2006). Certainly, the idea of settler colonialism itself was already a staple of Global South thought (Gurmendi Dunkelberg 2024b), and Israel had long been characterized as a settler-colonial state (Sayegh 1965: 21–38; Rodinson 1973). This interpretative framework was "consolidated among Palestinian intellectuals in the 1960s and 1970s, years before this term took hold in international academic discussions" (Sabbagh-Khoury 2023). But it was only after Wolfe and others (e.g. Barta 1987; Moses 2000) started to frame settler colonialism in genocide terms that the "Israel–genocide" connection began to be more widely discussed (Docker 2012; Rashed & Short 2012; Rashed, Short & Docker 2014).

My 2010 article took the issue of Palestinian genocide beyond settler colonialism, considering it in a wider historical as well as conceptual perspective. This chapter substantially extends the original case. First, it argues that genocide has always been part of the Palestine question, in so far as the genocide of the Jews was important for the establishment of Israel and its dispossession of the Palestinians; therefore it should not be surprising that we also examine the latter's genocidal dimensions. Second, it examines the conceptual and comparative foundations for treating the Nakba as a case of genocide, as well as the debate about 1948 itself. Third, it addresses how Israeli policies from 1948 to 2023 extended the Nakba, examining the genocidal logic of the military occupation in and de facto annexation of the West Bank, East Jerusalem and Gaza during the long period since 1967. Fourth, I address the idea of Israel as an apartheid state, which has also been widely advanced in the intervening years, arguing that Israeli apartheid always had a much stronger genocidal dimension than the South African prototype. Finally, I address genocide in Palestine as a whole and the significance of the Gaza genocide for its *longue durée*.

The argument thus follows the original direction, but much of the analysis is new. I make an important change to the framing of the Palestinian genocide as a whole: I argue that the Zionist state-project created a potentially genocidal *structure* of relations in Palestine, which the violence and large-scale dispossession of the Nakba *activated* and the subsequent occupation of the Palestinian territories *deepened*. It was this structure that Hamas embraced with its massacres of Israeli civilians and which Israel's response has brought to a terrible climax, in which "genocide" has been widely recognized.

"Genocide" as part of the Israel–Palestine conflict

In 2010, I felt that I had to begin by justifying why one should "introduce" the "inevitably controversial" discourse of genocide into the debate about Israel-Palestine. The special place that Israel and its defence occupied in academia had rendered Palestine one of the most divisive issues of our time, but it had not yet created the space for resistance that exists today (Alqaisiya & Perugini 2024).

My first answer was that genocide was already part of the political debate. Israeli advocates had long contended, after all, that the Arabs in 1948 aimed at genocide of the Jewish people – "to throw them into the sea", as they said – and behind this lay the actual genocide of European Jews at the hands of the Nazis. Despite Zionism's earlier roots, Israel itself was substantially the result of Jewish persecution in Europe in the 1930s and 1940s. Nazi extermination and the plight of the survivors spurred the UN great powers – still unwilling themselves to take in large numbers of Jews – to propose the partition of Palestine and the creation of a (disproportionately large) Jewish state, in the face of Palestinian and wider Arab opposition to both. The UN adopted the partition proposal while it was drafting the Genocide Convention.

Therefore, genocide was fundamental to the establishment of Israel, even if it was not its original driver. Soon, the Holocaust became central to the identities of both the state and the global Jewish community, which led to Israel-Palestine being widely represented as a similarly existential question of Jewish survival. Every perceived Arab or Muslim threat to Israel tended to be presented as genocidal, as shown by the campaign to represent remarks by the Iranian president, Mahmoud Ahmadinejad, in 2005 – that "the occupying regime" in Palestine must collapse – as a claim that Israel must be "wiped off the map". Following this, the IAGS passed a resolution alleging that they constituted early warning signs of genocide (International Association of Genocide Scholars 2006). Ahmadinejad's words were ambiguous and it was unclear that they had more than a rhetorical function, but since he was a high-profile proponent of Holocaust denial and antisemitism, in political terms there was enough to establish the case.

Equally, the fact that Israel's critics argued that it used the Holocaust to validate its mistreatment of the Palestinians (e.g. Finkelstein 2000) demonstrated the significance of genocide. For them, it seemed reasonable to ask whether the state's dispossession and violent repression of the Palestinians, from the Nakba to the first major attack on Gaza in 2009, could also be described as genocide. It was beginning to be understood that if the Nakba constituted genocide and Israel threatened new genocidal assaults, Palestinian advocates could then oppose their own genocide story to Israel's foundational myth. However, these arguments had hardly been examined in the academic genocide field.

Conceptual and comparative discussion

I also offered a more fundamental justification for adopting a genocide perspective. Genocide is an important concept of social and historical analysis, and applying this perspective could help us to explore and explain the Palestinian crisis. But for a genocide perspective to fulfil this role, it was necessary to discuss what genocide meant and how it should be used in historical analysis.

As a genocide theorist who was not an Israel-Palestine specialist, I argued that we needed to examine these questions in general before we could seriously approach the specific case. One reason for this was that both the general field and the Palestine debate were overladen with political and ideological preconceptions. Moreover, one could not establish the significance of genocide for Israel-Palestine simply by comparing it to other cases, and particularly not to the very different circumstances of the Holocaust. Rather, it was necessary first to establish clear *general* conceptual, analytical and historical frameworks.

The problem was that while "genocide" was always intended to have a general applicability in historical understanding, it was developed in a specific context and distorted by beliefs about its relationship to this context. Lemkin coined the term in a study of the Nazi genocide, which was later widely narrowed down to the extermination of the Jews. Yet while he defined genocide as "the destruction of a nation or of an ethnic group", he warned against a narrow interpretation:

> Generally speaking genocide does not necessarily mean the immediate destruction of a nation, except when accomplished by mass killings of all members of a nation. It is intended rather to signify a coordinated plan of different actions aiming at the destruction of essential foundations of the life of national groups, with the aim of annihilating the groups themselves. (1944: 79)

The nuances of the defining word, "destruction", were indicated here by the difference between "immediate destruction" of a nation and "destruction of essential foundations" of its life. Lemkin was clear that genocide referred *generally* to the latter; "immediate" destruction in the sense of "mass killings of all members of a nation", which the Nazis practised against the Jews, was a specific type but did not *define* genocide.

Clearly, both Lemkin and the UN drafters were heavily influenced by the legacy of Nazism but in different ways. Lemkin, although he grew up in a Zionist environment and remained sympathetic to Zionism, did not separate Jewish victimization from the wider destruction of national societies and cultures that Germany perpetrated across occupied Europe. Instead, his was a broad concept and he believed that many populations had suffered, albeit to very different extents, from Nazi genocide.

The UN Convention maintained the core of Lemkin's broad approach, but it created the ambiguity about the role of "physical" destruction that I discussed in Chapter 4. The later move by some scholars to narrow the meaning of genocide towards simple mass killing also corresponded to a growing tendency to view Nazi genocide itself solely in terms of the "Final Solution", although as that terminology suggested, extermination was the conclusion of a longer genocidal project.

Clearly the academic study of genocide needed to resolve these divergences, and the confusion they created as to the proper use of the term, in a coherent and consistent way that enabled us to apply it to a range of cases. A maximalist concept that equated genocide simply with mass killing was sociologically deficient, because this was only one *means* by which armed power organizations (states, parties, regimes, armies, militia, etc.) sought to destroy largely civilian social groups; it was more coherent to focus on the *aim* of destroying a group that informed their actions. While the finality of death for the individual seemed to make killing the ultimate form of violence, it was not self-evident that it was actually more defining of genocide than other methods such as rape, torture and expulsion. Nor was it clear that other coercive means, such as economic, political and cultural dispossession, all of which Lemkin emphasized, were any less significant for the destruction of a group.

What was clear, however, was that if the genocide concept was to be useful, we needed ways of delimiting it from other types of action and conflict. First, we needed to distinguish it from other violence, such as that of war. The key distinction here was that in genocide, an essentially *civilian* group or population is the *enemy* targeted for violence, whereas in war the enemy is another armed actor. Second, we needed to distinguish genocide from forms of *oppression or repression* that fall short of genocide. The distinction here can only be the *destructive* character of the genocidal policy, which aims not just to contain, control or subordinate a population but also to shatter and break up its social existence.

These definitions still left genocide a broad and complex concept. Group destruction would always be multifaceted, and the methods would vary between cases. They also left us with complex analytical tasks: for even if we distinguish genocide from war and repression, in historical reality they are usually closely related. Genocide is often entwined with war and is often preceded or succeeded by non-genocidal oppression. How genocide and war are related, and how repressive policies are transformed into genocide and back again, are constant tensions in any study of the problem. However, little of this intellectual context had been related to the Israel-Palestine case.

Genocide in modern history

I followed this general discussion of the scope of genocide with a discussion of how the development of the academic field had posed issues that were relevant to Palestine. It had became characterized as one of "comparative" study, but there was dissatisfaction with this comparative framework. Historians such as Donald Bloxham (2005; 2009) had shown that it was more fruitful to study genocide within specific historical contexts, rather than transhistorically.

Two major areas of historical enquiry were relevant. The first, of course, was the growing area of colonial genocide studies. Leo Kuper's pioneering work (1981) had emphasized the links between colonialism and genocide, and recent scholarship had greatly reinforced these. However, empire and colonialism were large topics and it was clear that neither phenomenon was universally or generally genocidal. In specifying the linkages, *settler* colonialism was seen as particularly significant, linked as it had been to projects of *displacing* rather than merely *dominating* pre-existing populations, with a greater tendency to deliberately break up established societies than other types of imperial venture.

Thus Dirk Moses (2000), analysing Australia, argued that settler colonialism was structurally prone to genocide, the process tending to involve serial "genocidal moments" in which settlers and militia rather than imperial authorities were the main perpetrators. Michael Mann (who used the term "murderous cleansing") concluded from a broader historical survey: "The more settlers controlled colonial institutions, the more murderous the cleansing. ... It is the most direct relationship I have found between democratic regimes and mass murder" (2005: 4). In the European colonization of the Americas, patterns of genocidal violence occurred at various times across several centuries but without a single centre or driver (Levene 2005a; Mann 2005; Kiernan 2007).

The other major area in which new research directions emerged concerned European genocide in the first half of the twentieth century. Holocaust research was, of course, the largest single area and its strength predated the growth of genocide studies. However, there was an important new trend to relink these fields (e.g. Stone 2007), with two major dimensions. The first was a new recognition of the imperial and colonial character of the Nazi project: the creation of a pan-European empire and grand plans for the German colonization of the East (Mazower 2009). In this perspective, the Holocaust appeared not as an entirely distinct anti-Jewish project but as the most extreme expression of the complex Nazi plans for enslaving the population as a whole, Slavs as well as Jews. This perspective returned us to Lemkin, for whom the genocide was always part of the new order that the Nazis were inflicting across occupied Europe.

This perspective was also important in that it corrected a tendency to distort the history of Nazi anti-Jewish policy itself. When early "intentionalist" accounts of the Holocaust, which read it back to Hitler's earliest antisemitic rhetoric, were countered by "functionalist" narratives that examined how the Final Solution emerged from the changing circumstantial logics of war and occupation, there was a tendency to lose the continuity of the genocidal frame in Nazi anti-Jewish policy. The title of Christopher Browning's important study, *The Path to Genocide* (1991), for example, suggested that only with the Final Solution did Nazi policy towards the Jews become fully genocidal.

This focus on mass murder obscured the fact that the Nazis consistently pursued a general aim of destroying Jewish society, first in Germany and then across Europe. If this aim was not completely clear in the early years – although the persecution and marginalization of German Jews was always designed in part to reduce the Jewish population if only through flight – it had become increasingly so by 1938 when anti-Jewish violence during the Austrian *Anschluss* was followed by *Kristallnacht* (11 November). With the invasion of Poland in September 1939, Nazi policy was immediately directed towards the expulsion of both Jews and non-Jewish Poles from western Poland. Their determined destruction of Jewish and Polish communities led to the concentration of the Jews in closed ghettos where the Nazis ensured that they had totally inadequate conditions of life.

By Lemkin's standards, these developments showed that Nazi policies were already genocidal, towards Poles as well as Jews. The later stages of socially destructive Nazi policies were more extensively murderous, leading through several turns to the extermination camps, but these were *developments of, not towards*, genocide.

The second dimension of the new approaches was the demonstration that Nazi Germany was not alone in implementing genocide in Europe in this period, which was the culmination of half a century in which genocide had been common in the eastern half of the continent (Bloxham 2008; 2009). And although Nazi genocide had its own dynamics, it was implemented in a war in which genocide was becoming an increasingly general tendency.

In particular, although the Stalinist regime, whose genocidal history (Werth 2007; Naimark 2010) already included the "liquidation" of the *kulaks* and the terror-famine, had no special antisemitic animus, when it conquered eastern Poland, it aimed – like the Nazis in the west – to empty large parts of its new territory of Poles and Jews. From mid-1941, when Hitler attacked the USSR, Nazi and Soviet policies developed antagonistically rather than in cooperation, but Stalin's regime developed new genocidal thrusts, brutally deporting whole peoples such as the Chechens, Ingush and Tartars. And Soviet plans for the conclusion of the war increasingly envisaged the expulsion of all Germans from the USSR and its new satellite states, as well as of Poles from areas of Poland annexed to the USSR.

It could therefore be argued that both the major protagonists of the Eastern Front, the Nazi and Stalinist empires, were engaged in genocidal war, partly against each other's core nationalities and partly against third nationalities. And this was not the limit of European genocide: the other Axis powers all had genocidal objectives – Romania to remove the Jews and Hungarians; Croatia to destroy the Serbs; Italy to clear Slovenes and Croats from the Dalmatian coast – while the Allied governments-in-exile of Czechoslovakia and Poland developed, with the approval of their British hosts, plans to expel, in countergenocidal revenge, their remaining German populations, which were seen as complicit in Nazi crimes (Ahonen *et al.* 2008; Brandes 2008).

In the concluding months of the war and afterwards, the USSR, together with the new Czechoslovak and Polish regimes, forced large-scale population movements including the expulsion of over ten million Germans, of whom at least half a million died in the process (Bloxham, 2008: 122). These policies were ratified by the Western Allies at the Potsdam conference in 1945 and resulted in a destruction of German society in the East almost as comprehensive, if not nearly as murderous, as the destruction of historic Jewish society.

The Second World War was therefore, especially in eastern Europe, a generally genocidal war. And this was not an exceptional phase of the modern international system. On the contrary, as Bloxham (2005) showed, this period followed from the earlier "great game of genocide", arising from the crisis of the Ottoman Empire, culminating in the Armenian genocide of 1915.

Zionism's incipiently genocidal mentality of "transfer"

How is this larger genocide history relevant to Palestine? Most of the Jewish population arrived in the late nineteenth and early twentieth centuries as European settler colonialism was reaching its global climax, so that the policies of the Zionist movement and Israeli state towards the Palestinian Arabs can certainly be examined as part of this pattern. Yet this suggests a modification of this perspective: we also need to pay attention to the prevalent genocidal mentality among nationalist elites in eastern Europe, the milieu in which Zionism was formed. Zionist colonization was an answer not to the problems of Palestine but to those "wrought by European modernity", as Areej Sabbagh-Khoury (2023: 10) puts it.

In eastern Europe it had become normal for nationalists to envisage removing populations that did not fit their proposed ethnically homogenous state. Outside the context of war, such projects were often proposed as involving voluntary "transfers" or "exchanges" of populations and in the aftermath of the First World War, and the USA, Britain and France had endorsed the proposals for an exchange between Greece and Turkey. Yet the reality of the uprooting and expulsion of populations was often much more brutal than euphemisms such as "exchange" suggested. The proposal here is, therefore, that we should view Israel's destruction of Palestinian society not simply through the settler-colonial lens but also as an extension of the exclusivist nationalism that had recently brought about extensive genocidal violence in the European war.

Early twentieth-century Zionism was therefore "a very particular colonial project", as Rashid Khalidi (2020: 9) argues; there was even a distinctive nexus of colonialism and socialism (Sabbagh-Khoury 2023). But from the movement's inception, its leaders envisaged displacing the Arab population, initially in gradual terms as Theodore Herzl advocated in 1895: "We must expropriate gently ... Both the process of expropriation and the removal of the poor must be carried out discretely and circumspectly" (Morris 2004: 41). As Benny Morris documented, ideas of removal were kept largely private and in the background, as "the Zionist public catechism ... remained that there was room enough in Palestine for both peoples ... There was no need for a transfer of the Arabs" (2004: 43).

In the early decades, Zionist thinking certainly included more enlightened strands, and its eliminationist ideology was not obviously genocidal: "fantasies of compulsory transfer were rare, and killing as a mechanism of elimination was absent from political discourse" (Sorek 2025: 2). As Mark Levene comments, "drawing a straight line from Herzl through David Ben-Gurion, to Ariel Sharon and beyond, accusing them of aiming to get rid of the Palestinians, elides all manner of Zionist thinking and practice which has been more circumspect, cautious, and often energized by the potential for a Zionist-Arab relationship in which the two peoples might live together" (2007: 676–7).

The ultimate Zionist rejection of coexistence was also conditioned by Palestinian resistance, beginning with attacks on Jewish communities during the 1929 and 1936–9 uprisings (Levene 2007: 676). As Sorek (2025: 2) puts it, "[t]he realization by Zionist settlers that Palestinians violently resisted the Zionist colonial settler project, coupled with the anxiety this resistance provoked, is critical to understanding the evolution of the genocidal imagination".

Nevertheless, the idea of "transfer" was increasingly dominant in Zionist ideology: as Morris (2004: 44) puts it, "by the early 1930s a full-throated near-consensus in support of the idea began to emerge among the movement's leaders". Zionists argued that the process could be benevolent, ironically describing Palestinian Arabs in terms reminiscent of the antisemites who denied that eastern Europe was really a "homeland" for its Jews. Zionists believed, Nur Masalha (1997: x) noted, that

> the uprooting and transfer of the Palestinians to Arab countries would constitute a mere relocation from one district to another; that the Palestinians would have no difficulty in accepting Jordan, Syria, or Iraq as their homeland; that the Palestinian Arabs had little emotional attachment and few real ties to the particular soil in Palestine and would be just as content outside the "Land of Israel"; that the Palestinian Arabs were marginal to the Arab nation and their problems might be facilitated by a "benevolent" and "humanitarian" policy of "helping people to leave".

As Morris (2004: 43, 60) argues, for Zionists "the logic of a transfer solution to the 'Arab problem' remained ineluctable; without some sort of massive displacement of Arabs from the area of the Jewish state-to-be, there could be no viable Jewish state". Transfer was "inevitable and inbuilt into Zionism – because it sought to transform a land which was 'Arab' into a 'Jewish' state and a Jewish state could not have arisen without a major displacement of Arab population". Interestingly, the Hebrew word *tihur* (transfer) is closer in meaning to "purification" or "cleansing", emphasizing the idea's affinity with the "cleansing" and "racial purification" ideologies typical of genocidal projects.

And if Zionist ideology envisaged voluntary dislocation, there was little doubt that the implementation of "transfer" would require coercion. The reality was that forced population movements were universally destructive: Giorgio Balladore Pallieri reported in 1952 that among 20 "transfer" treaties between 1913 and 1945, "there has never been a truly voluntary transfer of populations" (Schabas 2000: 195–6). How could it be otherwise? However variable populations' attachments to national ideas and territories, their attachment to *their* land, homes, villages and towns could hardly be doubted. For example, Jewish populations in Europe, often rejected as outsiders, had serious attachments to the places in which they lived (Cesarani, Kushner & Milton 2009). In fixed agrarian societies, and by extension in urban concentrations, communities were closely embedded in territorial settings.

Therefore, to propose breaking up communities was to threaten their destruction and the ideology of transfer pointed in a genocidal direction. Even if it were the case, as Morris (2004: 60) contends, that the pre-war Zionist consensus for transfer "was not tantamount to pre-planning and did not issue in the production of a policy or master-plan for expulsion", it nevertheless expressed an *incipiently genocidal mentality* towards Arab society, in the manner of many European nationalist ideologies of the time. As Tamir Sorek puts it, the genocidal mentality of the 2020s is "deeply rooted in the eliminatory imagination of transfer – a concept preached and practised by the founding fathers of Secular Zionism – and in annihilatory rhetoric employed by Secular Zionists as early as the 1930s" (2025: 2).

Zionist leaders developed their thoughts very much in the light of European developments. Morris (2001: 45) summarizes Ben-Gurion's discussion of "transfer" in his 1941 diary:

> a complete transfer of the bulk of the Arab population could only be carried out by force, by "ruthless compulsion", in Ben-Gurion's phrase. However recent European history, Ben-Gurion pointed out, had demonstrated that a massive, compulsory transfer of populations was possible – and the ongoing world war had made the idea of transfer even more popular as the surest and most practical way to solve the difficult and dangerous problem of national minorities. The postwar settlement in Europe, he envisioned, would include massive transformation transfers.

Similarly, Chaim Weizmann, president of the Zionist Organisation, even discussed forced removals with Ivan Maisky, Stalin's ambassador to London, in January 1941, while the USSR was removing the Jewish population from eastern Poland. Weizmann seemed unconcerned with this, instead canvassing Maisky on the prospects of moving the Palestinian Arabs "into Iraq or Transjordan". He said that "if half a million Arabs could be transferred, two million Jews could be put in their place". However, he did explain "that they were unable to deal with [the Arabs] as, for instance, the Russian authorities would deal with a backward element in their population in the USSR. Nor would they desire to do so" (Morris 2001: 46).

Thus Zionist leaders had a good grasp of the contemporary politics of population removal. This was the wider historical context in which the Nakba developed, and events in 1948 suggest that, when it came to putting "transfer" into practice, Israel's attitude was closer to Stalin's than to Weizmann's. The illusion of "voluntary transfer" could never survive implementation, especially not in circumstances of war.

The Nakba: the intentional destruction of Palestinian society

The events of 1948 have been widely discussed among specialists, and there remains substantial disagreement. In 2010, what I believed I could do as a non-specialist was to indicate the way in which a genocide perspective related to the disputed issues, and this remains the approach in the following discussion. I was over-reliant on Israeli rather than Palestinian historians, partly because they had produced some of the essential research, but also because I believed that by showing that Israeli work supported my argument that genocide had been committed, it would be easier to rebut the inevitable accusations of antisemitism.

Morris, who among the "revisionist" historians presented the view that suggested the least degree of Israeli planning for the destruction of Arab society, argued that "the Yishuv [the Jewish community] and its military forces did not enter the 1948 war, which was initiated by the Arab side, with a policy or plan for expulsion" (2004: 60). Rather, he suggested in his first book, *The Birth of the Palestinian Refugee Problem, 1947–1949* (1986), that the circumstances of the war brought about the flight of much of the Arab population, although Israeli forces did coerce and deliberately expel some Palestinians.

This view was challenged by Nur Masalha (1992: 180), who argued that it was "difficult – in light of the systematic nature of the 'clearing out' operations and the sheer magnitude of the exodus (not to mention the careful efforts to prevent the return of the refugees) – not to see a policy at work". Laila Parsons (2001) pointed to the discrimination within Israeli policies towards the population, so that the Druze, whose leaders allied themselves with the Zionists, were generally spared the general destruction; she argued that this provided evidence that purposeful Israeli policies lay behind the removal of the Arab population.

In the revised version of his book, Morris (2004) also acknowledged a substantially greater role for Israeli force in the destruction of Palestinian society. However, he still argued that there was no overarching plan; rather the war provided a situation in which the Israeli forces were able to secure the removal of the Arabs that was required by the logic of their project, taking advantage of the opportunities presented in the war.

In contrast, Pappé's *Ethnic Cleansing of Palestine* (2007) provided sustained evidence of systematic preparations for the dispossession of the Arabs by Ben-Gurion's leadership group, the Consultancy, prior to the war, and how these were implemented during it. On his account, it was clear that there had been extensive collection of information concerning the Arab population with a view to removing most of them from the areas allocated to Israel under the UN proposals, so as to achieve a Jewish majority. It was also clear that the removal of Palestinians had begun even before the war, and was pursued by the leadership during it, even if its implementation was influenced by decisions on the ground.

Mark Levene (2007: 678), while criticizing Pappé for understating the role of Arab resistance, agreed that he

> unequivocally demonstrates that the drive towards the removal of the Palestinians came from the top. Demotic elements there are: land-hungry kibbutniks intent on grabbing as much neighbouring Arab land as they can; greedy Tel-Aviv townies quick to recognize the once-in-a-lifetime opportunities to be had from the flight of Jaffa neighbours and the rapid seizure of their property and assets. But, as in so many similar examples worldwide, such despicable behaviour is not cause but effect ... The drive for *tihur* – cleansing – emanated from the Consultancy.

Levene concluded that "on all this, only one verdict is available, and it is the one that Pappé uses: ethnic cleansing" (2007: 680).

Yet Pappé adopted what can only be described as a naïve approach to his central concept, relying on definitions provided by dictionaries, Wikipedia and the United Nations High Commissioner for Refugees, and ignoring even academic writers who had utilized this term (Bell-Fialkoff 1996; Naimark 2001; Mann 2005). Pappé regarded "ethnic cleansing" as a "well-defined concept" and "paradigm", when in reality it was difficult and contested. And when Pappé and Levene compared Israeli "cleansing" with Serbian policies in Bosnia-Herzegovina, they failed to acknowledge that these were also often regarded as genocide, at the time as well as in the subsequent literature (Markusen 2003).

"Ethnic cleansing" and genocide

This is not the place for a full history of the "ethnic cleansing" idea. Suffice it to say that it was present throughout the twentieth century in ethnic expulsions in the Balkans and re-emerged during the 1990s. However, the term was not widely used outside the region until the Bosnian war, when it was adopted by Western media, international organizations, political leaders, international lawyers (although it is not a defined legal category) and scholars.

From the start, there were questions about ethnic cleansing's relationship to genocide. Population expulsion was clearly designed, in Bosnia as in eastern Europe and India decades earlier, to destroy particular ethnic or national communities, even if it did not necessarily entail the mass murder of all or most of their members. In this sense it certainly fell within the scope of Lemkin's and the Genocide Convention's definitions of genocide as the deliberate destruction of a group, although as we saw earlier, the latter's apparent conflation of "destruction" with its "physical" form, deepened in the international jurisprudence, confused the matter.

The proposal that expulsion of populations should be specified as a means of genocide had received short shrift during the convention drafting debates, because it was recognized that expulsion was being practised or approved on all sides, including by UN member states. Indeed, by the same token, during those years expulsion was the most common method of the "destruction" of population groups that was defined as genocide. Therefore, this was a fundamental, conscious lacuna, as Schabas (2000: 196) notes:

> There is no doubt that the drafters of the Convention quite deliberately resisted attempts to encompass the phenomenon of ethnic cleansing within the punishable acts. According to the comments accompanying the Secretariat draft, the proposed definition excluded "certain acts which may result in the total or partial destruction of a group of human beings ... namely ... mass displacements of population".

This decision created the ambiguous relationship of "ethnic cleansing" to the legal concept of genocide that repeatedly surfaced as international law began to be enforced in the 1990s. Some judges, such as the Cambridge lawyer Elihu Lauterpacht, nominated by the Bosnian Government as an ad hoc judge in the ICTY, considered "ethnic cleansing" to be a form of genocide (Shaw 2007: 50–51), because of its manifest fit with the overall idea of group destruction and because the means proscribed in the convention are commonly committed during expulsions. However, the majority of judges and legal authorities adopted narrower interpretations. The tribunal, for example, although on occasion ruling "ethnic cleansing" to be genocide, generally avoided this conclusion, as we have seen did the ICJ when it concluded that only the 1995 Srebrenica massacre constituted genocide while the "ethnic cleansing" of Serbian-occupied Bosnia between 1992 and 1995 did not (International Court of Justice 2007a). The Holocaust standard and the perception that forced removal was less serious fed the tendency to distinguish "cleansing" from genocide, and this continued over Darfur in 2003. This tendency served, of course, the political interest of governments and the UN in avoiding the recognition of genocide.

We cannot, however, see "ethnic cleansing" as an alternative to genocide. Even Bell-Fialkoff (1996: 3–4), who proposes the term, admits that its perpetrator meaning is a problem: "The term 'cleansing' itself is ambiguous. In everyday use it has positive connotations of cleanliness and purification ... But when applied to human populations it refers to refugees, deportation, and detention. It spells suffering. And that is why the term is widely used: it is a euphemism that hides the ugly truth." Similarly, Naimark (2001: 193) acknowledges: "There is nothing 'clean' about ethnic cleansing. It is shot through with violence and brutality in the most extreme form"; and Schabas (2001: 194), who argues that legally cleansing is not necessarily genocide, still calls it a "euphemism for genocide".

Indeed, organized violence against civilians cannot be genuinely cleansing, even for perpetrators, let alone for victims or society at large: if the language of dirt and cleanliness applies at all, it is surely the "cleansers" who foul social life, which needs purification from their violence. "Ethnic cleansing" is thus a euphemistic perpetrator term that has no place in social science or history, which is why I have kept it within inverted commas.

The question remains, however, whether shorn of this language the concept refers to a distinctive reality. Yet when advocates attempt to specify its content, there is more fuzziness. For Bell-Fialkoff (1996: 1), "[p]opulation cleansing [his broader version of the concept] ... defies easy definition. It covers a wide range of phenomena from genocide at one end to subtle pressure to emigrate at the other". Similarly, Naimark (2001: 3–4) is clear that the boundary between non-genocidal cleansing and genocide might be unreal:

> Further complicating the distinctions between ethnic cleansing and genocide is the fact that forced deportation seldom takes place without violence, often murderous violence. People do not leave their homes on their own ... They resist ... The result is that forced deportation often becomes genocidal, as people are violently ripped from their native towns and villages and killed when they try to stay. Even when forced deportation is not genocidal in its intent, it is often genocidal in its effects.

Indeed, how could mass "forced deportation" ever be achieved without extreme coercion or violence? How, indeed, can deportation not be forced? How could it not involve the destruction of a community, of the way of life that a group has enjoyed over a period of time? How could those who deported a group not *intend* this destruction, and how could people not resist? In what significant way is the forcible removal of a population from their homeland different from the destruction of a group? If the boundary between "cleansing" and genocide is unreal, why police it?

The Nakba as a genocide

No one contends that in 1948 Israel intended to commit the extensive mass murder of the Palestinians: the Nakba was not a new Final Solution. However, earlier episodes in the Nazi genocide of the Jews, such as the 1939–40 expulsion from western Poland into ghettos in central Poland, provide more debatable comparisons. More obviously, Palestine in 1948 was like Bosnia-Herzegovina, where a *minority* of the non-Serb population was murdered as part of a campaign to terrorize the *majority* of the population into leaving the territory controlled by Republika Srpska, the statelet that the Serbian nationalists carved out of Bosnia rather as the Zionists carved Israel out of Palestine.

However, one should not push any analogy too far. The question is whether, and if so how, a coherent, broad concept of genocide applies to Palestine. None of the "revisionist" historians who now dominate the field doubt that deliberate Israeli policies made a substantial contribution to the destruction of the larger part of historical Arab society in Palestine: not even Morris, who now justifies this as the only way in which a Jewish state could be created. This creates prima facie a strong case for considering the events within a genocide framework.

Equally, no serious scholar contends that Israel had a definite policy of destroying the *whole* of Palestinian Arab society. Even if Zionist leaders would have preferred an exclusively Jewish society in the whole of Palestine, they were operating under international surveillance. They were not actually implementing the partition plan; rather they were carrying out a unilateral secession from the Mandate territory of Palestine and took advantage of the war to extend the boundaries of their state beyond those allocated by the UN (Gurmendi Dunkelberg 2024a). Their aim was clearly to create as large as possible a state, with a large Jewish majority, expelling as many Arabs as possible.

Even on Morris's account, the widespread destruction of Arab society should be considered partly genocidal. Although some death and flight resulted fairly randomly from the war, much was the result of deliberate decisions by the Zionist political and military leaderships, local commanders and officials.

As Levene (2007: 678) says, as a case of ethnic expulsion, the story is familiar. Given

> that these operations occurred just two or three years after the end of the Holocaust, the ease with which they took on the aspect of a standard operating procedure is little short of sickening. After its onset in the initial tentative attacks, the general lack of Arab resistance provided a green light to a formula in which villages were surrounded, often at night or at dawn, and a range of ordnance loosed off to cause panic. The village having usually then surrendered, able men and boys were lined up, and sometimes shot – on the spot, or elsewhere. In worse cases, some where resistance had occurred, sometimes where it had not, a more general massacre ensued.

On Morris's account, this was a case in which, despite the ideology of "transfer", Israel's genocidal thrusts developed situationally and incrementally, in a partly decentred, networked genocide, developed in interaction with the enemy during the war. On Pappé's account, however, genocide was much more centrally planned and coordinated in practice, and resulted from a strong, coherent aim of the Zionist leadership to break up much of Arab society and drive most of the Arabs from Israeli-controlled land.

I originally argued that it was not necessary for me, as a non-specialist, to resolve these differences; what I could do was to place them in the context of comparative genocide research. The trend among scholars was to move away from the absolutist, singular conceptions of "intention", regarding these as historically and sociologically unrealistic. This trend was set in Holocaust studies: despite Hitler's undeniably genocidal ideology that can be traced to *Mein Kampf*, few now believed that the Nazis had a consistent aim of mass extermination before 1941, and all serious historians acknowledged that they developed policies in response to changing situations. Moreover, scholars were also less inclined to see genocide as a purely top-down affair: there is always a relation between different levels of state and society, involving some variant of Mann's typical trinity of elites, paramilitaries and core constituencies.

Thus to regard the Nakba as a case of genocide it was not necessary, I argued, to demonstrate a completely pre-formed, consistent intention on the part of Zionist leaders. On the contrary, it would be surprising if, in the context of a fast-moving political and military situation, their specific intentions and policies had *not* adapted in the light of new constraints and opportunities. Nor was it necessary to suggest that the various elements of the destruction of Arab society were decided only at the highest levels of Zionism, rather than in some combination of the Consultancy, various levels of military authority and local leaderships. The relationships between pre-formed policy and contingent adaptation, and between central leadership and other actors, were empirical questions, not criteria of genocide.

However, the intentional character of the destruction of Palestinian society was strikingly confirmed by the policies that Israel pursued after the removal of the population. As early as June 1948, Israel ruled out the return of those who had fled its terror in the previous months, while Palestinian villages that had been razed to the ground were rebuilt as Jewish settlements under new names. Although Israel was forced to accept a continuing Arab minority within its borders, this remained under military rule for two decades and was marginalized thereafter; the state was constructed with an overwhelmingly Jewish rather than an inclusive civic character.

The Nakba in comparative perspective

In comparative perspective, Israel's destruction of the larger part of Palestinian society in 1948 was not exceptionally murderous ("only" 5,000–10,000 Arabs were massacred). It was a case of genocidal expulsion in an era when this was occurring on a larger scale in both Europe and Asia, and it was not only in Palestine that it had lasting consequences. Nor was Israel unusual in having genocide in its past: Germany and other states in eastern and central Europe were heirs to the destruction of the Jews and various national minorities, while the states of the New World were also constructed through the destruction of indigenous communities. Not only in Israel but in most of these cases, histories were suppressed and their genocidal dimensions firmly denied.

Despite this, the consequences of the Nakba were distinctive. This is mainly because the Palestinians mostly survived and were able to develop their national movement, with support from the Arab world where nationalism was widely embedded. In contrast, most other settler-colonial genocides took place before or during earlier stages of the rise of nationalism, and their indigenous victims had not formed comparable movements. Therefore, while other settler states were able to consolidate their genocides in a relatively uncontested fashion and indigenous voices often became prominent only long after this had taken place, Israel was unable to achieve such uncontested dominance. The Palestinians never became reconciled to the effects of the Nakba, and whatever other concessions Israel was at times prepared to offer in return for peace, it never acknowledged the consequences of this terrible foundational event, for example by recognizing a Palestinian right of return.

This suggests that we should view the Nakba as *more than* a settler-colonial genocide and a product of modern nationalism. It was also a *genocide of decolonization*, the worldwide process of change in the period following the Second World War. Edward Said noted that "[b]etween 1922 and 1947 the great issue witnessed by the world in Palestine was not, as a Palestinian would like to imagine, the struggle between natives and new colonists, but a struggle presented as being between Britain and the Zionists" (1992: 51). However, in reality the Zionists were competing with the emerging Palestinian national movement to run Palestine when the British departed.

The most appropriate comparisons are not, therefore, earlier indigenous genocides in the Americas and Australasia, most of which concluded with the establishment of independent settler states before the First World War. Rather, we should compare Israel with the other post-1945 cases in which settler and indigenous nationalist movements competed to succeed the imperial power. In Algeria, nationalists fought a brutal and at times genocidal war of decolonization with France, which attempted to protect the settlers' dominance; this concluded with an exodus of the colonists. In Rhodesia, another war led to the defeat of the settler regime and Zimbabwe's independence. In South Africa, the apartheid regime, established to consolidate settler rule in the same year that Israel was formed, eventually avoided a full-scale war by conceding power to the national movement.

Thus Israel was the only case in which the settler movement retained power by expelling the majority of the indigenous population. In this, it was of course similar to earlier colonial cases, but in the era of decolonization and anticolonial nationalism this victory had a radically different significance. The Palestinians contested the Zionist victory through both civil resistance, most notably in the First Intifada, and armed struggle, which led Israel to present the conflict as a security issue and led to increasingly genocidal "permanent security" framings.

"Slow-motion" genocide: occupation, annexation, apartheid

In the succeeding decades, the Nakba became more potent and the conflict more severe because the results of 1948 were never enough for Israel's leaders. Their national project was always regarded as incomplete: the dispossession of the Palestinians continued after 1948 and the conquest of the West Bank, East Jerusalem, Gaza and the Golan Heights in 1967 profoundly changed the situation. Now Israel ruled over the entire territory of historic (Mandate) Palestine and all the Palestinians who remained within it.

The 1967 war was a moment of rapid acceleration in population removal. More than 300,000 more Palestinians – including many survivors of the 1948 expulsions who were living in refugee camps – fled or were expelled to Jordan and Egypt and, like those who fled in 1948, were prevented by Israel from returning (Masalha 2003: 178–217). In international law, occupation was supposed to be temporary and occupiers were not allowed to change local social realities or introduce settlers, but from the start Israel looked for a more or less permanent occupation and had little interest in finding a solution that would end it, while Zionist thinkers revived their ideas of "transfer" (Masalha 2003: 179–88).

In Lemkin's terms, Israel's leaders and ideologues saw the occupation as an opportunity to "impose its national pattern" and replace that of the occupied in the new territories, in order to progressively incorporate them into Israel. He had outlined two options for the genocidal occupier: imposing its pattern on the existing population, or on the territory alone without the population. In Ukraine after 2014, Russia effectively combined these options: it regarded Ukrainians as Russifiable and therefore accepted all who remained and voluntarily or otherwise accepted to be Russified, but it also imported settlers to fill the urban space emptied by the majority who left or were expelled.

Israel also combined the two methods but in a different way. It regarded Palestinians as members of a different ethnicity who could never be Judaized: even mixed marriages were banned. Israel accepted, on sufferance, the minority within the post-1948 state and eventually accorded them (second-class) citizenship, but the Palestinian population in the newly occupied territories was too large to be accommodated in this way – they would have threatened the Jewish majority in the population if given citizenship. Israel therefore opted for a distinctive version of the "territory alone" option: to impose its national pattern on the Palestinian population *in order to incrementally remove them* and colonize the territory with its own nationals. In the meantime, the Palestinians were to be contained through a combination of military, legal, bureaucratic and economic means.

The occupation therefore involved from the start what Saree Makdisi (2008) calls "slow-motion" genocide, extending and consolidating the mass expulsions of 1948 and 1967 in a piecemeal fashion. The "destructive" side of the process was clear: villages, houses and land were destroyed, property owners were evicted and residents were denied access to their neighbourhoods, while Israeli-only roads, checkpoints and the "separation wall" divided Palestinian areas from each other and individual Palestinians from family members and land that they owned. At the same time, the imposition of the Israeli pattern was embedded by the introduction of settlers and settlements, at first on a modest scale but by 2023 including a population of over 700,000, who increasingly contributed their own violence to the destructive process.

The idea of "slow-motion" genocide chimes with wider thinking: Sheri Rosenberg argues (2012) that genocide is "a process, not an event", and Pauline Wakeham (2021) argues that genocide studies' "prioritization of time-intense direct violence with explicit intent" has taken attention from the "slow violence" of settler colonialism.

The gradual erosion of Palestinian society, while illegal under the international law of occupation, was generally legalized by Israel's domestic law and supported by a large part of its state apparatus. While Israel never formally annexed the occupied territories, its practices amounted to annexation, as the ICJ recognized (International Court of Justice 2024d). Supporting the court's opinion, Ronit Levene-Schnur, Tamar Megiddo and Yael Berda (2025) argue that since formal annexation is internationally outlawed, from a legal point of view it is not appropriate to require a formal proclamation as evidence: rather, sociological analysis of power relations enables us to identify annexation. Since Israel has imposed its normative organizing framework, bureaucratic machinery and symbolic power on the territory, it has clearly incorporated the occupied territories into the state: most completely in East Jerusalem, very substantially in the West Bank and residually in Gaza.

Israel's annexation of the West Bank and East Jerusalem continued through the intermittent international negotiations of the 1970s to the 2000s. The negotiation period introduced, of course, the Palestinian Authority (PA) as a partially self-governing institution within the 22 per cent of Mandate Palestine over which Israel was prepared to cede some control: a minority of the West Bank, together with Gaza. However, Israel resisted any attempt to create a state even within these limits and, playing off Hamas against the PA, conspired to weaken further the structurally weak Palestinian institutions.

Indeed, the repeated negotiations amounted to "preventing Palestine", as Seth Anziska's eponymous book (2018) has it. For the Palestinians, the first talks at Camp David during 1977–8 were "a formative moment of disenchantment", and the principal "avenues for sovereignty" were closed down between then and Oslo in the 1990s (Anziska 2018: 2, 15). The further Camp David talks in 2000 failed, despite concerted US–Israeli attempts to blame the Palestinian Liberation Organization leader Yasser Arafat, because, Avi Shlaim (2024: 83–5) concludes, Israel was still unprepared to allow the return of Palestinian refugees or accept Palestinian sovereignty over the Muslim holy places in Jerusalem.

Despite the negotiations and because of their failure, the occupation accelerated in the new century as Palestinian resistance increasingly took an armed form and the far right and settler movements gained greater power in Israeli politics. Shlaim (2024: 107) cites Baruch Kimmerling's (2006) argument that Israel's consistent attempt to prevent a viable Palestinian entity amounted to "politicide", but taking this together with the incessant dismantling of Palestinian society, it represents a genocidal process in Israel–Palestine relations. Indeed, much of Lemkin's analysis of occupation as a context of genocide is directly relevant to the longest-running occupation of modern times. He wrote that:

> The confiscation of the property of nationals of an occupied area on the ground that they have left the country may be considered as a deprivation of their individual property rights. However, if the confiscations are ordered against individuals solely because they are Poles, Jews or Czechs, then the same confiscations tend in effect to weaken the national entities of which those persons are members. (1944: 79)

Substitute "Palestinians" and you have an analysis of expropriation in Palestine.

The idea of Israel as an "apartheid" regime raises similar issues. Alonso Gurmendi Dunkelberg (2025: 12) even suggests that "apartheid and other forms of structural racial domination" are "simply slow-moving genocides", but this formulation collapses the important distinction between colonial domination and destruction. While colonial rule generally transforms and undermines pre-existing indigenous societies and cultures, it doesn't always aim to destroy them, either instantly or gradually; it seems important to distinguish destruction policies, fast or slow, from situations in which colonial power incorporates indigenous societies and institutions. Thus, if Israel simply allowed Palestinian society to exist in a subordinate status under its dominion, its rule would constitute colonial oppression but it would not be genocidal. Israel is a genocidal, rather than simply an apartheid, state because its occupation regime is *designed to progressively destroy* Palestinian society and replace it by an ever-enhanced Israeli presence.

The difference can be understood by comparing Israeli apartheid to the South African prototype. Although Afrikaner nationalism, built on class domination and exploitation, incorporated non-whites *into* the state and assigned them distinct subordinate statuses, Zionism emphasized the separateness of the Jewish people. While content to exploit Arabs' labour, it was not interested in binding them into its rule through formal relationships. This is not to say that genocide had no role in South African apartheid. On the contrary, white rule was originally established through partially genocidal colonial wars that destroyed and subjugated indigenous peoples (Adhikari 2010; Penn 2013; Blackbeard 2015). The modern system of apartheid, inaugurated by the Nationalist Party in 1948, also consolidated Black subjugation through genocidal mass expulsions, notoriously at Sophiatown in 1955 (Shaw 2013: 116–17). However, while the Nationalists intended apartheid, once established, as a permanent system of racial dominion, Zionists did not see their version in this way.

Genocide has therefore been a more structural presence in Israeli than it was in South African rule. Israel's "slow-motion" version resembles South Africa's local destructions of non-white communities in the 1950s, but even before 2023, its violence in the occupied territories had taken it far beyond South Africa. Patrick Wolfe observed two decades ago that the West Bank and Gaza had "become less and less like Bantustans and more and more like reservations (or, for that matter, like the Warsaw Ghetto)" (2006: 404). Apartheid South Africa was notorious for its 1960 Sharpeville massacre in which 69 people died; from late 2023, Israel perpetrated a Sharpeville almost every day.

Here the "late" character of Israeli colonization is crucial. Israeli apartheid was established through a large genocidal event, the Nakba, which has no real comparator in twentieth-century South Africa. Likewise, the extension of Israeli rule entrenched a primarily military form of domination, where South African rule was enmeshed in economic power relations and enforced by the police as well as the army. Israel's openly military rule also provoked more persistent armed threats than South African apartheid ever faced (despite the African National Congress's rhetoric), so it responded more consistently with military force and violent civilian destruction. Nor was Israel's genocidal tendency restricted to the occupied territories: in 1982, in the Palestinian refugee camps of Sabra and Shatila, Israel's Lebanese allies committed under its supervision a notorious massacre in which a thousand died, which was widely recognized as genocide at the time (MacBride 1983).

The Gaza mini-wars and Israel's genocidal mentality

Even before 2023, Gaza presented the strongest case of the genocidal dynamics of Israeli rule. I wrote the original version of this chapter in the aftermath of Israel's first major military assault, Operation Cast Lead (2008–9), noting that within the IAGS, some who rebelled against its earlier pro-Israeli bias described the new war as genocide. At the time, I was unconvinced: it was not clear that Israel aimed to destroy Palestinian society in Gaza; rather, it seemed intent on imposing a severe collective punishment on that society for its support of Hamas, while attempting to destroy, physically as well as militarily, the organization itself. Ironically, it was the attempt to assassinate civilian Hamas members, killing their families, which seemed to me closer to genocide than the punishment of the general population.

After a decade and a half of further mini-wars that were, as Shlaim puts it (2024: 97), not "wars in the usual sense" but "one-sided massacres", this seems an unduly conservative interpretation. Certainly, taken overall, Israel's blockade from 2007 to 2023 was a form of repressing rather than destroying Gazan society; the difference is brought into relief now that we have seen what a fully destructive policy involves. Nevertheless, this "collective punishment" had much in common with genocide: it directed mass violence at a civilian population, as an enemy in itself, as well as at its Hamas rulers; and locally it was extremely destructive and murderous, as the 2023 campaign would be across the territory.

Therefore, with the benefit of hindsight we can see that 2009 was the harbinger of further major assaults in 2012, 2014 and 2021, which generalized the violence against the families and neighbours of Hamas militants into the razing of entire neighbourhoods. These episodes showed an increasing genocidal edge in the policy of repression, captured in the cruel euphemism "mowing the grass", which was even turned into a strategic doctrine (Inbar & Shamir 2014). Israel also responded with violence to the Great March of Return in 2018. The blockade could not really be understood apart from the way in which it was periodically enforced, which clearly pointed towards even greater violence if the situation was not resolved.

Israel's rhetoric also radicalized in a genocidal direction. As early as 1980, the Rabbi of Bar-Ilan University, Israel Hess, had published an article titled "The Genocide Commandment in the Torah", unambiguously stating: "In a war between Israel and Amalek, it is a commandment to kill and annihilate infants and babies. And who is Amalek? Anyone who launches a war against the Jews" (Sorek 2025). There was remarkably little pushback from other religious Zionists, and this was the rhetoric that Netanyahu himself would reference in 2023.

This mentality became more explicit with the Gaza wars. In 2008 a deputy defence minister, Matan Vilnai, warning that the state was close to launching a huge military operation in Gaza (which it soon did), said that Palestinians would bring on themselves a "bigger shoah", using the Hebrew word usually reserved for the Holocaust. Although he tried to play down his language, saying he meant only "disaster" and "did not mean to make any allusion to the genocide", Vilnai's rhetoric was suggestive of the trend in Israeli thinking.

In 2014, another minister, Ayelet Shaked, wrote on Facebook that the Palestinian people were the enemy and all who supported enemy armed fighters were combatants: their mothers, too, "should go, as should the physical homes in which they raised the snakes. Otherwise, more little snakes will be raised there" (Abunimah 2014). Genocidal rhetoric was becoming bolder (a better example of Moses' idea of permanent security would be hard to find) and Shaked, far from paying a price, was later promoted to both justice and interior minister. In 2009, and even in 2014, such ideas did not seem to fully inform Israel's policies, but by 2023, there was little doubt that they did.

This extreme rhetoric was combined, especially in mainstream US and other Western milieux, with the more fundamental Israeli ideology of anti-antisemitism, which as we have seen was codified in the International Holocaust Remembrance Alliance's (2016) definition of antisemitism and the campaign to diffuse this definition through international institutions.

With each new assault that Israel made on Gaza, increases in classical antisemitic acts and rhetoric were recorded in many countries, as well as the more widespread anti-Zionism that was misleading characterized as antisemitic.

Both were used to legitimate claims that Israel's violence was protecting Jews from antisemitism. What was also happening, however, within both Israel and Western societies, was that anti-Palestinian, anti-Arab and anti-Muslim racism were stimulated, equally serving to legitimate Israeli violence. It was hardly unusual for war to stimulate racist characterizations of "enemy" populations, but where the Israel–Palestine conflict was concerned, the structural production of anti-Palestinian racism *alongside* antisemitism mostly went unremarked in mainstream Western accounts, although the consequences for Palestinians were far more severe than for Jews (Shaw 2015).

Gaza and the structure of genocide in Palestine

In 2010, I drew the conclusion that a state and society founded in the circumstances of 1948, which was continuing to extend its genocidal expulsions and had not come to terms with their enduring injustice, would continue to resort to degenerate war as a method of keeping the Palestinians in their place. We now know that they would go far beyond that.

The "return of genocide" must therefore now include a reassessment of the Israel-Palestine history as a whole, taking account of how Palestinian writers are framing their experience. Although "genocide" was not as central before 2023 as it has now become, two accounts in particular lend themselves to a reformulation of the genocide perspective that I originally proposed. First, Rashid Khalidi (2020) has described the *longue durée* as a "century of war" against Palestine. But as I have shown, it is not far-fetched to think of the same history as a century of genocide, so long as we understand that this threat has often been partial or potential rather than widely realized, as in 1948 and 2023.

Second, developing an insight first expressed by Hanan Ashrawi in 2001, when she described the accelerating dispossession as an "ongoing Nakba", Ardi Imseis (2023) has analysed the Nakba as "a structure, not an event". The idea of structure has largely been marginal in genocide theory, but as we have seen Tony Barta (1987) seminally used it to describe the long process of colonial dispossession of indigenous peoples, seeing Australia as a structurally genocidal society. Later, Patrick Wolfe (2008: 119–21) argued that elimination, a "larger category" than genocide, was a structural proclivity of settler colonialism, which amounted to "structural genocide". I also made the reconciliation of structure and agency central to my reformulation of the concept (Shaw 2015: 103–27).

Combining these ideas, we can argue that early Zionism, because it aimed to create a Jewish state in a territory inhabited by Palestinians, initiated *a structural potential for genocide*, indicated by its incipiently genocidal ideology. Yet this idea of structure does not imply that particular outcomes were predetermined:

as Areej Sabbagh-Khoury (2023: 15) argues, "at every step, events could have gone differently". It does mean, however, that the Zionist project shaped a field of possibility for the replacement of Palestinians by Jews, which would develop – in a path-dependent way – in response to both the conflict in Palestine and the international context.

Through this lens, the Nakba was the moment in which the Zionist movement first widely realized the genocidal structure it had initiated. Taking this argument further, Israel's victories in 1948 and 1967 turned the Nakba into structural realities: territorial and social. The Palestinians were unlikely to overturn these, and the Palestine Liberation Organization eventually accepted them as even Hamas did at times. However, the dominant trend, strengthened in the present century, remained the determination of Israel's leaders and institutions, supported by much of the population and urged on by the settler movement and the far right, to extend their control over historic Palestine and progressively eliminate the Palestinian presence, in this sense to complete the Nakba. The ongoing genocidal expropriation of the Palestinians that I have analysed became ineluctable, and its territorial annexation was identified by the ICJ as a key feature of the occupation's illegality (International Court of Justice 2024d).

Events after 7 October 2023 transformed this latent and intermittently visible genocidal structure in Israel–Palestine relations into one that was clear and dominant. It was Hamas that brought this structure into the open with its massacres of Israeli civilians, but it was the Israeli state that deepened and radicalized it by pulverizing Gazan society in its entirety and escalating its violence in the West Bank.

In mid-2025, it is unclear where this will end. Bartov had argued that using the word "genocide" would "delegitimize" Israel, but Israeli leaders themselves now seemed to have done everything possible to bring the state's genocidal character into the open. In the short term, Israel is in no danger of "going down", as Bartov put it, but in the medium term its loss of international legitimacy could prove fundamental.

PART III

Conceptual and historical challenges

7
IN DEFENCE OF THE GENOCIDE IDEA: A CRITIQUE OF DIRK MOSES

The return of the genocide idea triggered by Israel's assault on Gaza has critical implications for the academic field of genocide studies and particularly for its discussions of the idea's meaning and value. As we have seen, ever since the field emerged, the core concept has been a matter of controversy. While much scholarship has sidestepped the difficulties of "genocide" – either by pragmatically following the Genocide Convention's definition or by introducing additional concepts, such as "ethnic cleansing" (Bell-Fialkoff 1996) and a range of further "cide" terms ranging from "politicide" (Harff & Gurr 1988) to "gendercide" (Jones 2000) – the debate about the meaning and scope of the central concept has remained fundamental (Kuper 1981; Fein 1990; Chalk & Jonassohn 1990; Andreopoulos 1994; Straus 2006; Moses 2008b).

However, as we saw in Chapter 1, no stable consensus developed, and Dirk Moses published an influential study (2021a) arguing that the "problems of genocide" are so deep-rooted that a new master concept, "permanent security", should replace the idea not only in historical and social research but also as an international crime. His radical challenge is directed principally at the political discourse surrounding violence against civilians, but it also has implications for the mainstream of comparative genocide studies, which he criticizes, and even for the "critical genocide studies" of which he was a principal advocate (Moses 2008c). In this chapter, I argue that while the "permanent security" idea is an important contribution to the explanation of mass atrocities, it should not, indeed cannot, replace "genocide".

Moses' case is, first, that the idea of genocide is unstable – and crucially, "inherently" unstable – because of the way that Lemkin and the convention defined it, and second, that a specific type of security imagination, "concerned not only with eliminating immediate threats but also future threats" and governed by "a logic of prevention" and "preemption" rather than racial hatred, is the fundamental problem in modern anti-civilian violence. Moses is not alone in seeing security politics as relevant to genocide, but his idea of "permanent security" – adapted, not "adopted", from SS-Führer Otto Ohlendorf's rationale for his troops' mass murders of Jews (Moses 2021a: 34–6) – suggests a distortion of the "normal" security ideas that others see as implicated (de Graaf 2021; Leader Maynard 2022). Systematic violence against civilians, he argues, is the consequence of "the striving of states, and armed groups seeking to found states, to make themselves invulnerable to threats" in the longer term (Moses 2021a: 1).

Moses argues that such totalizing, future-proofing ideas of security are the major driver not only of those policies and civilian harms that are classified as genocide but also of those that are treated as military violence, so that a coherent distinction between these two categories is unsustainable. He examines the history of thinking about particular episodes and types of violence, but his historical claims lead to a conceptual conclusion: "the genocide keyword evolved from the early-modern period to (mis)name the phenomenon of permanent security that underlay the imperial violence intrinsic to the growth of the European state" (2021a: 45).

Moses identifies as a historian "at the social science end of the spectrum" who engages in "conceptual development and even theory building" (2021b: 408), and offers not only a revisionist conceptual history (which extends other recent work, e.g. Meiches 2019) but also an exercise in conceptual critique and concept formation. In approaching his argument, we should therefore ask about not only the viability of his historical narrative but also how far this exercise meets the requirements of conceptual analysis in historical and social research.

While arguing that "genocide" misnames permanent security, Moses also suggests that "we should develop an alternative category to *name and explain* the criminality that the genocide concept only partially captures" (2021a: 34, emphasis added). This implies that there are *two distinct* conceptual issues, and taking this formulation seriously, this chapter questions whether Moses sufficiently distinguishes between these objectives that his category is designed to address, and therefore whether the redundancy of genocide is necessarily entailed by the new concept.

Addressing the requirements for concept formation in studies of violence against civilians through the lens of Max Weber's arguments and how these have been developed in social theory, this chapter explores the implications of treating permanent security as a different type of idea, an *explanatory* concept, from genocide which may be considered a *descriptive* concept of a category of violence and harm. In this sense, I ask whether the idea of permanent security can really be an alternative to genocide, or is it actually a type of explanation that can be combined with it in historical analysis?

The chapter also draws particular attention to the fact that in insisting on a conceptual choice, Moses sidelines not only the innovations that have been introduced to address the historic issues of the concept of genocide but also much of the established conceptual apparatus addressing armed violence that centres on "war". Although his book aims to integrate the treatment of anti-civilian violence named as military with that named as genocide, war is taken for granted: he does not examine ideas about it, referring to them only indirectly through the subsidiary notion of "military necessity". Yet the salience of military violence requires a treatment of this wider conceptual landscape, within which the ideas of genocide and permanent security are located.

From this perspective, the chapter discusses whether genocide, which Moses contends was *initially* an unstable concept, can be made adequate and coherent by understanding its relationships with the concept of war, which I argue *has become unstable* as anti-civilian violence has undermined its traditional rationale. The chapter concludes, therefore, by proposing that the value of the "permanent security" idea is enhanced if it is combined with the established concepts of genocide and war, critically understood in a "war and genocide" perspective.

Genocide: an inherently unstable concept?

While this chapter is primarily concerned with Moses' conceptual thinking, it is important to understand how this is underpinned by his historical arguments, and especially his conceptual history. Having shown first how the history of the language of transgression during colonization laid their foundations, he turns to the motives, parameters and contradictions of Lemkin's project and the Genocide Convention, the development of which he locates within a comprehensive account of thinking about anti-civilian violence in the 1940s. On this foundation, he builds a wide-ranging account of "permanent security in history", covering topics including colonial conquest, settlement and counterinsurgency; the Nazi empire; human rights, partitions and population "transfers" in India and Palestine; Lemkin's later campaigning; Hannah Arendt and Holocaust "uniqueness"; and the comparative genocide field.

These rich discussions spanning 500 pages explore the development of ideas in the context of the developments in extreme violence with which thinkers were engaging. Arguing that violence against civilians was carried out with the aim of future-proofing states and nations against imagined threats from populations, Moses contends that as well as the "illiberal", racist, fascist and authoritarian forms with which genocide is typically equated, this has had "liberal", Western, democratic variants that are typically rationalized in terms of universal, humanitarian principles and global policing. In contemporary "forever wars", he argues, "the continuous killing of civilians becomes the norm rather than confined to occasional wars" (2021a: 3).

Moses also contends that the equation of genocide with racial hatred, which he finds in the thinking of Lemkin and Arendt as well as in genocide studies, depoliticizes anti-civilian violence while justifying a view of genocide as a "crime of crimes" that is worse than merely military killing. This equation, he argues, elides the common motives for "illiberal" ethnic destruction, which is labelled genocide and explained in terms of hatred, and "liberal" military attacks on civilian populations, which are labelled as war or counterinsurgency and conventionally explained in "political" security terms. In contrast, Moses identifies both "security" drivers in genocides and quasi-genocidal, "paranoid" security thinking in military campaigns. He shows that ideas of permanent security, and even the term itself, have a powerful lineage in the thinking of perpetrators of violence, from colonial settlers to US strategists in Vietnam and Ohlendorf's rationale for the Holocaust.

Moses argues that Lemkin's idea of genocide and his ambitions for it were strongly rooted in his Zionist-influenced, group- or small nation-centric view of the world. While his account of Zionist influences has been criticized by Omer Bartov (2021), Moses develops a scrupulously documented case, drawing on recent sources (e.g. Loeffler 2017). Lemkin formulated the concept, he argues, in order to contribute to the international debate about Nazi war crimes trials, hoping to ensure that the Allies included the Jews in their trial calculations, and to embed it in international law. In line with these essentially political aims, Moses believes that his achievement was to "contrive a conceptual artifice that enabled a politically effective coalition ... combining the 'crippling' and 'extermination' of nations in a generic notion". The 1907 Hague Conventions did not protect "nations", so inventing genocide as a broad concept of national destruction created a bridge between the "extermination" of the Jews and the "crippling" of nations such as the Poles.

However, this bridging was, Moses argues, at a conceptual cost, leading to a contradictory and ambiguous formulation. He shows how, on the one hand, Lemkin "proposed an expansive notion" that entertained the idea that genocide could occur without mass killing, while on the other hand, he argued that "it contained an irreducible biological dimension, signalled ... by the word 'annihilation'" (Moses 2021a: 214). The notion of "the destruction of nations" through which Lemkin defined genocide was, Moses argues, itself "as intrinsically vague a notion as 'nations' itself. Are they primarily 'spiritual' or 'biological' entities? If a combination of the two, when do attacks on the former reach a genocidal threshold? In other words, at what point ... does the violation of honour" become "destruction"? Ultimately, "the relationship between persecution and the cultural and biological in the destruction of nations was never clearly articulated", and Lemkin's concept therefore represented "an unstable synthesis" of different ideas (Moses 2021a: 214).

Moses (2021a: 221) also shows that in order to secure genocide's status as an international crime, Lemkin took the initiative in narrowing it from his original formulation, both by excluding "political groups" from its scope and by limiting the methods recognized as genocide. In the drafting of the Genocide Convention, in which he participated, cultural genocide and population expulsion were sidelined according to a logic in which civilian harm "was not genocide if not physical destruction akin to the Holocaust" (Moses 2021a: 226). In this way, Moses contends, "genocide" surpassed the alternative legal concept of crimes against humanity "in rhetorical force", but it was now "understood in terms of its archetype the Holocaust, increasingly understood as a unique, depoliticized hate crime".

Indeed, Moses argues that the concept as the convention formulated it was triply "depoliticized": it was not a political offence; political groups were removed from its scope; and political motives were excluded (Moses 2021a: 203–4). The idea that genocide was bound up with fascism and Nazism suited the Western powers as well as the Soviet Union, since this threshold for genocide screened out the logic of military necessity, making "permanent security", liberal repression and destruction "all the easier" to legitimate as non-genocidal (Moses 2021a: 238). Moses concludes that as a result of these contradictions within and between Lemkin's original and the adopted legal definition, they together transmitted an unstable synthesis to later discourse.

That several decades of debate have manifestly not resolved the question of the meaning of genocide, and that writers continue to advance alternative concepts for phenomena that in principle are covered by these early versions, certainly implies space for Moses' view that the concept is redundant. However, this conclusion ultimately depends on another, more ambitious version of his thesis, namely that Lemkin's idea was not only originally unstable but also created "*inherent* concept instability" for genocide (Moses 2021a: 238). The two arguments are not clearly distinguished, since Moses argues for "inherent instability" on the same grounds (the "deliberate ambiguity" of Lemkin's formulations, etc.) which support his more limited claim.

However, the idea of "inherent" instability implies something extra: that the concept *cannot be made adequate* through further development. To evaluate this argument we need to consider not only the original incoherence that Moses analyses but also whether rigorous conceptual development could overcome this. His case would be more convincing, therefore, if he addressed not only the early formulations of the idea of genocide but also later attempts to rectify its perceived weaknesses. While Moses criticizes comparative genocide studies, his conceptual history stops short of systematically constructing how historians and social scientists have deployed the concept, although it is evident that they have often used the idea differently from the founding political actors.

Historians have not always given the idea itself particularly close attention but social scientists have often done so, usually recognizing in principle (albeit to varying extents in practice) that an adequate sociological concept will differ from Lemkin's and the UN's (e.g. Kuper 1981; Horowitz 1976; Fein 1990; Chalk & Jonassohn 1990). Understanding the purposes of scholarship as different from those of international law and politics (even if they intersect), they have therefore elaborated new definitions. My critical examination of some of the more prominent proposals showed that, while there was certainly a tendency to paraphrase the international legal definition, significant changes had also been proposed in attempts to address the latter's widely acknowledged deficiencies (Shaw 2015: 42–65). If it is understandable that Moses' already lengthy volume was not extended to cover these developments, this absence leaves his most ambitious claim insufficiently supported.

The problem is exacerbated by the method he uses to propose "permanent security" as an alternative category (Moses 2021a: 34), treating it largely as a concept that can be identified in the thought, motives and actions of the practitioners of violence themselves. While this approach is theoretically suggestive, "one always has to distinguish", Beatrice de Graaf notes, "between 'security' as an analytical concept in the hands of a historian, and 'security' as the political or semantic instrument of the historical actors under scrutiny" (2021: 385).

The permanent security concept entails, indeed, the same issue that already faces scholars using the idea of genocide, that is, how can we develop, starting from the ideas and actions of the actors, a theoretically adequate general concept that can inform a field of historical, sociological and legal research? For Moses, there is also the question of how the idea of permanent security can be made adequate to define a new international crime, since this is the sense in which he proposes it, just as Lemkin advanced genocide. We are faced with the flawed, inconsistent and self-interested ideas that practitioners have developed: how do we turn them into concepts that are adequate, coherent and (in the sense of not being identified with the interests of specific actors) disinterested?

From conceptual critique to concept formation

This is, of course, a general problem of the historical, social and legal sciences. Since scholars are also part of the social contexts they analyse, concepts generally *both* develop out of the thinking of social actors and the implicit meanings of their action *and* help inform their further thought and action. As the social theorist Anthony Giddens argued (1976: 162), social phenomena are subject to a "double hermeneutic" since they are twice interpreted, first by participants in action and then by scholars. However, the movement from everyday thinking to adequate research concepts raises methodological issues that in principle should be addressed as a specific task, before concepts are used in analysis.

In relation to genocide, I have argued that Max Weber's approach to concept formation offers insights that are particularly relevant to this task. His well-known proposal to take as a starting point the understanding of actors' subjective orientations (*verstehen*) aligns with the common assumption, derived from genocide's legal origins, that perpetrators' intentions are central (Shaw 2015: 103–27). Since Moses uses perpetrator ideas as a significant source of "permanent security", he appears to have used a similar approach in defining his new concept.

Weber's fullest exposition is contained in a 1904 essay, translated into English four decades later (1949) and built upon by later methodological thinkers in sociology such as Thomas Burger (1987) and John Drysdale (1996). The latter – whose account I mainly follow since it addresses some issues in Burger's formulations – argues that Weber's ideas provide "a reasonably coherent, if incomplete, theory of concept formation", which in his own commentary he represents more systematically than Weber does himself (Drysdale 1996: 71).

Weber offers a reflexive approach to classificatory concepts, opposing the dogmatism that often accompanies their use and viewing the relation between concept and reality as inherently problematic and subject to revision. In particular, he rejects the "naturalist" (positivist) idea that the aim of the cultural sciences should be "to construct a closed system of concepts, in which reality is synthesized in some sort of permanently and universally valid classification" (Drysdale 1996: 76). He would probably have agreed, therefore, with Moses' assertion that "[c]oncepts like genocide, crimes against humanity, and war crimes do not possess ontological status … [t]hey are products of history: of particular conjunctures of ideas and interests" (2021a: 27).

Sociological concepts, according to Weber, refer to an object or a phenomenon but accentuate, interpret and idealize it through the selection of relevant traits; hence his notion of a concept is often called an "ideal type". Congruent with Moses' idea that the critique of genocide leads to a double task, to "name and explain" anti-civilian violence, Weber distinguishes between "concepts" in the strict sense and what he calls "judgements" or explanatory hypotheses. Concepts name phenomena, are (relatively) simple and are means towards the more complex task of judgement or explanation, which is the principal goal of socio-historical knowledge. Concepts need to identify relevant traits and adequately demonstrate the meaning of the phenomenon, and they are judged on their adequacy; judgements concern causal explanation and are evaluated on their validity or accuracy. Both need to conform as far as possible to the phenomenon, but concepts are appraised on their cultural and social-scientific significance, judgements on their coherence and logical consistency (Drysdale 1996: 79, figures 1 and 2).

Weber saw concepts and (explanatory) judgements working together dynamically in sociological and historical research, but his distinction of their roles is central. "The failure to see Weber's distinction between concept and judgement", Drysdale argues, "has misled many interpreters" (1996: 80–81) and represents a risk in any conceptual discussion where it is not acknowledged. Although in principle Moses recognizes the distinction, he does not follow it through systematically; rather, by proposing permanent security as a conceptual replacement for genocide, it can be argued that he collapses it. It is one thing to argue that the anti-civilian violence that is considered military and that which is considered genocidal may be driven by the same general type of permanent security thinking, and may therefore require similar explanations. It is another to argue that the distinction between genocide and other anti-civilian violence should not be made.

It would be more coherent in Weber's terms to treat permanent security as a type of explanation, with anti-civilian violence as the phenomenon that is being explained. Considered in this light, although Moses is right to stress that the concept of genocide has many problems arising from what Weber calls "cultural significance" – including its status as the "crime of crimes" and its linkage to the sacred evil of the Holocaust – his account is less persuasive as to what Weber would call its "scientific value relevance", that is, its adequacy at the level of meaning for the purposes of knowledge.

Moreover, his ambitious claims for the explanatory power of permanent security deserve detailed comparative scrutiny; although that is beyond the scope of this chapter, Ulrike von Hirschhausen (2021) is right to warn that it should not be treated as a "monocausal explanation". One element that needs to be taken into account is that genocidal violence often elicits genocidal responses, as we have seen in Gaza. When such "countergenocidal" dynamics develop, genocide ceases to be purely a naming category and also assumes explanatory significance.

Contradictions of military "necessity" and the growing instability of "war"

While the linkage of genocide with military violence suggests that the security framing is a cogent one, Moses' critique of the purely military framing of much harm alerts us to the problems of "war" as well as of "genocide". He focuses (2021a: 236–8) on how legal tribunals after the Second World War "rescued" the idea of "military necessity", accepting German campaigns involving the destruction of cities, towns and villages as based on a legitimate rationale and distinguishing them from the "racial" elements evident in German campaigns against Jews and gypsies, which were described as involving "massacre for its own sake" (Moses describes this as "a nonpolitical reason for genocide").

This distinction, he argues, enabled the courts to avoid dealing with the victors' own civilian killing in the same frame as the defeated's, leading them to conclude that Allied bombing was justified "because it ceased when the enemy surrendered, whereas the German pursuit of Jews would have persisted after the end of hostilities". The case hinged on "the temporal distinction between current and future threats rather than civilian destruction; killing hundreds of thousands of civilians was legitimate in the course of military operations, but not to avert a future threat" (Moses 2021a: 236–7).

But, Moses asks,

> what if necessity and genocide had been joined instead? What if the recourse to military necessity in which civilians are murdered, their villages destroyed, and remnant population expelled, were considered genocide as well, because it was driven not by racial hatred but by the quest that Ohlendorf called permanent security? Why is murder on apparent racial grounds the "worst of all possible motives" ... ?

Thus, although Moses treats war only indirectly, his arguments have implications for the concept: by arguing that liberal as well as illiberal military practice has been widely captured by permanent security ideas, he implies that the very legitimacy of the use of armed force has been undermined.

Moses' argument therefore points to a key contradiction that afflicts war in the late modern period: while its core meaning remains a contest of power and force between organized, armed actors, civilian harm has become ever more central to how it is understood. Political and strategic thought traditionally regarded this harm as secondary to the meaning of war, and even international law marginalized the problem: the Hague Regulations of 1907 contained no specific provisions to protect civilians, which were only introduced with the Geneva Conventions of 1949.

For more than a century now, critical thinking that insists on the centrality of civilian harm has increasingly challenged this assumption. This intellectual trend is not merely the response of a growing liberal conscience (Howard 1978) but also responds to the expanded destructive capacity of war, the threats of social, civilizational and even planetary destruction that it has produced, and the devastating effects of even the most "limited" wars. Late twentieth-century attempts to develop and justify new Western ways of war by both mitigating and obscuring civilian harm are further evidence of the threat that it poses to the legitimacy of military practice (Cohen 2002; der Derian 2001; Moyn 2021). The failures of these attempts to restore the scope for legitimate warfare – in Iraq, Afghanistan and elsewhere – have shown that, I argued two decades ago, this crisis of war's legitimacy has not been overcome (Shaw 2005: 98–129).

It can therefore be claimed that the real problem of conceptual "stability" is the opposite of the one that Moses identifies: while he argues the concept of genocide was *originally* unstable, his argument points us towards the tendency of the idea of war to *become* unstable, since the legitimacy and even practicability of its contemporary forms have become increasingly problematic when viewed from a civilian harm perspective.

Racialized and military violence

Moses' critique points up contradictions in the Nuremberg prosecutions, but his dependence on it also leads to difficulties for his own case. For to "join" the different sides of the Nazi campaigns in a single concept, whether "genocide" (as he suggests could have been done) or "permanent security" (his preferred option), either implies that they are for all intents and purposes identical or still requires distinct accounts of the two sides and how they are related.

In a key passage, Moses accepts that permanent security may be racialized, so that we may distinguish racialized and non-racialized permanent security:

> it is a praxis in which human groups – civilians – are targeted collectively and preventatively as security threats. When a "national, ethnical, racial or religious group," to use the UN Genocide Convention list, is targeted, its members are racialized by those who ascribe racial meaning to social, political, and cultural processes and events. Members of groups can also self-racialize. Permanent security implicates racialization when it is combined with securitization: identifying a group as threatening. Persecution does not occur without securitization even if victims experience their persecution as the outcome of hatred, because that is the emotion they discern in the perpetrators. The social fact of racial or religious difference or even prejudice does not cause genocidal violence, however. The securitization of groups, whether racialized or otherwise defined, is the driver of excessive violence. (2021a: 42)

However, Moses appears divided about the significance of this distinction. On the one hand, he minimizes it, as when he asks, "what is the experiential difference between a victim of genocide and a victim of collateral damage?" (2021a: 43), implying that because death obliterates meaning, perpetrator ideology doesn't matter. On the other hand, he implies that the problem is the privileging of racialized harm, in the idea that "the deliberate destruction of a people" is worse than "the foreseeable destruction of many people" (2021a: 25).

Both these arguments are problematic. Experiential difference may surely be different in the two cases, if we widen our view to include survivors, victims' families and broader communities: victimization that is perceived as the unintended consequence of action with which the victims sympathize (such as the harming of French civilians in Allied military campaigns to liberate their country) is likely to be regarded differently from that which is perceived as targeted at the group with which the victims identify (such as Jewish suffering as a result of Nazi violence). The perception that group identity is at stake is likely to be important both in the immediate responses of survivors (many French continued to support the Allied campaign, while some Jews joined anti-Nazi partisan groups) as well as the ideologies of wider nationalist communities over time.

Equally, while it is clearly true that the idea of genocide as racialized violence has been widely privileged in hierarchies of harm, the concept does not necessarily entail this; its core implication is that the destruction of people has a *distinct* character when it is driven by the aim of destroying *a* people. While some uses of the idea enable or exonerate military violence, it does not have to perform this function. Rather, because racialized conceptions are so deeply embodied in military policies and practices, the idea of racialization adds another layer of critique that deepens the problematic character of military action as a whole.

For example, while Moses treats the US attempt to separate Nazi "military" violence from its genocide as a successful rescue of military action, with the potential to protect future Western warmaking, this works only within the narrow confines of US military ideology. In any serious historical perspective, German warfare in the Second World War, including that which was justified through military necessity, was comprehensively racialized. All occupied populations were subjected to military violence during and repressive violence after conquest, and both were comprehensively inflected with the Nazis' varying racial conceptions of these populations. Repression was also accompanied by greater destructive violence in the cases of the racially "inferior" peoples, slated to be enslaved within the expanded Reich or even to be physically eliminated.

In this light, Moses' criticism of Lemkin's combination of the "crippling" of some nations and the physical "destruction" of others in his concept of the Nazi genocide also seems insufficient. Despite Lemkin's failure to provide a fully satisfactory rationale for his approach, in principle he was right to treat the Nazis' racialized occupation policies as a whole, given their common aims of disintegrating – albeit with large variations in the type and extent of violence – most existing national societies and group identities in Europe (Shaw 2015: 26–7). And whatever the early tactical significance of "genocide", Lemkin later treated it as a general concept with broad potential in historical analysis.

Critically for Moses' argument that the separation of genocidal from military violence exonerated and enabled the "liberal" Western Allies, the latter's own anti-civilian violence was also partially racialized. Certainly, the core of the policies that drove their destructions of German and Japanese cities was instrumental, as the original British notion of "strategic" bombing suggested, and they did cease with victory. But group ideas played important secondary roles. Racial conceptions permeated the US war against Japan and influenced policy from the beginning, when Japanese-Americans were interned en masse. They were also explicit in the Allied bombing of Germany, which targeted its cultural fabric, and ambitious racial-destructive ideas became prominent, as when Henry Morgenthau Jr, US secretary to the Treasury, proposed a plan – briefly accepted by Roosevelt and Churchill – to deindustrialize or "pastoralize" the country, based on a racial conception of the Germans who would be compelled to perform forced labour as part of reparations (Grayling 2006: 158–63). Even more extreme calls for the complete elimination of Germany and the systematic sterilization of Germans also gained an audience (Grayling 2006: 166).

It is important to trace these ways in which even states that were not driven by racial-nationalist ideology tended towards racialization: as Moses notes, when entire populations are "guilty by association with enemy combatants", we "verge on the mental world of genocide" (2021a: 4). These genocidal, anti-group mentalities did not play the same role in Allied policy as they did in the Nazis', but they certainly had practical consequences, facilitating both Allied populations' acceptance of the destruction of German and Japanese cities and Allied support for the removal of Germans from the Soviet Union, Poland, Czechoslovakia and Yugoslavia during 1945–9. Without a distinction between "military" and "genocidal" ideas, we would not be able to explain these important linkages.

Moses' critique also includes some questionable theoretical assertions. Although in the long passage quoted above he refers to racialized group identities as "ascribed", he also contends that genocide "presumes the *existence* of identity-based groups" (2021a: 12, emphasis added). This ignores the current widespread rejection – except perhaps in international courts – of the idea that groups exist in an objective sense. They are now more commonly understood in the subjective ideological sense proposed by Frank Chalk and Kurt Jonassohn (1990: 23), so that genocide involves the targeting of groups as they and their members "are defined by the perpetrators".

Developed in this way, the conceptual apparatus of genocide, however problematic its earlier lineage, renders visible an essential element of civilian harm. Not only do many if not most perpetrators frame their targeting at least partly through ideas of the group character of populations, and how they do this often makes a difference to the harm inflicted, but as we have seen, even "military" targeting tends to encourage racialized thinking. Recognition of the subjective group element does not mean privileging ideology, but it allows us to accord it its necessary weight in the understanding of anti-civilian violence. It is not sufficient to frame racialization as the projection of "emotion" in a fundamentally securitized project: rather, it seems likely that the greater the ideological racialization, the greater the "permanent" element of security thinking.

Therefore, if Moses is right to reject the simple dichotomy of genocidal and military violence conjured by international prosecutions of Nazi crimes, in principle these can and should be distinguished, and analysis needs to address the variation in relationships between them. As we have seen in Gaza, a "democracy" that regards a population as a group enemy is likely to perpetrate a different kind of violence from that entailed by the standard Western disregard for civilian lives in war.

Genocide and war as hybrid forms

Moses appears to reject the distinction of genocide from war, both in its non-international armed conflict (civil war) and international armed conflict (interstate war) forms (2021a: 7). Yet the distinction between these two types of violence, while enabling us to differentiate two general types of conflict, "genocides" and "wars", does not oblige us to categorize given historical episodes exclusively as one or the other. Rather, the twin concepts can be viewed as complementary tools for analysing the dynamics of conflict, and scholars of war often recognize that specific wars (which may be civil, international or mixed) combine different types of violence. In his influential work on civil war, Stathis Kalyvas (2005: 29, Table 1.1) identifies the "logic" of a particular type, which he calls "civil war violence", but he does not categorize all violence in civil wars in this way, nor does this labelling preclude the occurrence of this type in international wars. Indeed, Kalyvas also recognizes "genocide and mass deportation" as a type of violence in civil wars, even if he does not give it much attention in his analysis.

In historical analysis we find that, while we can distinguish episodes of genocide and of war, there are typically systematic linkages. Thus we can conceptualize "the Holocaust" as a gigantic episode of mass murder distinct from "the Second World War", but the extermination of the Jews was, at every stage, connected to and calibrated with Nazi Germany's war against its armed enemies, and the linkages fundamentally informed the development and character of each. The extermination of the Jews can be regarded as a war-conditioned genocide – that is, a genocidal campaign within, and largely enabled by, the Nazis' total and more broadly group-destructive war – and the Second World War as in significant part a genocidal war.

Nor is the Nazi case exceptional. The "Rwandan genocide" cannot be understood except together with the "Rwandan civil war", and the competing concepts of the conflict in Bosnia-Herzegovina in the early 1990s, the "Bosnian war" and "Bosnian genocide", capture two sides of the same conflict that was fought simultaneously between armed forces and involved violence by each of those forces against civilian populations connected to the others.

The normality of this kind of linkage should not lead us to abandon one of the conceptual terms, or to collapse it into the other, but rather to recognize war and genocide as generally hybrid phenomena, the spectrums of which exhibit great overlap. On the one hand, most large-scale and longer wars (interstate and/or civil) have genocidal dimensions, even if these vary considerably in form and extent; although civilian harm is a universal feature of warfare, there is a non-genocidal end to the spectrum. On the other, in the spectrum of genocide, most cases are implicated with or lead to wars, but there are also episodes that do not involve war, typically because they are purely internal to powerful states and/or the balance of power between perpetrators and the target population is so unequal as to inhibit counter-violence and third-party intervention.

Indeed, a coherent concept of genocide may well treat it as derivative of and subordinate to warfare, since the idea of regarding populations and groups as enemies, whose power is to be destroyed, is essentially the application to civilians of the core ideas that have long defined war against armed enemies (Shaw 2015: 34–57). Recognizing the variation in the relationships between war and genocide means, however, that a war and genocide framework requires the complex secondary conceptualization of its hybrid forms of which this discussion has provided some illustrations.

Permanent security as a new international crime

We can now approach Moses' proposal that permanent security is the "crime" with which we should be concerned in anti-civilian violence. The current range of international crimes – war crimes, crimes against humanity and genocide – resulted from how states, courts and humanitarian actors reconfigured international law in response to patterns of violence during the Second World War. While the last three decades of international trials have produced further legal advances – for example, the recognition of rape as both a crime against humanity and a means of genocide – overall the case law has done little to reduce either the partial incoherence that results from the overlaps of the three main categories (e.g. extermination as a crime against humanity as well as a means of genocide) or the specific weaknesses of the law of genocide (sociologically unsatisfactory concepts of intention, group, destruction, etc.).

In principle, therefore, a case can certainly be made for revising the legal framework, but in a historical perspective there is little in the conditions of the 2020s that would lead us to believe that the United Nations could produce a radical revision; even a proposed convention to codify crimes against humanity, adopted by the International Law Commission (United Nations 2019), appears to have stalled. The advances of the 1940s were the product of the upheaval at the end of the Second World War and the opportunities it offered for the development of the international order; today, while we understand violence against civilians much better than Lemkin, international conditions militate against change. In any case, Moses' argument that we should criminalize the pursuit of permanent security comes up against the legal assumption that it is acts, rather than motives, that are the appropriate subject of legal sanctions (a distinction that parallels Weber's conceptual distinction between naming and explanation).

Moses also underestimates the potential of the existing legal framework to catch violations. For example, he argues (Moses 2021a: 237) that the distinction between genocide and military violence "was necessary for the developing US security strategy in the incipient Cold War" so that its "aerial superiority and command of atomic weapons could not be criminalizable". However, the use of such weapons would necessarily violate major principles of the existing laws of war, such as proportionality; Moses himself quotes Richard Falk's view that the US military's strategy in Vietnam was "indiscriminate and thus illegal" (Moses 2021a: 427).

Nuclear weapons provide a further example of this issue. The laws of war were strengthened (through political struggles between the victorious powers similar to those which shaped the Genocide Convention) in the negotiations that led to the 1949 Geneva Conventions (van Dijk 2022). Subsequently, the ICJ, in an advisory opinion, averred that "the threat or use of nuclear weapons would generally be contrary to the rules of international law applicable in armed conflict, and in particular the principles and rules of humanitarian law" (International Court of Justice 1996). This opinion has greatly informed recent antinuclear activism, as I show in my recent history of it in Britain (Shaw 2024: 114–17).

Therefore, the problem is not principally the legal framework itself, which despite its imperfections can be interpreted to render much anti-civilian violence illegal, but its marginalization in practice. As Itamar Mann (2022) argues, international law as it stands "has the doctrinal toolbox" to deal with permanent security and strengthening international law enforcement is the more urgent task.

In this light, the political theorist Sinja Graf (2022) emphasizes the primarily symbolic potential of Moses' proposal, by helping to "chip away" at the "charismatic monopoly" of the genocide idea. Yet the symbolic role of "genocide" does not only have the downsides that Moses evokes. Gaza has shown that, in the hands of protestors as well as international judges, it also has powerful positive potential, recalling, indeed, earlier cases to which he himself has helped draw attention (Moses & Heerten 2018). As Lemkin realized, naming anti-group violence in a holistic way is a key to opposing as well as understanding a whole class of civilian harm. While scholars will gain much from *The Problems of Genocide*, it would be a mistake for them to accept its recommendation to abandon the concept.

8

"POLITICAL GROUPS", CLASS AND GENOCIDE

A major aspect of the depoliticization of genocide, of which Dirk Moses complains, is the neglect of how political collectivities have been targeted. Too many assume that because genocide often targets an entire nation or ethnic group and is carried out in the name of another ethnicity or nationality, it is a phenomenon of ethno-national relations. Yet genocide is invariably a political project arising from political conflict, often as we have seen in a war or security context; when nationality and ethnicity become focal points of genocide, they are invariably politicized. Yet sometimes the perpetrators directly conceptualize their targets in political terms, or entwine ethnicity and politics so that it becomes difficult to separate them. And often, regimes that target ethnic enemies also apply specific destructive violence to political opponents who share their own ethnicity.

These issues were discussed in the UN drafting debates under the rubric of "political groups" as a target of genocide, and the terminology has stuck. However, they were notoriously resolved by excluding these groups from the final Genocide Convention, leaving a fundamental lacuna to which critics have returned ever since. In this chapter, I take this question beyond the debate about the convention's omission, arguing that as well as the political interests involved, it reflects fundamental weaknesses in the consensus on the scope of the genocide, which chronically underestimates political targeting. I explore the implications of this issue in a wide-ranging historical discussion, but I also argue that in the new era of authoritarian far-right politics, the question of politically targeted genocide may have renewed significance.

The exclusion of political groups and social classes

The immediate reason for the UN's rejection of "political groups" appears to have been the perception that their inclusion threatened the interests of great powers such as the Soviet Union (from victims of its political persecution in eastern Europe) and the British Empire (from the rising tide of anticolonial revolt).

However, it can also be argued that there were more fundamental reasons why the scope of genocide was restricted in this way. By the time that Lemkin formulated the idea in 1944, political conflict on a global scale had culminated in the holistic subordination of nations by mega-imperial powers: he focused on Nazi Germany's domination of Europe, but Japan's conquests in Asia involved a similar pattern of destruction and control. In these circumstances, it made sense to consider the violent destruction of populations and groups as primarily a national or ethnic phenomenon.

Moreover, this formulation of genocide reflected a wider normalization of national thinking about societies in mid-century. Lemkin expressed this in his idea of the nation or *genos* as the core "contributor" to a common human culture, but it reflected the holistic academic anthropology and sociology of this period, articulated by writers such as Bronisław Malinowski and Talcott Parsons. Indeed, there was a widely influential collectivist current in social thought during and after the Second World War, in Western as well as Communist states (Shaw 2015: 24–5).

Despite these trends, the homogeneity of national "groups" could not really be taken for granted in this period, as the Soviet and British anxieties demonstrated. Nor was it true, in a historical perspective, that destructive violence against populations had always taken the form of violence against "whole" national or ethnic groups. As the inclusion of "religious groups" in the convention recognized, violence had often been targeted against a section of a population on the grounds of its beliefs. Indeed, while the Jews – the archetypal genocidal victims – might be considered a "whole" ethno-religious group, they constituted minorities within the societies from which the Nazis had taken them for extermination.

The idea that political groups might also be targeted for destruction was therefore all too meaningful in the period in which the idea of genocide emerged, and its omission duly became a consistent theme of critics of the convention. Yet politically targeted violence has remained consistently marginal to the actual concerns of genocide scholarship, which have remained focused on violence against "whole" ethnic and national groups, even as "critical" genocide studies developed. Indeed, even today's return of the genocide idea in Gaza reinforces the holistic national group problematic.

This chapter therefore offers a disruptive perspective on the significance of political division for genocide. Its focus, after an initial review of the literature on political groups, is the partially submerged history of politically targeted destruction. I challenge dominant historical assumptions about twentieth-century genocide, arguing that "political" genocide was historically the necessary precursor of the holistic national destruction of the Second World War period. I contend that any adequate overview of this classical context of genocide needs to examine the relationships between successive historical waves: from politically targeted violence during the interwar period to ethnically targeted violence, culminating in the Holocaust, during the Second World War.

In addition, the chapter brings into focus the extent to which the idea of "political groups" is itself insufficient. It can be largely considered, I propose, a surrogate for social classes as targets of anti-population violence; the marginalization of political groups is also the marginalization of class. In this chapter, I therefore distinguish between "ethnic-national" and "class-political" targeting and argue that a history of modern genocide must centre the dynamic relationships of these two types.

By "ethnic-national" genocide, I mean cases in which populations are primarily identified as targets via their presumed ethnic and/or national identities, and by "class-political" genocide I mean cases where they are chiefly identified via class and/or political identities. To be clear, both types are political in the sense that group destruction is invariably a political project, and each type usually incorporates the other: class-political genocide typically has ethnic and national dimensions, while ethno-national genocide has class-political dimensions. Indeed, Michael Mann argues that ethnic genocide has an essentially class character: groups are targeted when one group can be represented as exploiting the other, so that "class sentiments are displaced onto ethnic group relations" (2005: 31).

The purpose of this discussion is therefore to challenge received interpretations of genocide as idea and history, but the argument is also topical. The rise of the far right in the early twenty-first century has not only involved hostility, discrimination and violence towards ethnic, national and religious minorities. It has also aroused hostility and violence towards their liberal and left-wing political opponents, and this could radicalize further.

Political groups and the Genocide Convention

The exclusion of "political groups" from the Genocide Convention was part, David Nersessian (2010: 109) argues, of a "negotiated political compromise" around the definition, in which the vulnerabilities of the great powers to which we have referred were taken into account. While William Schabas (2000: 134) considers this outcome acceptable – arguing that crimes against political groups can be considered through other legal categories – Nersessian (2010: 76–85) presents a broad legal and historical case that incorporating these collectivities within the crime of genocide would be more coherent.

This exclusion has also been justified sociologically, notably in Helen Fein's claim (1990: 23) that political groups are not a "basic class, kind or subfamily of humanity" in the way that ethnic and national groups are. For Fein, political groups are voluntary subdivisions of more organic collectivities, and membership in them is "achieved" rather than, as with ethnicity and nationality, "ascribed". However, this distinction is unsustainable: while formal membership of political parties is indeed typically voluntary, this is also true of religious denominations, the inclusion of which in the convention is universally accepted. Moreover, as in the religious case, the emphasis on the "voluntary" character of political allegiances obscures their often deep social embedding. Political loyalties are often inherited through family, class and communal tradition in similar ways to – and often overlapping with – ethnic, national and religious loyalties. Likewise, if individuals can choose to alter their political allegiances, they can also renounce their given ethnic and national affiliations. Therefore the supposed sociological differences do not add up to a serious case for separating class-political from ethnic-national genocide.

Nor do the assumptions about "groups" embedded in the convention and Fein's sociology fit well with contemporary understandings of human collectivities. The idea of "basic" subgroups of humanity is problematic, since types of human collectivity have mutated throughout history. Thus "race" – the convention category that Schabas (2000: 132–3) sees as most solid – is now widely acknowledged as an ideological construct that does not correspond to actual social collectivities, since these are not biologically based; indeed, Max Weber, who died in 1920, pointed this out even before Lemkin invented "genocide" (Weber 1964: 138).

The foundational claims that Lemkin made for his "genocentric" approach have also not been upheld, even in the genocide field. Far from introducing a fundamental "new element" into the study of history, as he claimed, the idea of "the *genos* (group) as the source of cultural creation, tension and conflict" has few supporters today. "Genos" has not entered common usage and Lemkin's claim that the idea "permits the investigation of the genocentric elements of history which are sometimes even more determinative than the elements of state and empire" (Lemkin 2012: 9) has not been upheld by scholars.

In contrast, the terminology of "groups" has survived in genocide law and analysis, as a catch-all way of referring to populations belonging to particular social categories. Yet Dirk Moses (2010: 22) also criticizes Lemkin's stronger version for what Rogers Brubaker (2004: 35) calls "groupism", that is, "the tendency to treat ethnic groups, nations, and races as substantial entities to which interests and agency can be attributed". It is mistaken, Brubaker argues, to treat these as "internally homogeneous, external bounded groups, even unitary collective actors with common purposes".

Therefore, the original conceptual basis for excluding political groups has not been sustained, and Lemkin's overemphasis on ethnic and national groups has,

Adam Jones (2010: 11) argues, proved "vexing for subsequent generations". In the historiography of genocide, the exclusion of political groups has been partly superseded during recent decades. Influential works have increasingly considered "politically" targeted violence, for example by both Communist (Kiernan 2006; Naimark 2010) and anti-Communist regimes (Esparza, Huttenbach & Feierstein 2010; Feierstein 2014).

Nevertheless, this accommodation of political genocide has not led to a fundamental historical or conceptual reappraisal; rather, it has been added on to a paradigm that remains ethno-nationally defined. Some have argued for adding "political groups" to the groups protected by the convention: Nersessian (2010: 206) proposes that this could be achieved in international law through a new "optional protocol". However, this idea has not become mainstream, and even if it had the chances of its being adopted in twenty-first-century international circumstances are minimal. More fundamentally, since such an amendment would simply multiply the types of groupism, a more appropriate solution to the definitional quandary is a generic definition of genocidal targets as: "social collectivities", as Lemkin (1933) originally proposed; "aggregate populations" to which perpetrators ascribe group characteristics, as Levene (2005a: 36) suggests; or (as I have argued) "civilian social groups" (Shaw 2015).

Accommodating political genocide to the Genocide Convention

Although Donald Bloxham has argued that recognizing genocide "should be a 'by-product' of the historian's work, not its ultimate aim or underpinning" (2003: 189), much academic study is driven by recognition, often for political reasons. None of the solutions just discussed, which take us beyond the conventional understanding of the Genocide Convention, will satisfy those for whom a major aim is to enable legal action against "political" perpetrators. Instead, creative interpretations of the convention's ethnic and national categories have been pursued, in order to accommodate within their framework targeting that appears prima facie incompatible.

In the case of Cambodia, the idea of "auto-genocide" was invented to encompass the full range of Khmer Rouge violence between 1975 and 1979 within a single "Cambodian genocide", rather than limiting the genocide to the targeting of the Vietnamese and other ethnic groups as a literal interpretation of the convention would entail. This idea presents Cambodia as an anomalous case: since the genocidists had the same ethnicity as their targets, this must be classified as a self-genocide of the Khmer group (Schabas 2000: 118). Yet the fact that a "Khmer" regime targeted people of Khmer ethnicity actually suggests that they did so on grounds *other than* ethnicity: class, education, politics, religion, etc.

While the idea of "auto-genocide" ticks the convention's box, it does little to help us understand what happened.

There have also been sustained attempts to include the 1970s killing of leftists by the Argentinian military junta within the framework of the convention. These have been more sophisticated, focusing on the political ideology of the perpetrators rather than their ethnicity. In a case in which Argentinian officers were charged with killing Spanish citizens, the Spanish judge Baltasar Garzón argued that the killings of presumed leftists by the dictatorship constituted genocide because they were targeted as part of a project to impose a new definition of the nation. The sociologist Daniel Feierstein builds on this case, arguing that the military were pursuing a type that he calls "reorganizing genocide" (of which Nazism is the prototype), in which the targeting of political groups is part of a broader attempt to reorder the entire national society (Feierstein 2014: 19–20, 48, 60). The victims were therefore targeted, Feierstein argues, as part of a national group, and the violence of the military regime comes within the scope of the convention.

Yet as a definitional exercise this appears unsatisfactory because, despite the Argentinian dictatorship's national-reorganizing *rationale* for its violence, its targets were *identified* through their presumed political affiliations and beliefs, and this therefore remains a case about political rather than national groups. Using the Nazi case, to which Feierstein compares Argentina, this point becomes clearer. The Nazis variously identified their targets as Jews, Slavs, Roma and Sinti, physical and mental "degenerates", "anti-socials", Communists and Socialists, etc., but all these targetings were developed within their larger project to forge a racialized nation, state and empire. Jews, for example, were targeted not only because of a core Nazi antisemitism but also because at specific points in the development of this project, they were identified as obstacles to expanding German power.

In a case such as this, where the perpetrators have multiple and evolving targets, Feierstein's approach points to the need to examine the dynamic relationships of types of targeting. Except from a legal point of view, it is unnecessary to treat political targets in Argentina as part of the "national group"; rather, we need to grasp the role the targeting of leftists played in the nationalist project, and how different targetings were dynamically related in the development of the project and its outcomes.

Class-political genocide from the French to the Russian Revolution

I now turn to examine how analysing the combination of class-political with ethnic-national targeting can be used to reinterpret twentieth-century European genocide. Although most of the literature treats episodes in that history largely in isolation from each other, there have been significant attempts to address the history as a whole. Donald Bloxham (2005; 2009) and Mark Levene (2005a; 2005b; 2014a; 2014b) have written major parts of it in a broad world-regional perspective, encompassing multiple and interacting perpetrators. However, even this literature has barely explored the role of class-political targeting in the overall pattern. In particular, the role of the wave of class-political violence of the interwar period in creating the conditions for the ethno-national genocide of the Second World War has not been clearly addressed.

Levene does, however, make a major contribution to putting political genocide into our historical understanding, beginning with his account of an early modern episode: the destruction of the rural Vendée by the French revolutionary regime in 1794. This arose, he argues, from a "dialectic of revolution–counterrevolution" in which the new French revolutionary nation was consolidated through the bloody suppression of religious- and royalist-inspired counter-revolution. In response to a "Catholic and Royal" insurgent army, the revolutionary regime set out "to wipe out an entire community systematically with a longer-term view to repopulating the territory with its 'own' loyal followers" (Levene 2005b: 115). The Vendéens were identified as an enemy through a political rather than an ethnic lens: as David A. Bell argues (2020: 22), this was "a campaign of political killing" aimed at enemies of the revolution and extended to all (including women and children) who did not clearly support its cause. It had echoes in the suppression of rebellion in Ireland in 1798 (Malcolm 2013).

The Vendée counter-revolution also had an implicit anti-peasant class dimension. The regime saw the Vendéen political threat as the ultimate expression of the peasant localism and archaism that it aimed to combat, representing an exceptionally destructive instance of the nationalizing process that the French state pursued across rural society for a century after 1789, usually by "turning peasants into Frenchmen" (Weber 1976) rather than by massacring them. In this sense, too, France was a model for national homogenization across Europe, through which peasant societies were transformed into modern nations and states. Where, especially in the east, nationalization took the radical form that is now called "ethnic cleansing" (Ther 2014), this also mostly involved the destruction of peasant communities.

Yet while Levene highlights the Vendée, he does not present it as of general significance for the evolution of genocide. It remains atypical, being sandwiched between two colonial and imperial periods: the genocides of European colonization from the fifteenth to the eighteenth century, and the consolidation of new and contraction of old empires in the nineteenth and early twentieth centuries.

However, the wider significance of class is apparent if we recognize that while the Vendée events were distinctive in Europe, the French Revolution stimulated another important episode in Haiti in 1802–4, following a decade of conflict triggered by a major slave revolt. Philippe Girard shows how this extremely murderous case entwined a political struggle and war between ex-slaves and the French with a social conflict over the restoration or permanent abolition of slavery. Although he calls this a "racial war" (Girard 2007), he also writes that the French agenda, never fully realized, "was aimed more at a rebel social class than a given race" (Girard 2013: 133).

Haiti, like the Vendée, shows that the metropolitan–colonial link, more commonly made in relation to later developments, can also be made at the beginning of the modern era, and in a class-political as well as an ethno-national sense. Haiti was also a harbinger of the widespread genocidal violence during colonial rebellions and counterinsurgency. This is usually regarded as ethno-nationally targeted, but conflicts between rebels and imperial power were primarily about political control and colonial socio-economic hierarchies.

Meanwhile, during the nineteenth century, class conflict in Europe began to became the explicit focus of the "political" genocide that the Vendée prefigured. While the revolutionary idea of the nation continued to play an important role – undergoing, as Levene (2005b: 166) puts it, "a series of mutations into more virulent forms" – the rise of nations was increasingly entwined with that of classes. As Mann (2005) argues, "nations are not the opposite of classes, since they rose up together, both (to varying degrees) the product of modernizing churches, commercial capitalism, militarism and the rise of the modern state".

The emergence of working-class movements was a key manifestation of these changes. The working class increasingly formed an imagined community *within* the nation in many countries – E. P. Thompson (1965) provides a classical exploration of its "making" in Britain – and its emergence was deeply challenging to the authoritarian regimes that still dominated Europe in the nineteenth century. As class-based social movements became more important, so did the state's violent repression of workers' movements, from the massacre of the Manchester working class at Peterloo in 1819 (Poole 2019) to the bloody suppression of the Paris Commune in 1871 (Merriman 2014), which became a consistent pattern (Goldstein 1983).

Yet this nineteenth-century violence has been ignored in the history of genocide, as though attempts to destroy workers' movements and communities were less significant than those aimed at ethnic groups. This may be partly explained by the fact that by the end of the century, class violence in western European countries seemed to have been contained. Indeed, in a rare treatment of this in the genocide literature, Donald Bloxham (2009: 144–5) argues that by the end of the nineteenth century, the consolidation of working-class organization in stable party and trade union organizations increasingly led to its "incorporation" into the state. Yet, as Bloxham notes, this incorporation did not last, since it was undermined by the upheavals of the First World War. While war initially increased class integration, in Germany ultimately "social schisms opened and became cavernous", he argues, and the pattern was echoed elsewhere. In this context, a dialectic of "revolution–counterrevolution" like that which Levene identified in the Vendée developed across Europe, with the 1917 Russian Revolution as its catalyst.

Class-political genocide between the wars: the Soviet Union

The class-political polarization issuing from the First World War and the Russian Revolution rapidly produced violence against civilian populations across the continent, with both "right"- and "left"-wing variants. Yet although Europe in the first half of the twentieth century is the classic locus of genocide and its culmination, the Nazi genocide, the paradigmatic case, the academic field has barely recognized this pattern. At best, scholars have added particular class-political cases to an ethno-nationally defined canon, almost always with question marks over whether these are "really" cases of genocide and emphasizing their entwined ethnic dimensions in order to accommodate them to the dominant paradigm.

Once again, it is Levene who has given the closest attention to the beginnings of this violence in the early aftermath of the Russian Revolution, arguing that there were two "Russian Vendées" during the 1918–21 civil war, during which revolutionary forces, attacking "counterrevolutionary bandits", engaged in "the mass excision of troublesome populations and the colonization of their regions by other, supposedly loyal, communal groups". Like the French revolutionaries before them, the Bolsheviks treated whole populations as political enemies, so that certain ethnic groups became "class enemies" in their Marxist framing (Levene 2014a: 216).

Other writers have also emphasized the ethnic dimensions of the targeting. Manus Midlarsky (2005: 45, 264–5) draws attention to how "peasant hostility toward the Jews" was channelled into highly murderous pogroms in Ukraine during 1919–20, which he sees as a precursor of the Nazis' later extermination in the same regions. Brendan McGeever (2019) explores the intertwining of different rationales for violence within these conflicts. Arguing that "class and ethnic categories could not be easily separated", he shows that "the terms 'Ukrainian' and 'Jew' simultaneously bore both class *and* ethnic overdeterminations: 'Ukrainians' were 'true' and 'honest' 'toilers' who put their hands to 'productive' labour. 'The Jew', in addition to being a 'Communist', was a 'non-labourer', a 'speculator'." In other words, the categories Bolshevik leaders deployed in their class analysis – "bourgeois", "toiler", "the people", "exploiter" and "exploited" – were, on the ground, "understood in profoundly complex and racialized ways".

Later Soviet violence, after Stalin consolidated total power after 1929, has received more attention, perhaps because, rather than occurring during a messy civil war, it was the product of a "totalitarian" regime, fitting the narrative that linked genocide to dictatorship (Harff 1986). Stalin orchestrated violence against a population over which he ruled almost without challenge, yet, extending the civil war mindset, he saw potential enemies everywhere, not least because the Soviet Union faced first a possible and then an actual military threat from Germany. "Stalin's genocides", as Norman Naimark (2010) calls them, were therefore products of extreme, militarized campaigns to consolidate and maintain his regime's total control over society as well as the party and state.

Yet as Stalin consolidated his rule, it was the problem of the peasantry as a class that shaped his first mass anti-population campaigns. Ever since they took power, the Bolsheviks had seen the 90 per cent peasant majority as a locus of opposition (Lewin 1975), and by the time Lenin (the founder of the Soviet Union) died in 1924, the aim of collectivizing agriculture was becoming the centre of a debate between a "left" faction under Leon Trotsky, which advocated accelerating the process, and a "right" led by Nikolai Bukharin, who advocated more gradual change. However, both opposition factions were crushed by Stalin.

Stalin's own solution was to eliminate resistance through an extreme programme of agricultural collectivization. In 1929, he launched a campaign, implemented through violence and deportations, to "liquidate the *kulaks*" – this pseudo-scientific term, denoting a wealthier peasant, defined a section of the peasantry as a political and class enemy. In reality, the campaign was directed against the peasant class as a whole: as Levene (2014a: 321) summarizes, "*dekulakization*'s primary purpose was ... to provide a smokescreen and pretext for ... the transformation of Russian society by way of the blanket super-exploitation of its peasant aggregate man". As the conflict between the regime and the peasantry deepened, during 1932–3 Stalin presided over a "terror-famine" (Conquest 1986), during which the regime confiscated food, refused starving peasants access to stored grain and perpetrated extensive violence. These episodes have been widely recognized in the genocide literature, primarily because their death tolls had, as Bloxham (2009: 108) puts it, "some ethnicized characteristics". The famine has largely been interpreted through its anti-Ukrainian dimension ("The Holodomor"), although it was by no means confined to Ukraine.

Thus it has proved difficult – despite widespread dissatisfaction with exclusionary definitions – to recognize the Stalinist regime's early policies in their primary class rather than secondary national frame. In theory, Levene (2014a: 333) suggests, "collectivization was not supposed to have an ethnic dimension; [but] in practice it quickly developed one", so its genocidal significance is mainly interpreted in this way. Some writers have acknowledged the centrality of class to dekulakization and the famine, but have then excluded these episodes from the genocide category: Mann categorizes them as "classicides" (2005: 17, 318–52).

There remains the question of how to understand the linkages of Stalin's policies against different population groups and the regime's overall relationship to genocide. Naimark, despite describing four different genocidal episodes in the 1930s and proposing that Stalin's regime was "was genocidal by [its] very character" (2010: 129), nevertheless fails to offer a coherent account of the pattern. Bloxham (2009: 108) argues that the Stalinist regime was "only deliberately murderous at specific points", apparently emphasizing Stalinism's divergence from Nazism, although the judgement could also apply in that case. Levene (2014b: 308) similarly notes that "the Soviet path to genocide ... remained *sui generis*" and only addresses the question of whether Stalin's policies were genocidal in the terms of the Genocide Convention.

In such accounts, the later deportations of whole "unreliable nations" within the Soviet Union – which began in the late 1930s in response to perceived threats of German and Japanese invasion and continued after the Nazis actually invaded in 1941 – are the strand connecting Stalin's policies to the "norm" of ethno-national genocide that Lemkin codified, or at least to "ethnic cleansing". Importantly, Bloxham adds, in addition to the domestic episodes described by Naimark, Stalin's international projection of violence against Poles and Baltic peoples in the early stages of the Second World War and against Germans and others at the end, noting that after the Nazis, "the other main agent of ethnic cleansing in Europe from outside Axis ranks was the USSR" (Bloxham 2008: 170).

Yet this emphasis is insufficient to define Stalinist anti-population policies as a whole. The deportations of nationalities were certainly a major strand, which could be traced back to the 1919–21 civil war, but they only became the dominant element in the build-up to, during and at the end of the Second World War. Earlier in the 1930s, we have seen, destructive violence against the peasantry (and party-state elites) predominated. This sequencing reflected Stalin's initial need to first consolidate his internal rule, by crippling the main source of potential social resistance, the huge peasant class, as well as totally dominating the party and state apparatuses. The shift in the targeting of violence towards nationalities from the late 1930s onwards reflected his shift to facing external enemies, especially Nazi Germany and Japan, for whom he saw them as surrogates.

Class-political genocide and Europe's right-wing dictatorships

It is poorly appreciated that Stalin's shift from predominantly class-political to ethno-national genocide is mirrored in the trajectories of the counterrevolutionary right-wing regimes in the interwar period, including the Nazis. Indeed, even before Stalin had come to power and launched his anti-peasant violence, Benito Mussolini had already pioneered in Italy the strategy of destroying the social world of the organized working class that Hitler would follow a decade later. Rather than interpreting Stalinist class-political violence through the prism of later Nazi ethnic genocide, as Lemkin's approach entails, it is more coherent to see it and Mussolini's violence as precursors of Nazism's trajectory. Yet it is a curiosity of contemporary historiography that the class-political violence of the right-wing dictatorships, including the Nazis', has been even more neglected than that of Stalinism in narratives of European genocide.

Italian fascism's destruction of the working class

Mussolini's fascist regime has barely been recognized as a genocidal actor, and then only through the external power projection that followed its violent suppression of the working class in Italy itself. It is the large-scale massacre in Addis Adaba during the conquest of Ethiopia in 1937 (Campbell 2017) that leads Levene to comment that analysing "Italian fascism in its broader colonial behaviour would necessarily include discussion of genocide" (2014a: 471, *n*10). Similarly, "ethnic cleansing" in the areas that Italy occupied during the Second World War has also been noted (Ahonen *et al.* 2008: 43–8), as has an ethno-national "cultural genocide" within Italy itself, with the forcible acculturation of ethnic Slovenes and Croats in the Venezia Giulia region (Hametz 2010).

Certainly, it is the imperial murderousness "on the periphery, temporarily and geographically removed from the Fascist regime that ruled the Italian peninsula and its people between 1922 and 1943", as Michael Ebner (2011: 11) puts it, which is most obviously seen as genocidal, contributing most of the estimated million civilian deaths attributed to Italian fascism. However, because of this many have minimized fascist violence within Italy itself: as Ebner summarizes, the view of many scholars is that "Italy under Mussolini was a more or less 'normal' police state that often governed with the consent of its citizens. Not since the 1920s has a book on Mussolini's Italy featured the term *terror*" (2011: 11). Among genocide scholars, only Levene appears to have acknowledged fascist coercion and violence, but he may also minimize its genocidal significance when writing that "dictatorship ... cannot in itself be assumed to be more *inherently* genocidal than liberal democracy. Any more than the label 'fascist' ... automatically denotes a polity intent on annihilatory extirpation of *domestic* ethnic or religious targets" (2014a: 243, emphasis in original).

Yet the genocide studies focus on the later ethnic targets distorts the historical pattern of genocidal violence in Italy, as it does in the Soviet case. As Ebner argues, "any assessment of the role of violence under Fascism must take into consideration the initial terror upon which Mussolini established his dictatorship" (2011: 47). The initial targets were primarily domestic and class-political, and it was only after this social opposition had been eliminated that the regime could project ethnicized imperial violence.

Mussolini came to power through the systematic violence of fascist "squads" against the working class and Socialist movements; the Marxist theoretician Antonio Gramsci, comparing this to anti-Jewish violence, "often referred to fascist and nationalist violence as a form of pogrom" (Foot 2022: 347). During the high tide of *squadrismo,* "the fascists mobilized tens, even hundreds, of thousands of Italian men, who carried out thousands of acts of brutal violence within their own communities and neighbouring cities, towns, villages and hamlets" (Ebner 2011: 25). Provocations, including acts of violence, by some of the left were characterized as "red chaos" and quickly exploited in vastly greater "fascist revenge, mass arrests and repression", leading to the "collapse of the institutions controlled by the left", before the fascists seized central political power. In the build-up to the March on Rome in autumn 1922, the fascists committed "proletarian massacres" (Foot 2022: 101, 46, 90). For them, the Socialists "were the *enemy,* they had to be annihilated – every trace of them had to be wiped out" (Foot 2022: 111–12, emphasis in original).

Fascism used this violence to wreck the Socialist "state within a state", which had been consolidated during the working-class upsurge from 1918 to 1920, following the end of the First World War. However, its attack was also more fundamental: it aimed to cripple the entire infrastructure of the working-class community created over a longer period – networks of trade unions, peasant leagues, cooperatives, labour halls and social clubs – as well as the Socialists' political infrastructure: local offices, newspapers and cultural and social organizations. Cyclical violence directed against local leaders prevented the Socialists from reorganizing. By the mid-1920s, the fascists had destroyed the political, economic and cultural existence of the working class as a collectivity.

Once this task was completed, fascist violence changed. Mussolini repressed the squads, as Hitler would the Sturmabteilung (SA), and promoted more surgical violence. Ebner argues that "the Mussolinian economy of violence that emerged out of the seizure of power represented a synthesis between the dictator's strategy of carefully calibrated state repression and the *squadrist* ethos for spontaneous punishment of 'internal enemies'" (2011: 46). However, "the novelty the fascists had introduced into modern politics the armed party, the combination of political and military action" (Foot 2022: 115) would be echoed in genocidal regimes across Europe, and especially in Nazi Germany.

Nazism's destruction of the German working class

Although Lemkin described a pan-European genocide against the "occupied" peoples, in general the Nazi genocide has subsequently been recognized through the extermination of the European Jews. This tendency has mainly been controversial because it has obscured other ethno-national persecutions such as those of the Roma and Sinti (Hancock 2001), and in recent work that has returned the field closer to Lemkin's original conception, attention has been given to the wider ethno-nationally targeted violence of both Nazi Germany and its allies during the Second World War (Segal 2016; Bartov 2018). But little attention has been given by genocide scholars to violence in Germany itself between 1933 and 1939, which laid the foundation for the more extensive genocide of 1939–45.

In fact, Nazism followed a similar trajectory to that of Stalinism and Italian fascism. The wartime genocide that Lemkin analysed was premised on the earlier destruction of internal class-political enemies that he (and most subsequent genocide historians) ignored. Therefore, if we examine the Nazis' genocide in the light of the full span of the regime's rise and rule, class-politically targeted violence should not need to be added in, since it was present from the moment they seized power. While "Hitler and his inner circle ... were stumbling and in the dark as to how they might *systematically* implement their intended attack on the Jews", as Levene puts it, "the SS and SA ... were able to declare open season on all suspected political opponents of whatever hue, the consequences of which were that several hundred thousand were taken into custody, beaten up, and terrorized across the length and breadth of Germany" (2014a: 394, 391).

Levene sees this period as "a time of 'wild' actions, of arbitrary terror", but Richard J. Evans in his fuller account (2005: e.g. 113, 55) portrays a more deliberate (if certainly improvised) policy: the Communist and Social Democratic parties and trade union organizations "were ruthlessly swept aside", with "near-universal violence". Evans (2005: 87) argues that "Jews so far did not form a separate category: the aim was to purge the *German* race, as Hitler and Himmler understood it, of undesirable and degenerate elements". Levene agrees: "Where were the Jews in the equation? Practically nowhere. To be sure, there were some Jews among activists in the KPD [German Communist Party], trade unions, and other parties", but he concludes: "what the spring of 1933 proved unequivocally was the entirely chimerical nature of the supposed Jewish *threat* [and] the frailty of general German dissent" (2014a: 399, emphasis in original).

Yet the unrestrained violence that the Nazis used to defeat the working-class movement suggests that "frailty" is an overstatement. They arrested over 100,000 political opponents, mostly Communists, Socialists and trade unionists, many of whom were incarcerated in newly created concentration camps, tortured or killed. National and local leaders of the left were the primary victims of treason indictments and a rapid expansion of capital punishment. Compared to later episodes of Nazi violence, the death toll was limited, yet, Evans (2004: 348) concludes, this was "a massive, brutal and murderous assault", which lasted until 1935.

Indeed, Levene (2014a: 399) notes the "complete pulverization of political opposition" and Bloxham (2009: 146) comments that "the organized representation of labour was shattered". The language of these judgements is obviously redolent of the idea of group "destruction" through which genocide has been defined. Yet the "group" involved here was not just "political", since left-wing parties and unions presided over the autonomous social world of the German working class, created over an even longer period than in Italy (Evans 1982). The Nazis aimed to destroy this in its entirety, incorporating workers as individuals into their own party-linked institutions. Yet in the period before 1939, Levene identifies genocide only in the Nazis' 1937 assault on Jehovah's Witnesses (2014a: 401), which was much more marginal to the regime's trajectory.

Nazism's class-political destruction was the culmination of a longer history. Counterrevolutionary violence had begun after the First World War with the Freikorps attacks that helped defeat social revolution in 1918 (Broué 2006) and continued with the terror of the Nazis' own paramilitary SA, which intimidated the left before 1933. The weakening of the working-class parties in these earlier struggles and the sharp division between them – in Stalin's ultra-left phase after 1929, the Communists regarded the Social Democrats rather than the Nazis as their principal enemies – probably avoided the need for Hitler to use even greater violence to crush them (Evans 2005: 13).

Of course, Nazism's class-political violence was carried out in tandem with the systematic segregation, comprehensive discrimination and individual violence that the Nazis practised against the Jews before 1939. But as Peter Longerich (2010: 20–132) shows, Nazi anti-Jewish policy only radicalized towards mass violence during the Austrian *Anschluss* and the so-called *Kristallnacht* pogrom in 1938, and open destruction of Jewish communities was only extensively carried out after the invasions of Poland in 1939 and the Soviet Union in 1941. In the Nazis' pre-war campaigns, it was class-political destruction that predominated.

The Nationalist destruction of the working class in Spain

In this pattern of right-wing destruction of working-class communities and parties, the most extreme case was that of the Nationalist forces led by Francisco Franco in Spain during and after the Civil War of 1936–9, which has received increasing attention as a result of Paul Preston's *The Spanish Holocaust* (2012). Viewed through the prism of the Nazis' Holocaust, Preston's terminology is confusing, but in fact he proposes no comparison with the extermination of the Jews; rather he uses "holocaust" (which of course is not an elaborated category like "genocide") in a more everyday sense, to describe the history of unremitting violence that he narrates.

There are echoes of Preston's approach in the genocide literature: Bloxham (2009: 104, 98) mentions Franco's dictatorship as an example of a "right-wing authoritarian regime", while Levene (2014a: 21) notes the "extraordinary violence and atrocity" of the Civil War; but no major narrative has given it the importance it deserves. Yet the class-political violence of the Spanish right constitutes the largest-scale violence of its kind before the devastation of Indonesian Communism in 1965: it is estimated that about 200,000 civilians died, three-quarters of whom were victims of the rightists, and other forms of violence were widespread.

The reason for the ferocity of the destruction in Spain was that, like the Italian and German right wing immediately after the First World War (but unlike the Nazis in the early 1930s), in the mid-1930s the Spanish right (the Church, military leadership and property-owning classes as well as right-wing parties) faced a working-class movement whose strength, confidence and ambitions for change had grown rapidly. During the "social war" that began after the declaration of the Second Republic in 1931, extensive landowner violence against rural workers anticipated the right's campaign in the Civil War (Preston 2012: 3–33).

Moreover, unlike in either Italy or Germany at the time of the rise of the far-right movements, in Spain the left's Popular Front government controlled the state, forcing the right to launch its political terror through a military rebellion. Constitutionalist traditions were weaker among workers in Spain than in Italy or Germany – anarchism was the strongest political force – and the rebellion provoked a revolutionary wave, which involved widespread violence against the clergy and landowners. This in turn fed the rightist violence, in the countergenocidal pattern that we have seen in colonial situations.

The right's campaign was therefore an attempt simultaneously to defeat the Republican government militarily and to destroy the working class as a social force, including its unions and social as well as political organizations. This continued, with extreme violence, throughout the Civil War in both the towns and the countryside (Preston 2012: 131–221). The military rebels stood for a racial, antisemitic, Christian, imperial view of Spain and applied to the Spanish working class the racial ideology and brutal methods of massacre and rape that the army had honed in the colonial subjugation of Morocco (Preston 2012: 34–51).

On both sides, the violence was predominantly class-political, but the Nationalists also attacked the Basque, Catalan and Galician nationalities that had gained autonomy under the Republic. Preston shows that Nationalist violence against civilians resulted from a deliberate campaign of extermination, while violence from the Republican side was chiefly reactive, spontaneous and committed by local actors rather than the Republican government, whose increasing control caused it to wane.

After the Civil War, Franco's victorious dictatorship continued the campaign of extermination against the left, but his regime was preoccupied with consolidating its rule after the disaster of the war and maintaining Spain's existing colonial empire. It did not, therefore, reproduce the external genocide of Nazism or, on a smaller scale, Italian fascism. This, together with the secondary importance of ethno-national targeting in this case, has contributed to the marginalization of the "Spanish Holocaust" in the genocide field. Yet it represents the most important example of the class-political variant in the overall pattern of European genocide during the second quarter of the twentieth century.

Class-political targeting in a general perspective on European genocide

Incorporating the class-political violence of the right-wing dictatorships in a perspective on European genocide leads to three main conclusions.

First, taken together, the destruction of working-class culture, social life and political and union organization in Italy, Germany and Spain represents the first large phase of the right-wing nationalist genocide that later climaxed in more extensive mass murder across the European continent. The destruction of the working class, especially in Germany, was the crucial precondition of this later pan-European genocide. Moreover, this was a general phenomenon: the destruction of working-class institutions was also accomplished in many eastern and southern European countries well before the war, if with less violence, since workers' movements were generally weaker. As Mark Mazower summarizes (1998: 27): "in most of Europe by the mid-1930s – outside the northern fringe – ... the organized Left had been smashed". In the north, autonomous labour parties and trade unions mostly survived until 1939–40, after which the Germans abolished them in all the occupied countries, including in France through the Vichy regime.

Second, considered together with Stalinist genocide, this violence also represents an important phase in the development of European genocide as a whole towards its climax during the Second World War. Across Europe, both left- and right-wing dictatorships first consolidated their power by destroying the countervailing political, economic and cultural power of the working class and peasantry, as well as all kinds of autonomous social and political institutions, through organized violence and coercion that varied according to national circumstances. Class-political genocide preceded and was the precondition for the ethno-national destruction that was carried out by the Soviet Union as well as Nazi Germany.

Third, the destruction of the working-class movements also represents a distinct, western European geographical arena of genocide. Levene (2014a: 34) writes of genocide's greater "geographical density within the rimlands" of the continent, and during the Second World War it did become concentrated in what Timothy Snyder (2010) calls the "bloodlands" between the Nazi and Stalinist empires. Yet genocide in the first half of the twentieth century was a genuinely pan-European phenomenon. Bloxham (2005) shows that it originated in decades of ethno-national conflict in southeastern Europe amid the decline of the Ottoman Empire, culminating in the 1915 Armenian genocide. He also recognizes a broader "European pattern" in the Nazi genocide, including a "western expansion" of the "final solution", as the Nazis collected Jews from across their empire to feed their industrialized killing machine in the east (2009: 212–60).

However, in the light of our discussion, it can be seen that this was not a "westward expansion" of genocide from eastern origins, but a *return* of genocide to western Europe, the region where it had originated in violence against the working class and its movements. In this light, the Spanish Holocaust, which involved the largest-scale killing and other violence against civilians in Europe anywhere to the west of Germany during the first half of the twentieth century, was the culmination of a seminal process of group destruction in the west that played a pivotal role in the continental escalation.

A final conclusion from this reconsideration of European genocide is conceptual and theoretical. Lemkin's original definition of barbarity (genocide) as acts of "extermination directed against the ethnic, religious *or social* collectivities" (1933, emphasis added), was a more adequate definition than his later "destruction of a nation or of an ethnic group" (Lemkin 1944: 79–80). Lemkin's 1944 study made virtually no reference to the suppression of working-class institutions in the occupied countries, let alone their prior destruction in Germany and other countries under dictatorial rule. Most of the genocide literature has followed this approach to Nazi and European genocide as well as to general definition. Adam Jones is a rare exception, but even he argues – while challenging the exclusion of political groups from genocide – that ethnic and national groups "predominated as victims in the decades in which Lemkin developed his frameworks (and in the historical examples he studied). However, by the end of the 1940s, it was clear that political groups were often targeted for extermination" (Jones 2010: 11). Jones has reversed the historical order, as his example, the "liquidation of the *kulaks*" – which preceded the ethnic-national targeting, of which Lemkin wrote, by a full decade – shows.

In the genocide literature, Bloxham (2009: 37) alone provides a more general historical rationale for ethno-national bias: "Of all the forces unleashed by urbanization, industrialization, population growth, improved literacy, and ideas of emancipation, the one that acquired most venom in the final analysis was that of nationalities." Yet while it is true – if we measure "venom" through body counts

– that Nazi violence was ultimately most venomous towards nationalities, in Europe overall the victims of class-targeted destruction, especially peasants at the hands of the Stalinist regime, were similarly numerous; they were certainly counted in the millions (Conquest 1986: 306) even if the precise numbers may never be established (Viola 1999: 28).

In any case, body counts are hardly the whole story, and the victim category that is ultimately the most numerous is not the only one that matters. Christopher Browning (1991: ix) argues that

> if the Nazi regime had suddenly ceased to exist in the first half of 1941, its most notorious achievements in human destruction would have been the "euthanasia" killing of 70–80,000 German mentally ill and the systematic murder of the Polish intelligentsia. If the regime had disappeared in the spring of 1942, its historical infamy would have rested on the "war of destruction" against the Soviet Union, the mass death of two million prisoners of war in nine months and the killing of 0.5 million Jews in the same period.

We can add to this that if Nazism had ceased to exist in 1939, its class-political violence of 1933–5 would have figured most prominently. The Nazis' ultimate violence may have been against ethno-national groups, but from the most meaningful ultimate standpoint – that of historical understanding – the pattern of violence against multiple targets, including its dynamics through the whole period, is more important than the calculus of deaths.

Global and theoretical implications

The role of class-political targeting in European genocide needs to be located within a longer and wider perspective. It would continue to be very significant after the Second World War, as the primary locus of genocide shifted away from Europe.

Although genocidal violence in the widespread conflicts over decolonization and secession was often ethno-nationally or religiously targeted, Cold War ideology framed much of this violence in terms of the same dialectic of revolution and counter-revolution that had been seen in Europe (Chamberlin 2018). Both Communists and anti-Communists carried out huge campaigns of violence with hundreds of thousands of victims, against enemies defined largely in class-political terms, often targeting each other's social class bases. Examples include the violence of both sides in the Chinese and Korean civil wars of the 1940s and early 1950s; the Mao Zedong regime's targeting of the peasantry during the state-produced famine of the Great Leap Forward in 1958–61 and the educated middle class in the Cultural Revolution of 1966–76; the Indonesian military's and their allies' targeting of Communists in 1965; the Khmer Rouge's targeting of *ancien régime* personnel, the educated and the middle class in Cambodia during 1975–9; and the violence of right-wing military dictatorships and their allies against leftists in Chile, Argentina, Guatemala and Colombia in the final quarter of the century (Shaw 2013: 98–123). The Chinese regime's suppression of the student movement in Tiananmen Square in 1989 was also in this tradition.

Many of these campaigns had of course important ethno-national dimensions: the Great Leap Forward hit particularly hard in Tibet, where it continued the suppression of national identity begun in 1950; the Indonesian violence disproportionately affected ethnic Chinese; the Khmer Rouge heavily targeted ethnic minorities (Kiernan 2006: 252–313), even if they were only a "small proportion" of the victims (Midlarsky 2005: 309); and the Guatemalan genocide was the largest of the Latin American episodes because it was widely directed at rural indigenous people, the Maya, rather than mainly at urban leftists as in Argentina and Chile. While it is important to distinguish the class-political and ethno-national strands, it is not appropriate to separate them in a categorical sense, as in arguments such as Midlarsky's that in Cambodia, "the vast majority died in a politicide" while only the Vietnamese and other ethnic minorities were victims of a "genocide" (2005: 310). Rather, the idea of a single "Cambodian genocide" accurately captures the idea of an episode of extraordinary regime violence against an entire population, even if targeting differentially affected the groups within it.

Taking this twentieth-century history of class-political violence as a whole, it is more plausible to see it as the outcome of what Eric Hobsbawm (1994) called "the age of extremes" than as a projection of the "genocentric" dynamic that Lemkin proposed. In finally giving class its proper emphasis, genocide research does not need to replace Lemkin with Marx, but it does need to address how the intellectual formation of the genocide field has contributed to the elision of class-political genocide.

The parameters of Lemkin's own approach have been discussed: his upbringing in the minority Jewish community in Poland, where nationalism and antisemitism were strong (and class identity was weaker than in western European societies); his "forgotten" Zionism (Loeffler 2017); his interest in the Ottoman destruction of the Armenians in 1915; his formation as an international lawyer that predisposed him to view questions in terms of national–international relations; and the influence of the holistic and functionalist thinking of Malinowski (Moses 2010: 22–5; Butcher 2013).

The crucial question is why the sociology and historiography of genocide in recent decades have largely accepted, rather than challenged, Lemkin's assumption of the primacy of the ethno-national, even if they have not fully embraced his wider intellectual agenda. By the time the field emerged, not only had Nazism's "final" solution long eclipsed its class violence but also the Communist regimes in Russia and Eastern Europe had become authoritarian rather than totalitarian states. Even the regimes responsible for the late anti-Communist violence in Latin America were disappearing in the democratization of the 1990s. The "age of extremes" appeared to have ended.

Perhaps most importantly, by the 1990s the industrial working class was declining as a political force. Although there had been an upsurge of workers' movements in the late 1960s and 1970s, many working-class institutions once more appeared "incorporated" in Western democratic societies. Class conflict no longer took extensively violent forms, and class was increasingly seen by sociologists as only one dimension of complex social stratification, intersecting with race and gender. After the Cold War, class-political genocide increasingly appeared to be a thing of the past, and its absence in the present may have fostered the assumption that historically, too, it had been of minor importance.

Alongside these developments, Marxism – which had revived as an intellectual paradigm and informing much historical as well as sociological writing in the 1960s and 1970s – was also largely eclipsed, despite the critical relationship to Communist states of most academic Marxists. Of the major genocide scholars only Levene (2005a), who dedicates his *The Rise of the West and the Coming of Genocide* to E. P. Thompson, seems to have been significantly influenced by class-centric Marxism; while the insights of the tradition undoubtedly informed his insights, they were not explicitly integrated into his history.

Instead, Lemkin's "genocentric" focus, if not all his theoretical assumptions, fitted the preoccupations of different groups of scholars. On the one hand, many in the generation of social scientists who pioneered the genocide field in the 1980s were North Americans of Jewish and Armenian origin, whose thinking was particularly influenced by their communities' experiences in the Holocaust and the Armenian genocide. On the other hand, the younger European, Australian and other historians who followed them were primarily concerned with colonial genocides, their relationships to European empires and the Second World War; these too lent themselves to being seen primarily as ethno-national cases.

In the twenty-first century, genocidal targeting has also mostly appeared to be ethno-national, but political identities remain important even if they have been largely deanchored from class. People are attacked not only because of their ethnic, national or religious identity but also for how this is politically articulated. In a partially democratized world, "ethnic" and "party" identities are often intertwined in electoral politics, and therefore in the ideologies of perpetrators of post-election violence, in ways that make it difficult to conclusively establish priority (Shaw 2013: 55–60).

The Syrian case shows how such combined targeting can be important. Most explicit "genocide" debate has focused on IS's persecution of the Yezidis: UN special advisers on genocide and on human rights made public statements on Syria and Iraq, and the IAGS passed a resolution concerning the "crimes of ISIS" (International Association of Genocide Scholars 2014), a group they identified by their religion. Yet during the civil war as a whole, the Bashar-al-Assad regime was estimated to be responsible for over 90 per cent of deaths. Unlike IS, the regime did not initially rationalize its attacks on civilians through ethnic or religious identities; the overt rationale was political since the war continued the repression of mass protests. However, the regime increasingly identified its political enemies in sectarian terms, since most opposition supporters were Sunni Muslims, whereas the regime's support was mainly drawn from the Alawites and other minorities, and the war was sectarianized as the secular opposition was increasingly superseded by armed Islamists (Hashemi & Postel 2017).

The new far right and political genocide

In the last decade, sharp new polarizations have developed around authoritarian far-right nationalism, in both its illiberal "radical" right and openly anti-democratic "extreme" right forms (Mudde 2019), as well as in historic right-wing parties such as the US Republicans that have been taken over by far-right forces. The principal animus of the new far right's repression and violence is what I have called "political racism" (Shaw 2022a), directed mainly at migrants and minorities seen as "outside" the racialized nation. Both state and popular violence resulting from the new far right have been directed principally at these groups and have been limited by historical standards. Yet the far right also orchestrates hostility against liberal and left-wing political enemies "within" the nation, and it is not inconceivable that the far right in Western democracies will mobilize significant violence against such enemies, as the attack on the US Capitol on 6 January 2021 showed. In the authoritarian playbook, the two types of repression work together: for example, in 2025 the new Trump administration used anti-Palestinian racism to intimidate students, academics and the left as well as Palestinians, Muslims and Arabs.

Greater violence has already occurred elsewhere. In India in 2020, Hindu nationalist paramilitaries of the Rashtriya Swayamsevak Sangh inflicted violence on the opposition, after the Bharatiya Janata Party government of Narendra Modi achieved a parliamentary majority in the previous year. As Modi introduced a discriminatory citizenship scheme that aroused large-scale protests, his paramilitary allies launched a state-condoned pogrom, dubbed the worst since 1950, going on the offensive "not only against Muslims but against large sections of the democratic opposition", including a violent rampage against students at Jawarhalal Nehru University in early 2020 (Agraval 2020; Ahmad 2020: 22). Even more extreme forms of repression have happened in other countries: in Egypt in 2013, opposition supporters were massacred during and after Abdel Fattah El-Sisi's seizure of power; and in the Philippines in 2018, President Rodrigo Duterte ordered the military to "destroy" the left by emulating the 1965 mass killings of the Indonesian Communists (Simangan & Melvin 2019).

It is too early to know how widely the rise of the far right will stimulate the rise of such violence. Despite some obvious similarities, there is not a simple revival of classical fascism: radicalized far-right parties are creating authoritarian regimes, but unlike their predecessors most have not (yet) mobilized very large paramilitary movements or aimed at outright dictatorship. Yet this new far right also often displays a genocidal mentality, and is at home with the language of genocide, which it subverts in ideas such as that of a "white genocide" centred on the "replacement" of whites in Western populations (Moses 2019). Under certain conditions, far-right regimes could tip from repressive to truly destructive violence. Understanding this danger will help genocide research to prepare its readership for the worst that the new far right may bring.

9
BRITAIN AND GENOCIDE: STRUCTURES OF COMPLICITY

The Gaza genocide and its denial have been international Western affairs, but they have also been heavily mediated by national political relations. Attention has largely focused on the USA, which has been central to Israel's campaign, but it is important that attention is also given to the roles of other states. This is particularly true of the UK, which provided important support to Israel that continued long after the extent of its atrocities was clear and the ICJ ruled that there was a plausible risk of genocide, which should have triggering the UK's duty to prevent it, as a signatory to the Genocide Convention, if its own prior knowledge had not already done so.

There appears to be a serious justification for the British Palestinian Committee's allegation (2025: 3), that the UK was "not simply failing in its third party responsibilities to uphold international law, but [was] actively complicit in genocidal acts perpetrated against the Palestinian people". A UK–Israel Military Cooperation Agreement had been concluded in 2020, and Britain gave Israel military support that probably contributed, at least indirectly, to its genocide. Speaking at the Royal Air Force (RAF) base at Akrotiri in Cyprus on 9 December 2024, Prime Minister Keir Starmer told RAF personnel: "Quite a bit of what goes on here can't necessarily be talked about all of the time ... we can't necessarily tell the world what you're doing." This could have been a reference to the force's reconnaissance flights over Gaza, reportedly a majority of all such flights in the first year of war, which are believed to have supplied intelligence to Israel: supposedly to help its campaign to rescue its hostages but almost certainly contributing to its violence against Palestinians, since Israel hardly distinguished between the two types of operation (Yusuf & Miller 2024). The UK also provided parts for F-35 bombers, which Israel used to attack Gaza, despite knowing that this probably contravened IHL: the excuse, revealed in the High Court in November 2024, was a higher priority for multinational collaboration in the F-35 programme, euphemistically proclaimed as necessary for "international peace and security". After Labour took power in July 2024, it imposed an embargo on some weapons sales, but limited this so as not to step too far out of line with the USA (Abdul 2024).

The UK, which regarded Israel as an "ally", also supplied legal and political support. The Conservative government, in office for the first nine months after October 2023, presented Hamas' attacks as an "existential threat" to Israel, endorsed its "absolute" right to defend itself, presented Palestinians killed by Israel as victims of Hamas and conjured a threat to British Jews from pro-Palestinian demonstrations (Sunak 2023a; 2023b). In the early months, the government, supported by the Labour opposition, opposed calls for a ceasefire; later it also opposed South Africa's ICJ case and attempted to block the proposed ICC prosecution of Israeli leaders (House of Commons Library 2024: 33–7). Foreign Secretary David Cameron, a former prime minister, even threatened that the UK would defund and withdraw from the ICC if charges were brought against Israeli leaders (Hearst & Mulla 2025).

Although opposition to the ICC prosecutions was withdrawn by Labour when it was elected in July 2024, Starmer and other ministers repeatedly denied that genocide was being committed. His own denial was particularly striking since he had taken part, as a lawyer, in Croatia's 2014 genocide case against Serbia in the ICJ, describing the destruction of Vukovar in 1991, in which over a thousand civilians died, in terms that clearly fitted the much greater destruction of Gaza in late 2024: "not an armed conflict directed at military objectives, but a radically disproportionate attack, deliberately intended to devastate the town and its civilian population" (Proudfoot 2024). Indeed, even as Labour leader, Starmer had tweeted in 2021: "genocide can never be met with indifference, impunity or inaction", a statement that was now quoted against him by by pro-Palestinian activists (North Herts PSC 2024). In January 2025, he told a Holocaust Memorial Day event, "it is on all of us to make 'never again' mean what it says: Never again", but his speech completely failed to mention Gaza, while his foreign secretary held a reception together with the Israeli ambassador, an outspoken advocate of her state's assault (Shaw 2025).

These official stances were overwhelmingly reinforced by mainstream British media, including the BBC, which offered few challenges to the state's complicity and largely reproduced the culture of denial, promoting the idea that antisemitism was the major challenge in the crisis, reporting only a small proportion of Israel's atrocities, avoiding the word genocide and failing to platform the voices of Palestinians and their supporters (Centre for Media Monitoring 2024; Jones 2024). British universities mostly avoided the extremes of "anti-antisemitic" repression seen in the USA and Germany (Streeck 2024), but they also often reflected the general elite climate and several attempted to discipline student protestors.

Understanding "Britain and genocide"

This experience had particular sources in the historical relationships of the British state, politics and society to Israel-Palestine, to which this chapter will return. Yet it also reflected general British self-images, largely shaped by the representation of the Second World War in collective memory. Regarded as the foundational event of the modern nation, the war came to be represented almost exclusively as a fight against Nazism, itself identified with the Holocaust, in which Britain led the forces of good.

This was the context in which, in 1997, prime minister Tony Blair proclaimed an annual Holocaust Memorial Day: although promised as a commemoration of genocide in general, it enshrined a particular place in the national culture and politics for the archetypal genocide that Britain claimed to have played a major role in ending. This particular institutionalization of genocide memory was almost designed to block critical reflection on Britain's own history; as Tom Lawson (2014: 441) noted, the country had "no official means for the memorialization of its colonial genocides". It was largely shared across the political spectrum and disseminated in national media, popular historical literature and the school curriculum: Nazism and the Holocaust were the only international history topics that most pupils could be assumed to have studied. It even influenced protest movements, for example in the idea that Britain had a unique capacity to provide global moral leadership over nuclear weapons (Hinton 1989).

Official memorialization of the Holocaust sustained a myth that genocide is something that other nations commit and Britain fights against: the country is always part of the solution to genocide, never of the problem. Gaza is not the first event since 1945 to bring this narrative into question, but it particularly holds up a mirror in which the entire British relationship to genocide needs to be re-examined. The longer history raises key questions: how widely have the state and other British actors committed genocide, been complicit in the genocides of others – or been genuine opponents of others' genocides as the national myth claims? Is the UK's active complicity in Gaza a departure from the historical pattern or a continuation of it?

These are the issues this chapter explores. The interpretative frames that the growing genocide literature has forged have never been systematically applied to British history, which is a striking omission, especially when we consider the seminal importance of British imperialism and colonization for the "colonial turn" in genocide studies during the 2000s. British and Commonwealth scholars have been prominent in this decolonization of genocide research, but there has been far more attention to colonial societies and states than to the imperial core. The neglect of Britain as both a structural factor and an actor (or set of actors) is even more striking if we recognize that many of the postcolonial situations that have been examined by genocide scholars in recent years – the violence of the Indian Partition, the Nakba, the Biafran war and the war of Bengali independence, to name but a few – have also arisen in states that were formerly parts of the British Empire where the UK continued to play a significant role.

I became aware of this paradox two decades ago and delivered the first version of this argument in the annual War Studies lecture at King's College, London, in 2010 (Shaw 2011). "Postcolonial" studies had long emerged by this point but the idea of "decolonizing" academia had not. However, it seemed to me that while empire and colonization would necessarily be central themes in a genocide critique of the British state and society, they would not – at least in the ways they are generally understood – be the whole story. In particular, the involvement of Britain in the two world wars was also more problematic than the national myth suggested: although Britain's enemies – the Ottomans during the first war, the Nazis in the second – were classical perpetrators, the country's own involvement demanded more critical accounting. "The *ambiguity* of Britain's response to Nazi tyranny and racism is lodged in our history", the Jewish historian David Cesarani concluded (2002: 2, emphasis in original).

Such ambiguity is pervasive in recent British relationships to genocide. The UK played an important role in the drafting of the Genocide Convention between 1947 and 1948, but, as we have seen, it is also often partly blamed for its omissions, such as that of political groups. And as a great power and permanent member of the Security Council since 1945, the UK has been involved in most of the genocidal crises of the postwar era, but by no means only and always as an upholder of international law.

In the original lecture, I challenged the core of the national ideology outlined above through a schematic outline of the role of genocide in British history. The idea of "bad/guilty" and "good/vigilant" nations belonged, I argued, more to genocidal thought than anti-genocidal understanding: nations never stand unequivocally on one side of the historical process. Complexity and ambiguity are the norm, and Britain had been part of the problem, possibly as much as or more often than it had been part of the solution. As British citizens and scholars, we had responsibilities to investigate the reasons why our politicians, state and social institutions had often been complicit in or indifferent to genocide. I also noted the weakness of genocide research in Britain compared to the USA or even Australia, and this remains true: genocide studies is still a Cinderella field in British academia. The intervening decade and a half has certainly seen a growth in critical studies of Britain's global roles, including in knowledge about Britain's role in genocide, on which I draw in this chapter, but they have not seen any new synthesis from a genocide standpoint, such as I attempted.

My original project therefore remains relevant, all the more so because of developments in British politics, which were substantially overtaken by reactionary racial-nationalist ideas as the United Kingdom Independence Party and successor far-right parties led by Nigel Farage pushed the whole spectrum in their direction during the 2010s. Brexit, a nationalist and pseudo-imperial fantasy project achieved through a racist anti-immigrant campaign (which I have analysed elsewhere: Shaw 2022a), led increasingly to far-right dominance in the Conservative Party and its media, and Labour was also affected. Almost a decade after the 2016 referendum, Brexit itself is almost universally acknowledged as a failure, but the far right is once again on the march, now through a new Farage party, Reform UK. While it continues the broad-spectrum "culture war" politics promoted by the far-righted Conservative government in the early 2020s (Satia 2021) – which also include anti-trans and anti-net zero campaigning – its core is a cluster of issues around imperialism and race (Lester 2022), and its resurgence since 2024 has been focused on these.

In this context, my aim of problematizing Britain's genocide history is all the more relevant. The argument is organized around five more or less chronological, but overlapping, historical structures of genocide in British history: its role in the development of the British state; the problem of genocide in the British Empire and its settler colonialism; Britain's relationships to twentieth-century European genocide; its roles in the genocidal violence of decolonization; and, finally, its involvement in the genocidal crises of the post-Cold War world. I conclude where I began, with Gaza.

Genocide in the formation of modern Britain

We have seen that genocide is implicated in the origins of many relatively new states, both in the colonized world (Moses 2000; 2004a; 2008a; Kiernan 2007; Levene 2005b) and in east-central Europe (Bloxham 2005; Bessell & Haake 2008; Ahonen 2008). The role of genocide in the origins of "old" states is not, however, a widely considered question. The British tend to regard theirs as formed by gradual processes of accretion, as an English state emerged out of regional Anglo-Saxon and Danish kingdoms, was conquered by the Normans, separated from their large possessions in modern France, conquered Wales, united with Scotland and incorporated Ireland to form the United Kingdom in 1801 – from which the Irish Republic separated in the twentieth century. Clearly there was, in this long history, no single foundational genocide as in other cases. Yet as we have seen genocide is not only a matter of large-scale, coordinated campaigns such as the Holocaust, but also of more episodic, localized genocidal massacres and expulsions, in the context of military campaigns and religious and political persecution. Of these there were plenty in the pre-modern history of the English and British states.

As early examples, consider two medieval episodes from my home county, Yorkshire. Here, Daniel Chirot and Clark McCauley (2006: 14) argue, the Norman dynasty owed its hegemony to an extensive destruction of the indigenous population:

> William the Conqueror ... commanded that Yorkshire be cleared of its population in order to break the ability of the Anglo-Saxon lords of that region to continue their resistance of the Norman Conquest. No one is sure how many died, but the systematic destruction of villages and crops, the widespread murder and flights into the surrounding mountains, where enslavement by Scottish tribes or starvation awaited the refugees, greatly reduced the population.

Yorkshire's hills are not generally regarded as mountains, but the point that a brutal counterinsurgency made the inhabitants victims of what would now be called genocide is well taken.

A century or so later, some of the English (as they were coming to regard themselves) were implicated in a different violent episode in roughly the same locale, against the Jewish population. The site of the violence was Clifford's Tower, the keep of the Norman castle in York, in whose shadow my mother was born and down whose steep, grassy hillside my own children later liked to roll. Yet in 1190, the wooden predecessor of the surviving stone edifice had been burned down together with about 150 Jews who had taken refuge in it from a mob; many of them took their own lives rather than be killed, while others were massacred. In 2010, the tower's tourist website linked this event, which we might now call a genocidal massacre, with the accession of Richard I, the Crusader king and an iconic figure in English history. It was Richard who promoted anti-Jewish sentiment, although the website reassured us that his chancellor "imposed a heavy fine on York's citizens" as punishment for the massacre. Yet before we build up an antiheroic version of *English* history, let us recall that while Richard was king of England, he hardly spoke English and spent most of his reign – when he was not fighting the Crusades, concerning which perhaps other questions of genocidal violence arise – in his Duchy of Aquitaine in modern France.

More directly pertinent to the role of genocide in the formation of the modern state is the long-controversial Cromwellian (re)conquest of Ireland in 1649–53, although as Robbie McVeigh (2008: 546–8) shows, settler as well as administrative colonialism – which raises at least questions of "cultural genocide" – can be traced over the previous half-millennium. There is no doubt that this was a brutal military campaign; but Cromwell's Irish policy was also, Mark Levene (2005b: 56) contends, "a conscious attempt to reduce a distinct ethnic population, not simply on the grounds of their religious disposition, but also for demonstrating their potential to challenge the mono-directional and monopolistic thrust of an Anglo-Protestant dominated British Isles. The genocidal process which emerged after 1651 was [not] simply a short-term military strategy … . It was a long-term political policy." The 1652 Act for the Settlement of Ireland is, he argues, "the nearest thing *on paper*, in the English and more broadly British domestic record, to a programme of state-sanctioned and systematic ethnic cleansing of another people. … The expropriated were to be required to move, on pain of death, to a designated area [in] the most westerly corner of Ireland and so make way for a massive new wave of Anglo-Scottish settlers who would supersede them" (emphasis in the original).

McVeigh (2008: 548–9) also notes that historians largely regard *An Gorta Mór*, the Great Famine of 1845–51 in Ireland in which up to two million starved and a similar number were forced to emigrate, to be a result of deliberate British policies; hence some have concluded that this too was genocide. Neither Cromwell's campaign nor the famine were extermination in the sense of the Final Solution, but the former was the eviction of "a troublesome population whose place within the national or colonial frame had been definitively and permanently revoked", comparable to "the Nazis' 1939–40 projected removal of Polish Jewry", Levene (2005b: 57) contends, while the famine certainly expressed the racist contempt of the British authorities towards the Irish people.

As in other colonial contexts, allegations of genocide have also been raised concerning violence against the settler population. A decade before Cromwell's campaign, in 1641–2, Irish insurgents in Ulster had killed between 4,000 and 12,000 Protestants who had settled on land whose former Catholic owners had been evicted. If these massacres "were magnified for propagandist purposes to justify Cromwell's subsequent genocide" (Coogan 1997: 6), nevertheless they demonstrate something that we have seen in recent cases: genocidal violence often begins in the resistance of "subaltern" peoples, only to be followed by the even greater violence of the imperial power (Moses 2008b; Jones & Robbins 2009). Moreover, even after the Good Friday agreement of 1999, a "genocidal imperative – 'Kill All Taigs' and 'Kill All Huns' – remained a commonplace grafitto in contemporary 'post-conflict', 'peaceful' Northern Ireland" (McVeigh 2008: 554).

As Michael Hechter (1975) argued, this Irish history anticipates the wider history of British empire and colonization; McVeigh (2008: 542–3) adds that it is an important case study of their connections with genocide. Within the British Isles, the closest comparison is the destruction of the Gaelic-speaking clan society in the Scottish Highlands between the mid-eighteenth and mid-nineteenth centuries, as a combination of anti-Jacobite repression, the suppression of traditional culture (seen as necessary for the consolidation of the Anglo-Scottish imperial state) and landlord dispossession hollowed out once-thriving communities (Richards 2000). If Levene (2005b: 58–9) is right to say that there was no singular genocidal policy of the kind practised in Ireland, this was a case, similar to later colonial experiences, in which the combination of different kinds of political and economic policies over time resulted in the destruction of traditional society. Indeed, even in England in the same period, brutal law enforcement was directed against the rural and urban poor (Thompson 1975), with sharp repression of the emergent trade union and Chartist movements.

Genocide in British imperialism and colonialism

It was only, therefore, from the second half of the nineteenth century that Britain even partially deserved the reputation for peaceful gradualism that has been central to its complacent national self-image. Yet despite the subduing of the state's internal foes, international violence continued, as Ireland showed. Indeed, Leon Trotsky argued that "the whole history of Great Britain is first of all the history of violent changes which the British governing classes have made in the life of *other* nations" (1970 [1925]: 17, emphasis in original), and the sentiment is echoed by contemporary imperial historian Caroline Elkins (2022: 46): "Violence was not just the British Empire's midwife: it was endemic to the structures and systems of British rule." An even more drastic verdict was proposed by the Native American scholar-activist Ward Churchill, for whom the English were "global leaders in genocidal activities" (Moses 2004a: 4). Whether or not this comparative judgement would survive a careful study of other European countries' colonial records, it challenges the benign view that has long led to a particular smugness about British imperialism.

Yet Churchill's invocation of "genocide" to describe parts of the British colonial legacy is still not widely followed, even by critical writers who have made major contributions in recent years (Gopal 2020; Sanghera 2021; Elkins 2022; Lester 2024). Part of the reason for this appears to be that genocide has been connected to a particular aspect of British imperial history: *settler* colonialism. Michael Mann (2005: 4) concludes from a broad historical survey: "The more settlers controlled colonial institutions, the more murderous the cleansing. … It is the most direct relationship I have found between democratic regimes and mass murder". Moses (2004b: 19) makes a similar argument about Australia, where about 600 indigenous cultural-linguistic groups, many of whom regarded themselves as separate peoples, were either wiped out or drastically reduced in numbers and displaced from their traditional lands. Although much Aboriginal decline was an indirect result of British settlement, he suggests that "each willed act of extermination by settlers and/or the state of an Aboriginal group could be regarded as genocide. In that case, many genocides took place in Australia, rather than [its] being the site of a single genocidal event."

Moses (2000) argues that settler colonialism was structurally prone to genocide and involved serial "genocidal moments". Settlers and local militia were the main perpetrators: "rarely can exterminatory intent be discerned in British authorities" yet "there was a greater degree of consciousness about the fatal impact of their presence" than defenders of the official role contended (Moses 2004b: 5). British authorities in London and the colonies willed settlement knowing that it foretold the often brutal removal of the indigenous inhabitants, even if they sometimes disapproved of the means that settlers adopted.

The identification of exterminatory violence with settlers meant that, even as questions of genocide began to be raised, British responsibility was minimized. While Australia has had a national debate on genocide – albeit with official acknowledgements that effectively amounted to denials (Barta 2008) – British commentators have mostly regarded this as a purely local affair, without implications for the "home country" from which most settlers came or, indeed, were sent as a matter of state policy (Stone 2006).

The other effect of the identification of genocide with settler colonialism is the sidelining of a broader range of questions about British imperial rule. It tends to be assumed, for example, that India, the largest component of the empire, where a small British ruling caste controlled hundreds of millions of Indians – which Adolf Hitler notoriously saw as a model for his empire in eastern Europe (Mazower 2009: 229) – did not experience the genocide issues that arose in settler colonies in North America and Australia.

If imperial rule in India was not genocidal as a whole, major questions arise about two types of episode. First, genocide research has highlighted the importance of war as the occasion of genocide: in the context of empire, this means that moments of conquest, insurgency and counterinsurgency were more dangerous than periods of relatively stable rule. In India, the Great Rebellion of 1857 (known in Britain as the Mutiny) demands attention, not only because of the murderous "subaltern" animus of the rebel soldiers towards British civilians (the subject of Victorian propaganda) but chiefly because of the countergenocidal brutality of the military repression, which went far beyond the defeat of the rebels to extensive massacres of Indian civilians (Dalrymple 2006). There were "hundreds of Britons slain and tens of thousands of Indians slaughtered", Priyamvada Gopal (2020: 49) points out, but the full history is virtually unknown in the UK. Indeed, even among genocide specialists, despite the attention given to later episodes in the subcontinent such as Partition and the East Pakistan war, 1857 has not been examined as a genocidal event. Part of the explanation for this may be a tendency for the events to be memorialized in India as "rebellion" rather than massacre, and how the 1923 Amritsar massacre has become then principal symbol of imperial violence (Condos 2022: 578–80).

Second, genocide research has highlighted the importance of large-scale famine. In cases such as the Stalinist "terror-famine" in the early 1930s and the even larger famine resulting from Mao Zedong's Great Leap Forward during 1958–61, it has been argued that state policy disastrously exacerbated the human consequences of climatic failures and that leaders who ignored peasant suffering effectively willed mass death (Conquest 1986; Dikötter 2010). Yet similar claims have also been made about famines in British India in the final quarter of the nineteenth century; in the "late Victorian holocausts", as Mike Davis (2001: 32) calls them, British policies exacerbated natural problems, causing millions to die: "those with the power to relieve famine convinced themselves that overly heroic exertions against implacable natural laws, whether of market prices or population growth, were worse than no effort at all". The same relationships between intentional state policies and wider sets of conditions could be seen in the 1943 Bengal famine (Ó Gráda 2009: 159–85).

Elsewhere, insurgencies and counter-insurgencies during decolonization in the third quarter of the twentieth century raise similar questions to the Indian rebellion. During the insurrection of the Land and Freedom Army (known in Britain as the Mau Mau) in Kenya from 1952 to 1960, the British detained 160,000 "suspected terrorists" in camps, while concentrating almost the entire Kikuyu population of 1.5 million in villages ringed with barbed wire. Counterinsurgency methods included summary executions, electric shock, mass deportations, slave labour, the burning down of villages and similar collective punishments, starvation and rape. Tens of thousands died from the combined effects of exhaustion, disease, starvation and systemic physical brutality. In contrast, the "savage" insurgents killed about 1,800 Kenyan loyalists as well as 32 settlers out of a total of 95 "Europeans" (Elkins 2005: 36; Anderson 2005).

Here, as often before and since, degenerate counterinsurgency war, much more than insurgency itself, breached the borderline between extreme repression and genocide, with the deliberate partial destruction of the indigenous society. Yet this aroused little opposition in 1950s Britain: as Stephen Howe (2005) commented, there was nothing like "the engagement of Sartre, Camus and others with France's crimes in Algeria. Liberal Britain's muted reaction to the Kenyan crisis remains puzzling, and shaming." And in today's Britain, despite the recent scholarly attention, it is almost forgotten.

To draw some interim conclusions: clearly the literature does not support facile equations of British imperialism everywhere and always with genocide. Nor does it suggest that central authorities in the British state developed *overall* genocidal policies: rather, genocidal moments seem to have been mainly the direct responsibility of settlers, local administrations and military commanders. But it does suggest that genocide was a repeated, structural problem of British (as of other European) imperial and colonial expansions, in which the imperial centre was often implicated.

Britain's role in twentieth-century European genocide

The rivalries of the European and other world empires, in the context of which colonial genocide was committed over half a millennium, led to interimperial war and the classical modern genocides. As we have seen, Europe was the locus not only of the Holocaust and the wider Nazi genocide but of complex, multicentred genocidal dynamics. Indeed, as Bloxham (2008) argues, genocide was endemic in important parts of the European international system between roughly 1875 and 1949, from the Balkans before the First World War to eastern and central Europe as a whole in the Second World War. Britain did not commit genocide in Europe, but as a repeatedly victorious great power was implicated in various ways in these European developments.

There was what Bloxham calls a "great game of genocide" in southeastern Europe during the final crisis of the Ottoman Empire: the 1915 Armenian genocide was the nadir of a half-century of genocidal expulsions by both the empire and the emergent nation-states. During this set of conflicts, the British espoused "humanitarian" principles, while tacitly encouraging Armenian and other Christian nationalists against the Ottomans, to the point of condoning their expulsions of Muslims and helping provoke Ottoman atrocities. In British responses to the Armenian genocide, as later with the Holocaust, "the warning of punishment for the chief perpetrators substituted for any overall policy of assistance to the victims" (Bloxham 2005: 138).

Following the First World War, the British government of David Lloyd George was central, with the USA and France, to the attempt to manage nationalist "population politics" that dominated the Paris settlement (Weitz 2008). However, this process stimulated the national conflicts it was meant to control: states and nationalist movements manoeuvred militarily to secure conditions on the ground prior to international agreement, often through violent means.

Notoriously, Britain supported the Greek army when it invaded Anatolia in 1919, provoking intercommunal atrocities in which the Greeks were the greater perpetrators, only to be beaten back by the Turkish army, which in its turn brutally attacked the historic Greek populations, especially at Smryna (Izmir) in 1922. The fate of orthodox archbishop Chrystosomos was emblematic: having blessed the disembarking Greek troops in 1919, he was torn to pieces by a Turkish mob: "such", Donald Bloxham writes, "was the outcome of Greco-British imperialism in Anatolia" (2005: 165). The conclusion to this episode was the 1923 Lausanne treaty through which the new Turkey completed, with great power legitimation, the process of ethnic homogenization begun in the 1915 genocide. The Greco-Turkish "population exchange" may have been agreed between the two states, but it represented the destruction of historic communities on both sides.

Moreover, "majority" national states and movements used the Paris framework to press home their advantages over minorities, even to the point of violent expulsion; and the provisions were as successful in provoking powerful nationalists as in protecting minorities; Hitler invoked these provisions to justify his invasion of the Czech Sudetenland in 1938. It would be facile to primarily blame British politicians for these outcomes, but it would be equally so to see Britain as outside the increasingly genocidal logic of much continental politics.

This conclusion is borne out by an examination of British policies during the Second World War. Winston Churchill's well-known reluctance to prioritize action to stop the Holocaust is one side of this story (Cohen 2003: 261–305). As Cesarani (2002: 2) concludes:

> Documents show that the British Government knew about the slaughter of the Jews from the moment it began, but did not issue any official condemnation of the genocide until very late. There was no attempt to prevent the genocide, even when counter-measures were feasible. Nor were restrictions on refugee immigration to Britain or Palestine eased. British policy was to defeat the Nazis without paying too much attention to distractions such as the persecution and mass murder of the Jews, or wasting resources on humanitarian initiatives.

Britain's other implication in wartime genocide lay in its support for allies' proposals for countergenocidal policies against the German minorities in their countries, seen as implicated in Nazi rule. In 1942 the exiled president of Czechoslovakia, Edvard Beneš, suggested expelling the remaining ethnic German population from the country after the war; the British foreign secretary, Sir Anthony Eden, conveyed his government's approval (Brandes 2008: 286–7). When Stalin proposed pushing Poles westwards into former German territories and expelling Germans from the USSR as well as Czechoslovakia and Poland, the British and Americans argued over the extent, but not the principle, of this territorial revision and expulsion (Brandes 2008: 290–91).

Similarly, when, in the concluding stages of the war and afterwards, the Soviet Union, Czechoslovakia, Poland, Romania, Hungary and Yugoslavia implemented expulsions of their German populations, the Western Allies did little to ensure that these were "orderly and humane", as their Potsdam agreement with Stalin had required (de Zayas 1979). Over ten million Germans were forced out at the cost of half a million lives, with the British, Americans and French receiving many into their occupation zones (Bloxham 2008: 122). The destruction of German society in these countries avenged, of course, the Nazis' destructive policies towards the Slavic and other east-central European peoples, rather than their extermination of the Jews, which was of less concern to the postwar central

European governments; indeed, in Poland at least, antisemitic persecution continued (Gross 2006).

There was some British resistance to these developments, and even Winston Churchill was discomfited by the atrocity reports (Frank 2008); a few prominent individuals outside government, Bertrand Russell for example, protested strongly (de Zayas 1979: 108). However, for most British people, these expulsions, which destroyed historic communities on a scale – if not with a murderousness – comparable to that of the destruction of Jewish communities in the same regions, barely registered. Like the Soviet, Czechoslovak and Polish leaders, many tacitly accepted the assumption of collective responsibility that made all Germans guilty of Nazi crimes, although this was exactly how Nazism itself viewed Jews, Russians, Czechs, Poles and others.

The principle of collective punishment also provided secondary justification for the most problematic of Britain's own wartime policies: the extensive bombing of German cities. The mass killing of civilians was fully intended: Britain's "primary object", an Air Staff directive specified in 1942, "should now be focused on the morale of the civilian population" (Grayling 2006: 50). This was civilian destruction as a means of defeating the German state, rather than because the civilian population was seen as an enemy in itself. But if in this sense the British campaign might not be regarded as genocide, nevertheless the methods had much in common with overtly genocidal policies, as A. C. Grayling shows: "terror-bombing", "dehousing" entire populations, destroying whole towns and many of their inhabitants by flooding, fire and burying them under their ruined buildings (2006: 59, 72, 82–91, 159–62).

Likewise the mentality: if it was the US secretary of the Treasury, Henry Morgenthau Jr, who notoriously articulated the idea of "pastoralizing" Germany by permanently destroying its cultural and industrial fabric, it was Britain's Bomber Command that "continued to act in ways that gave every impression of trying to bring about such a result" (Grayling 2006: 168). For the RAF had begun its campaign to destroy Germany's cities by attacking their historic centres and continued with "a concerted smashing of as much of Germany, its people and its cultural heritage as possible". The British campaign was similar in scope to the US bombing of Japan, which culminated in the atomic destruction of Hiroshima and Nagasaki: both are testimony to the general degeneration of warfare and to its close affinity with the specifically genocidal developments of the same period.

Britain's role in the genocidal violence of decolonization

Britain continued to be complicit in genocide committed by others after the Second World War. However, important general changes were taking place in the late 1940s, a major turning point in the history of genocide. First, the phenomenon was named by Lemkin and criminalized by the United Nations. Second, after three-quarters of a century during which genocide had become an increasingly central strand in European history, it disappeared from the continent for four decades.

This shift hardly resulted from the UN Genocide Convention. In reality, both the convention and the end of European genocide were results of the definitive Allied victory, which in east-central Europe involved the triumph of Soviet over Nazi genocidal policies, and the subsequent Cold War confirmed the shift. Indeed, the progress involved in these developments appears even more doubtful when viewed in its historical context. As we saw in Chapter 8, one of the main authors of the convention, the Soviet Union, could be regarded as a genocidal state: both its wartime deportations of "treasonable" peoples and the expulsions of Germans fell within its definition.

Crucially, the late 1940s saw major new genocidal violence outside Europe, which was to continue through and beyond the Cold War period. The new waves were chiefly but not only in Asia, where the war's shake-up of old imperial arrangements caused new conflicts. As the UN drafted the convention and the Soviets concluded the elimination of Germans from central Europe, Mao Zedong's Communists came to power in China with the aid of large-scale killing of "class enemies" (Chang & Halliday 2005), which the Nationalists reciprocated. Similar violence, initiated by the anti-Communist right with which the USA and Britain were allied, occurred on a large scale in the Korean civil war.

Meanwhile in India, where the war shifted power away from Britain, the triumph of the national movement was soured by the massive violence of Partition that occurred under British imperial control: the numbers expelled or forced to flee (estimated at 12 million) and the numbers of deaths (at least a quarter of a million) roughly matched those in the expulsions of the Germans (Khan 2008: 6). Clearly these events were not orchestrated by a central party or state machine, but the actions (and failures to act) of the leaders of the Indian National Congress, the Muslim League (the ruling party of the emergent Pakistan) and the British under their viceroy, Lord Mountbatten, fatefully influenced these events. Indeed, the first large massacres predated the partition plan by nine months, but the imperial authorities still drew it up with disregard for its probable consequences and, like the nationalist leaderships, continued with their course although the outcomes were disastrous. Nor were these spontaneous outpourings of violence: "Everywhere there was an element of planning and organization involved and a sense of immunity from the governing provincial party – whether League or Congress." Khan (2008: 7) charges Mountbatten with "almost breathtaking callousness" in seeing renewed violence as helping to influence political leaders to accept his plan.

In this sense, the Indian massacres have rightly been seen as genocidal actions, carried out by militia and party organizations with British complicity (Brass 2003: 75; Talbot 2007). The Partition manifested a new, postcolonial model of genocide: partial in its attack on the "enemy" population; localized and regionalized in the scope of its destruction; decentralized in its political leadership; implemented by paramilitaries rather than regular forces or central state institutions; and yet the product of conflict over the postcolonial state at the national level, informed by ethnic or religious politics in a context of electoral democracy and approved by global powers. This model appeared in the moment of transition from the imperial order and was replicated in some later decolonizations.

The 1948 Nakba was the other major genocidal situation in which the contracting empire was involved. Britain had long been central to actualizing the danger to Palestinian society, through the 1917 Balfour Declaration, the violent suppression of the 1936 Palestinian revolt, the 1937 Peel Commission partition plan and its general promotion of Zionism. As Avi Shlaim argues, hostility to the Palestinians was "a constant and defining factor in British foreign policy from 1947 to 1949", and without British support, "the Zionist movement could not have achieved the degree of success that it did in its quest for statehood" (2024: 31, 23). But here there was also a new element: Britain acted partly in the context of the United Nations' own partition plan, and its role was changing from an autonomous empire to a component of a global power conglomerate centred on the UN and dominated by the USA. Responsibility for the catastrophe was internationalized, even if Britain retained the largest share.

Britain and the genocidal crises of the post-Cold War world

In the aftermath of empire, the UK continued to claim great power status through its possession of nuclear weapons and permanent membership of the Security Council, but it was evidently diminished. While allegations of genocide were made against the policies of states that were allies of the UK and other Western states as well as those that were not, these generally arose from conflicts that were not regarded as involving strategic British interests. Indeed, genocide sometimes became an issue for British policy only when sectors of domestic public opinion became concerned, rather than because policy-makers proactively involved themselves. Yet some of the most important genocidal crises of the Cold War era arose in Britain's former territories in Africa and South Asia; the UK was not directly responsible as it had been in the Indian and Palestinian cases, but legacies of its rule were contributory factors and historic linkages gave British roles particular salience.

The first to receive wide attention was the 1967–70 war in Nigeria's Eastern Region, whose military ruler announced its secession, as "Biafra", following a genocidal massacre of thousands of Igbos (the main group in the east) in northern Nigeria in autumn 1966. The UK initially wavered in its support, but Cold War and oil interests increasingly led it, and the USA, to back the federal Nigerian state against Biafra: the UK also feared the consequences of successful secession for other postcolonial states in Africa (Heerten & Moses 2014: 174; Smith 2014: 250). Nevertheless, the "genocide" debate promoted by Biafra's supporters had a strong impact in Britain, especially as a federal blockade caused famine in the secessionist region, and public opposition affected government policy (Smith 2014: 251–5). Biafra was also a major moment in the emergence of a wider "genocide" discourse, even if most early genocide scholars, influenced by the Holocaust paradigm, rejected it as a case, as Lasse Heerten and Dirk Moses (2014: 178–85) show.

In the 1971 war of East Pakistan's secession from Pakistan, neither Cold War nor economic interests were as determining, and the UK remained neutral, reflecting "concerns for its regional interests, Cold War geopolitical paralysis, and [a] sense of powerlessness and distance" (Debnath 2011: 442). Much of the British opposition and media accused Pakistani forces of violating human rights and even genocide, and the Foreign Office recognized that Pakistan was in breach of the Genocide Convention, but the UK government paid "only superficial attention to reports of state atrocities" and – anticipating the stance it would take over Bosnia two decades later – declared it would not interfere in the "hideous atrocities ... being committed on both sides" in what it described as a civil war (Debnath 2011: 444, 421). Anti-civilian violence was indeed multidirectional (Bose 2011), but the UK government used this fact to avoid addressing the Pakistani state's primary responsibility.

Even where genocide was committed by regimes with which the UK had no attachment, governments were prone to overlook campaigns that were widely regarded as genocide. In 1963, despite officials privately regarding a Ba'athist offensive against the Kurdish minority in Iraq as genocide, the UK supported the regime (Ali 2023). Even in the case of the Khmer Rouge regime in Cambodia during 1975–9, the British government had to be pressured by public opinion into protesting about what was widely recognized as genocide. Moreover, the UK shifted, for Cold War reasons, to a tacitly pro-Khmer Rouge position after it became clear that military action by Vietnam, an ally of the USSR, was ending Khmer Rouge rule, and continued to support the latter's retention of the country's UN seat even after its overthrow (Waddington 2024).

After the Cold War ended in 1989–91, genocide became an increasingly prominent international issue, first in former Yugoslavia from 1991 and then in Rwanda in 1994. Samantha Power would famously argue in her study of "America in the age of genocide" that policy-makers, journalists and citizens alike were "extremely slow" to reckon with genocide and "spun themselves" about the nature of the violence that was occurring, usually rendering it "two-sided and inevitable, not genocidal" (2003: xvii–xviii). Leaders interpreted societal silence as indifference, trusted in negotiations and diplomacy, urged ceasefires and donated humanitarian aid. Power concluded that the failure to prevent genocide was structural: there was a "consistent policy of nonintervention in the face of genocide", which offered "sad testimony not to a broken American political system but to one that is ruthlessly effective" (2003: xxi).

While Power's work gathered international attention, Brendan Simms (2001) had already critiqued British policy in the Balkans in similar terms. After Serbian forces began to "cleanse" Croatia in 1991 and Bosnia-Herzegovina in 1992, the UK's Conservative government manoeuvred to avoid committing forces to stop them, aiming to maintain "impartiality" between the principal perpetrators and their victims. In what Simms calls its "unfinest hour", the UK "sat astride the international management of the Bosnian war like an enormous dog in the manger, by turns resentful and self-congratulatory, firmly blocking any attempt at an alternative strategy". Moreover, "Britain's failure over Bosnia was not confined to government. Unlike their American counterparts, parliament and the opposition failed to mount any significant challenge to the executive" (Simms 2001: 339–41).

No special shame was later attached to the UK for the denouement of these policies, the 1995 Srebrenica massacre that even the ICJ would later recognize as genocide, after Dutch troops handed over thousands of Bosnian Muslims to Bosnian-Serbian forces. However, the failure was one of the UN command as a whole, in Sarajevo and New York as well as on the ground, and the UK was a major part of that; indeed, British special forces observers had "stood aside, powerless" as the Serbians overran the enclave (Simms 2001: 317).

Only after the massacre, when President Clinton (who for three years had defaulted on his election campaign concern for Bosnia) finally decided for action as a new US election loomed, did British forces play a part in lifting the siege of Sarajevo and breaking the deadlock. Even then, the West was in tacit alliance with Croatia, which by 1995 was carrying out its own destructive expulsions of Serb communities from the reconquered "Krajina" region. And the 1996 Dayton settlement that Clinton brokered allowed the Serbian entity established through the genocide, Republika Srpska, to maintain its autonomy within an internationally supervised Bosnian state.

International, including UK, responses to the 1994 Rwanda genocide were even weaker. James Woods, US deputy assistant secretary of defence under Clinton, said that "it was ... a ... spectacle of the US in disarray and retreat, leading the international community away from doing the right things and I think that everybody was perfectly happy to follow our lead – in retreat" (Simms 2001: 339). In fact, not everybody was happy – there were dissenting voices among the non-permanent members of the Security Council – but the UK seems to have been. As Michael Barnett (2002: 171) recorded, "Britain fought against the initial push for intervention in April, and then shifted position in May when it had overwhelming evidence of the genocide. Still, it contributed no real resources." Even a year afterwards, the Foreign Office did not accept that genocide had been committed, calling discussion of the question "sterile" (Melvern 2000: 230).

Reacting against this Conservative record and its own weakness in opposition, Labour under Tony Blair took different stances after 1997. The government leaned substantially into a rhetoric of Britain as a bulwark against genocide: having adopted a foreign policy with an "ethical dimension", in 1997 it proclaimed an annual Holocaust Memorial Day to commemorate all genocide. The UK also became one of the post-genocide Rwandan Patriotic Front government's main donors, accepting its share of international guilt for the failure to halt the 1994 genocide. Yet this had a major downside: when the new Rwandan regime played a central role in internationalizing a new civil war in the Congo, Blair's overseas development minister, Clare Short, "was persuaded of the Rwandan regime's absolute innocence" despite evidence of its troops' violence against civilians (Prunier 2009: 219), which were later characterized as genocidal massacres by the office of the UN High Commissioner for Human Rights (2010).

Back in Yugoslavia, when Serbian repression grew in Kosovo during 1998–9, Blair was also a major advocate of NATO's initial bombing campaign to halt this; and when the bombing provoked Serbian president Slobodan Milošević to escalate his violence, killing thousands and terrorizing over a million into refugee camps in neighbouring countries – threatening a permanent genocidal expulsion as in Bosnia – Blair pushed the alliance to extend its campaign. The resulting escalation halted Serbia's destruction of Albanian communities, but NATO "fought" exclusively from the air since most of its 19 governments dared not risk soldiers on the ground. While this led to unprecedented successes in force protection (no NATO personnel died at Serbian hands), it condemned hundreds of Serb and Albanian civilians to immolation by bombing. Indeed, this was the paradigmatic case of the "risk transfer" that I identified as a structural feature of contemporary Western war (Shaw 2005). And although NATO's victory ensured the return of the expelled Albanians, it failed to prevent revenge expulsions of Serbs. Blair also sent troops to intervene in the genocidal civil war in Sierra Leone in the same year.

Of all the regions in which genocide arose, the Middle East was the one that most engaged Western interests, but this did not necessarily lead to a concern with genocide prevention. Indeed, since both the USA and UK tacitly supported the Iraqi regime of Saddam Hussein during its invasion of and war with Iran, they stood aside during his chemical massacre of Kurds at Halabja in 1988. They broke with Saddam after he invaded Kuwait in 1990 but allowed his regime to survive once they had forced its troops back to Iraq in the (Persian) Gulf War; yet their victory provoked further rebellions and a new genocidal crisis, as the regime terrorized most of the Kurdish population to flee into the mountains bordering Turkey. The British prime minister, John Major, asked if the West hadn't encouraged the rebels (which the US president George H. W. Bush had certainly done), responded: "I don't recall asking the Kurds to mount this particular insurrection" (Shaw 1996: 89). However, a campaign in the British media helped push Major to join the USA and France in creating a Kurdish "safe haven" in northern Iraq after Turkey refused to admit the Kurdish refugees (Shaw 1996: 79–96; Robinson 2002).

After 1991, the UK continued to have a major supporting role, alongside the USA, in Western policies towards Iraq. The two secured UN sanctions on Saddam's regime and helped maintain them even after it was clear that these were leading to widespread civilian deaths (Gordon 2010). Then, after 9/11 led George W. Bush to launch the "global war on terror", Blair was his principal international partner in the invasion of 2003. An overall civilian death toll of hundreds of thousands over the following decade followed from this intervention: in precipitating a political transition in which the majority Shia prevailed over the previously dominant Sunni minority, the US–UK coalition helped provoke a low-level genocidal conflict during 2005–7, as al-Qaida in Iraq and other Sunni-based militia fought opposing Shi'ite militia, terrorizing the other's populations out the areas of Baghdad that they controlled.

Britain and the Gaza genocide

In most of these situations, British and other Western politicians found themselves in a structural dilemma as genocide developed. While notionally committed to preventing genocide, they would nevertheless only use military power in ways determined by their perceptions of national interest, which were often calibrated by considerations of force protection inevitably enmeshed with electoral calculation. In this context, the interests of threatened civilians were often insufficient to produce action, and it was mainly their lives rather than those of their own military personnel that the British and other Western governments were prepared to risk in any intervention. The UK was guilty mostly of what Adam LeBor (2006: xi) calls the typical "passive complicity" of the UN and Western states.

Gaza after 2023 was radically different from all these cases: the complicity, as we have seen, was active as well as passive; the UK state was effectively a participant. Instead of facing genocide committed by hostile forces, secondary allies or third parties, the UK like other Western states found itself dealing with a genocide by a major military, political and economic ally. A long history dating back to the Balfour declaration linked the UK to Israel, and as Avi Shlaim put it, recent British policy exhibited a basic contradiction, "advocating a two-state solution but recognizing only one" (2024: 34). Although the USA was now Israel's principal support, the UK's deep integration into its world system of power – the UK depended on the USA for its nuclear weapons and other materiel – reinforced its pro-Israeli orientation. The UK followed its more powerful ally on most major international issues: the most notable exception to this pattern had been in 1956, when Britain joined Israel and France in the Suez invasion of which the USA disapproved.

During the Gaza genocide, both state and civil society remained fundamentally pro-Israeli until 2025, holding to this underlying commitment despite the mounting record of Israel's atrocities. In part, this was because the dynamics of British politics had strongly reinforced the pro-Israel traditions of the main parties over the previous decade. After Labour elected the pro-Palestinian Jeremy Corbyn as leader in 2015, his opponents weaponized evidence of antisemitism among some of the party's supporters, together with his failure to suppress this; this culminated in the far-right-leaning, anti-immigrant and anti-Muslim Conservatives successfully mobilizing anti-antisemitism as a form of "antiracism" in order to defeat Labour in the 2019 election (Shaw 2022a: 125–7). The link between anti-Zionism and antisemitism cemented in these years also reinforced strong pro-Israeli assumptions in the media and conservative sections of society, even if much of the left remained pro-Palestinian.

These trends meant that, as in the USA, Germany and elsewhere, Hamas' attacks on Israeli civilians were perfectly calibrated to reinforce an anti-antisemitism narrative in responses to Israel's campaign in Gaza. Their horrific character overdetermined Labour's pro-Israel position, which Starmer had quickly asserted in ill-judged remarks in October 2023, implying that Israel had the right to cut off water and power from Gaza; although he later denied that this was his intention, he failed to apologize and so fed mounting dismay by Muslim and left-wing voters.

Meanwhile, the Conservative government, seeing a chance to damage Labour, doubled down on its own uncritical support for Israel and took the lead in intervening against potential prosecutions of Israeli leaders by the ICC. This ploy did not prevent Labour winning the July 2024 election, but the party suffered serious side losses because of its Gaza stance. Hence in office, Labour attempted to balance its core support for Israel with gestures towards international law designed to placate pro-Palestinian supporters. Yet these did not involve the explicit support for the ICC's charges against Netanyahu that the government gave to those against Putin. Like Starmer himself, his foreign secretary, David Lammy, a fellow lawyer, contradicted his previous position on other genocides in order to defend Israel.

Lessons of Gaza

In historical perspective, British policies towards the Gaza genocide undermined the anti-genocidal credentials that its elites had long claimed, especially after Blair instituted Holocaust Memorial Day; although, as we have seen, the record was already far from sustaining these. Gaza especially challenged the underlying national myth, derived from Britain's role in the Second World War, that the problem of genocide lies with others and "we" are part of the solution.

In the original version of this chapter, I argued that while Britain did not have the special role in countering genocide born of moral superiority that the national myth assigned, it did have major responsibilities because of its centrality to global state networks, with overlapping memberships of the UN Security Council, NATO, the EU, G7, G20 and other major international organizations, and its high-profile soft-power roles in the global media, NGO and academic spheres. All of these meant that despite the country's secular decline relative to greater powers, British politicians, broadcasters, campaigners and even academics were well placed to influence wider responses.

In the test of Gaza, we can now see that the British state and institutions largely failed to fulfil their self-proclaimed anti-genocidal responsibilities. Despite the near-total knowledge that the UK possessed of Israel's campaign, its attitude was not far from that which it sometimes demonstrated in earlier centuries towards distant genocide in its empire: condoning and even facilitating the perpetrators' campaign, while periodically expressing muffled concern about possible excesses and humanitarian consequences. And it was not only the state that failed: with some honourable exceptions, denialism was pervasive and weakly challenged in civil society until 2025.

These failings were not, of course, uniquely British: support for Israel's atrocities and mobilizations of anti-antisemitism were even more extreme in the USA and Germany. Indeed, the claims of the whole edifice of genocide prevention, and of the West as its main support system, were deeply exposed by Israel's campaign. Even Samantha Power, who by 2024 was the Biden-appointed head of the US Agency for International Development, fell prey to the structure she had analysed two decades earlier and failed to acknowledged Israel's genocide (Beaucar Vlahos 2024). The stronger emergence of international courts as centres of accountability offset this record to a degree, but the backlash to which they were exposed only confirmed the shallowness of opposition to genocide across the West.

Indeed, Gaza appears to have shown that even in a global media gaze, genocide can succeed. The return of the idea, which this book propounds, needs to be accompanied by unremitting criticism of all the sources of power that enable this situation and a determination to change it.

10

CONCLUSION: THESES ON GENOCIDE THOUGHT AND ACTION AFTER GAZA

This book has argued that the return of genocide has changed the intellectual and political landscape around anti-civilian violence, and that it needs to inspire a clearer conceptual perspective on the problem. In conclusion, I offer some fundamental new rules for all who think about and act against genocide.

1. *Think sociologically and historically before you think legally.* Remember that genocide is first a matter of political, military and social relations and needs to be grasped in socio-historical terms before it is filtered through the categories of the Genocide Convention and international jurisprudence. Don't substitute legal for sociological categories.
2. *Don't think of genocide as a discrete crime.* Recall that Lemkin originally proposed genocide as a general crime that included many specific ones; it is wrong to think of genocide as another crime alongside war crimes and crimes against humanity, when in fact it is always a composite of many types of both. Likewise, in a sociological understanding, genocide is a general mode of anti-civilian action, comparable to war with which it is closely related, not a specific type of anti-civilian violence alongside others.
3. *Think holistically about anti-civilian violence.* Always ask Lemkin's question: how are different types of anti-civilian violence and coercion related in the campaign of a state or armed organization; does it have overall destructive aims towards the civilian population? Understand their violence in a strategic as well as a tactical sense.
4. *Resist the temptation to break up anti-civilian violence into disparate sociological categories.* Don't split genocide up, for example by labelling forced removal as "ethnic cleansing", the targeting of elites as "politicide" and mass rape as "gendercide". Rather, think of these and other methods (incarceration, torture, expropriation, etc.) as different means of genocide and examine how they are used in combination or sequentially.

5. *Think of genocide as a type of action and conflict, not in terms of a particular ideology or scale.* Remember that genocide has manifested in many different ways, with many different kinds of targeting and ideological rationales and at various scales. Recognize that different types of targeting (ethnic-national, religious, political, class, gender, etc.) are often combined, rather than privileging some of them to define genocide. Be alert to genocidal massacres as well as mega-genocides; recognize the historical specificity of particular events but look for patterns.
6. *Think of genocide together with war.* Start from "war and genocide", assuming that any war, civil or international, may lead to genocide; be alert to how even military operations that are not obviously genocidal may racialize groups; recognize the genocidal implications of military violence. Understand the paradox that war is largely illegal in international law but that all major states prepare for non-defensive war, and recognize that in our era, war is largely degenerate in the sense of systematically targeting civilians.
7. *Think of genocide as simultaneously international and domestic.* Don't look at genocide as typically something that states do to "their" subject populations; recognize that genocide can be projected both within and across borders; understand how both domestic and international support systems for genocide work; see how genocide can only be opposed in a multilevel way.
8. *Think of genocide historically and in terms of our new period.* Thinking about genocide understanding has been bedevilled as well as enriched by historical analogies; remember that the Holocaust should never be a general standard, that the genocides of the colonial and postcolonial eras have both been very different to it as well as to each other, and that we are now in a new historical period, in which the threats may not only resemble earlier threats but also take distinctive new forms.
9. *Don't rely on international institutions to stop genocide.* Remember that, although the UN adopted the Genocide Convention and most states have ratified it, both have breached its obligations more than they have honoured them, and that international courts have rarely remedied this situation. View all of these in terms of the power relations involved, in a historical and sociological perspective; mobilize practically and intellectually to influence them.
10. *Solidarize with victims, but do not be captive to nationalist agendas.* Place victims, irrespective of ethnicity, nationality or beliefs, at the centre of your genocide perspective; show solidarity with collectivities under attack, but do not became captive to particular nationalist or other

agendas in such a way as to deny solidarity to other victims; oppose all genocidal acts, large or small, by states or armed organizations,

11. *Analyse and organize.* Use our common intellectual resources to develop the fullest possible research on and understanding of genocide, and use our knowledge to fight against it.

GLOSSARY OF SOCIOLOGICAL DEFINITIONS

This glossary provides some basic definitions, adapted from those in my previous books. The relationship of these sociological definitions to legal definitions is also indicated.

War

War is conflict between two or more organized, armed actors in which each aims to destroy the other's power. War is generally legitimate in most societies and, provided tight conditions are met, under international law, but its practice often renders it illegitimate and illegal.

Civilians

The social organization and practice of war create the category of civilians, those who are non-combatants and non-members of armed organizations and are supposed not to be targeted. This category is central to the problems of war; when civilians are deliberately harmed, it is rendered illegitimate and often illegal, with war crimes and crimes against humanity being committed. When deliberate civilian harm is a systematic tendency, as in most modern war, war can be regarded as degenerate, departing fundamentally from the norm of legitimate war. The idea of the civilian is also central to genocide, since the common feature of the different types of the groups and populations which are attacked is that they are primarily civilian in character.

Genocide

As a type of social action, genocide is violence in which armed power organizations aim to destroy civilian social groups and populations, treating them as enemies in themselves whose real or putative social power must be destroyed. This action causes genocidal conflict, in which the attacked groups and other actors resist destruction. Genocide is by definition illegitimate, because civilian harm is central to its meaning and illegal under the Genocide Convention. A coherent sociological definition treats the deliberate destruction of all civilian groups and populations, not just the four categories listed in the convention, as genocide.

Means and episodes of genocide

As a general category, genocide includes many specific types of violence and coercion, directed against both collective features of group life and individuals whom perpetrators regard as members of the groups. Its typical means include some, such as torture, rape, forced removal and cultural destruction, which are not listed in the Genocide Convention. A large-scale episode, involving a substantial number of victims, may be regarded as *a genocide*, while more limited or localized episodes may be described as *genocidal violence*.

The general hybridity of war and genocide

War and genocide are centred on the same principal type of power, military power based on violence, and the same type of principal actor, armed power organizations, which include both state and non-state actors, while the category of civilian is central to the legitimacy of both. War and genocide are typically combined, so that from a sociological point of view, they can be considered a hybrid general domain of action and conflict, to be distinguished from, as well as analysed together with, other domains such as the political, economic and cultural.

Degenerate and genocidal war

The general hybridity of war and genocide is reflected in specific hybrid forms. In *degenerate war*, violence against civilians, constituting war crimes, is used systematically and instrumentally as a means of defeating the armed enemy. In *genocidal war*, genocidal violence or a genocide, targeted against a civilian population or group considered an enemy in itself, is combined with more conventional war against armed enemies.

REFERENCES

Abdul, G. 2024. "UK upheld some arms export licences to Israel to reassure US". *The Guardian*, 18 November. https://www.theguardian.com/world/2024/nov/18/uk-upheld-some-arms-export-licences-to-israel-to-reassure-us

Abunimah, A. 2014. "Israeli lawmaker's call for genocide of Palestinians gets thousands of Facebook likes". *The Electronic Intifada*, 7 July. https://electronicintifada.net/blogs/ali-abunimah/israeli-lawmakers-call-genocide-palestinians-gets-thousands-facebook-likes.

Addameer Prisoner Support and Human Rights Association. 2024. *Arrests and Prisons as an Extension of the Crime of Genocide*. Jerusalem/Ramallah: Addameer Prisoner Support and Human Rights Association.

Adhikari, M. 2010. "A total extinction confidently hoped for: the destruction of Cape San society under Dutch colonial rule, 1700–1795". *Journal of Genocide Research* 12(1/2), 19–44.

Agraval, R. 2020. "Why India's Muslims are in grave danger". *Foreign Policy*, 3 March. https://foreignpolicy.com/2020/03/02/india-muslims-delhi-riots-danger/.

Ahmad, A. 2020. "Strictly technical". *London Review of Books*, 19 March. https://www.lrb.co.uk/the-paper/v42/n06/aijaz-ahmad/strictly-technical.

Ahonen, P. *et al.* 2008. *People on the Move: Forced Population Movements in Europe in the Second World War and Its Aftermath*. Oxford: Berg.

Airwars 2024. *Patterns of Harm Analysis: Gaza, October 2023*. Exeter: Airwars.

Al-Haq. 2025. *How to Hide a Genocide: The Role of Evacuation Orders and Safe Zones in Israel's Genocidal Campaign in Gaza*. Ramallah: Al-Haq.

Albanese, F. 2024a. *Anatomy of a Genocide*. New York: UN General Assembly.

Albanese, F. 2024b. *Genocide as Colonial Erasure*. New York: UN General Assembly.

Alexander, J. 2002. "On the social construction of moral universals: the 'Holocaust' from war crime to trauma drama". *European Journal of Social Theory* 5(1), 5–85.

Ali, H. 2023. "Britain, Iraq, and the politics of genocide: the 1963 Ba'ath government campaign against the Kurds". *Journal of Genocide Research* 26(4), 355–77.

Alqaisiya, W. & N. Perugini 2024. "The academic question of Palestine". *Middle East Critique* 33(3), 299–311.

Ambos, K. 2010. "What does 'Intent to Destroy' in genocide mean?" *International Review of the Red Cross* 91(876), 833–58.

Ambos, K. 2016. "Karadzic's genocidal intent as the 'only reasonable inference'?". *EJIL: Talk!* Blog of the *European Journal of International Law*, 1 April. https://www.ejiltalk.org/karadzics-genocidal-intent-as-the-only-reasonable-inference/.

Amnesty International 2022. *"I Used to Have a Home": Older People's Experience of War, Displacement, and Access to Housing in Ukraine*. Report. London: Amnesty International.

Amnesty International 2024. *"You Feel Like You Are Subhuman": Israel's Genocide against Palestinians in Gaza*. Report. London: Amnesty International.

Anderson, B. 1983. *Imagined Communities: Reflections on the Origins and the Spread of Nationalism*. London: Verso.

Anderson, D. 2005. *Histories of the Hanged: Britain's Dirty War in Kenya and the End of Empire*. London: Weidenfeld & Nicolson.

Andreopoulos, G. (ed.) 1994. *Genocide: Conceptual Historical Dimensions*. Philadelphia: University of Pennsylvania Press.

Angel, A. 2024. "Leaving Zion". Interview. *New Left Review* 2(148), 23–40. https://newleftreview.org/issues/ii148/articles/arielle-angel-leaving-zion.

Anziska, S. 2018. *Preventing Palestine: A Political History from Camp David to Oslo*. Princeton, NJ: Princeton University Press.

Applebaum, A. 2017. *Red Famine: Stalin's War on Ukraine*. London: Penguin.

Arel, D. & J. Driscoll 2022. *Ukraine's Unnamed War: Before the Invasion of 2022*. Cambridge: Cambridge University Press.

Azarov, D. *et al.* 2022. "Genocide committed by the Russian Federation in Ukraine: legal reasoning and historical context". SSN Papers. https://papers.ssrn.com/sol3/papers.cfm?abstract_id=4217444.

Bachman, J. 2019. "A 'synchronized attack' on life: the Saudi-led coalition's 'hidden and holistic' genocide in Yemen and the shared responsibility of the US and the UK". *Third World Quarterly* 40(2), 298–316.

Bachman, J. & E. Brito Ruiz (eds) 2024. *A Modern History of Forgotten Genocides and Mass Atrocities*. Abingdon: Routledge.

Barnett, M. 2002. *Eye-Witness to a Genocide: The United Nations and Rwanda*. Ithaca, NY: Cornell University Press.

Barta, T. 1987. "Relations of genocide: land and lives in the colonization of Australia". In I. Wallman and N. Dobrowski (eds), *Genocide and the Modern Age: Etiology and Case Studies of Mass Death*, 237–51. New York: Greenwood.

Barta, T. 2008. "Sorry, and not sorry, in Australia: how the apology to the stolen generations buried a history of genocide". *Journal of Genocide Research* 10(2) 201–14.

Bartov, O. 2018. *Anatomy of a Genocide: The Life and Death of a Town Called Buczacz*. New York: Simon & Schuster.

Bartov, O. 2021. "Blind spots of genocide". *Journal of Modern European History* 19(4), 395–9.

Bartov, O. 2023. "What I believe as a historian of genocide". *New York Times*, 10 November. https://www.nytimes.com/2023/11/10/opinion/israel-gaza-genocide-war.html.

Bartov, O. 2024. "As a former IDF soldier and historian of genocide, I was deeply disturbed by my recent visit to Israel". *The Guardian*, 13 August. https://www.theguardian.com/

news/audio/2024/sep/13/as-a-former-idf-soldier-and-historian-of-genocide-i-was-deeply-disturbed-by-my-recent-visit-to-israel-podcast.

Beaucar Vlahos, K. 2024. "'Humanitarian superstar' Samantha Power admits Gaza is a loss". *Responsible Statecraft*, 19 December. https://responsiblestatecraft.org/samantha-power-gaza-2670499374/.

Becker, M. 2024. "Crisis in Gaza: *South Africa v Israel* at the International Court of Justice (or the unbearable lightness of provisional measures)". SSRN. https://papers.ssrn.com/sol3/papers.cfm?abstract_id=5018178.

Bell, D. 2020. "The French Revolution, the Vendée, and genocide". *Journal of Genocide Research* 22(1), 19–25.

Bell-Fialkoff, A. 1996. *Ethnic Cleansing*. Basingstoke: Macmillan.

Bellamy, A. 2009. *Responsibility to Protect: The Global Effort to End Mass Atrocities*. Cambridge: Polity.

Bessell, R. & C. Haake (eds) 2008. *Removing Peoples: Forced Removal in the Modern World*. Oxford: Oxford University Press.

Blackbeard, S. 2015. "Acts of severity: colonial settler massacre of amaXhosa and abaThembu on the eastern frontier of the Cape Colony, c.1826–47". *Journal of Genocide Research* 17(2), 107–32.

Bloxham, D. 2003. "The Armenian Genocide of 1915–1916: cumulative radicalization and the development of a destruction policy". *Past & Present* 181(1), 141–91.

Bloxham, D. 2005. *The Great Game of Genocide: Imperialism, Nationalism and the Destruction of the Ottoman Armenians*. Oxford: Oxford University Press.

Bloxham, D. 2008. "The Great Unweaving: the removal of peoples in Europe, 1875–1949". In R. Bessell & C. Haake (eds), *Removing Peoples*, 167–208. Oxford: Oxford University Press.

Bloxham, D. 2009. *The Final Solution: A Genocide*. Oxford: Oxford University Press.

Bloxham, D. 2025. "The 7 October atrocities and the annihilation of Gaza: causes and responsibilities". *Journal of Genocide Research*, 3 April. https://www.tandfonline.com/doi/full/10.1080/14623528.2025.2483546.

Borger, J. 2022. "'It has been machine guns lately': fighting intensifies in southern Kherson". *The Guardian*, 9 December. https://www.theguardian.com/world/2022/dec/08/it-has-been-machine-guns-lately-fighting-intensifies-in-southern-kherson-dnipro-kyiv.

Bose, S. 2011. "The question of genocide and the quest for justice in the 1971 war". *Journal of Genocide Research* 13(4), 393–419.

Brandes, D. 2008. "National and international planning of the 'transfer' of Germans from Czechoslovakia and Poland". In R. Bessell & C. Haake (eds), *Removing Peoples*, 281–96. Oxford: Oxford University Press.

Brass, P. 2003. "The partition of India and retributive genocide in the Punjab, 1946–47: means, methods, and purposes". *Journal of Genocide Research* 5(1), 71–101.

Breaking the Silence 2024. *The Silent Overhaul: Changing the Nature of Israeli Control in the West Bank (Analysis of the Israeli Government's Annexation Policy)*. Tel Aviv: Breaking the Silence.

British Palestinian Committee 2025. *British Military Collaboration with Israel*. London: British Palestinian Committee.

Broué, P. 2006. *German Revolution, 1917–23*. London: Haymarket.

Browning, C. 1991. *The Path to Genocide*. Cambridge: Cambridge University Press.

Brubaker, R. 2004. "Ethnicity without groups". In A. Wimmer *et al.* (eds), *Facing Ethnic Conflicts: Towards a New Realism*, 34–52. Lanham, MD: Roman & Littlefield.

Bugayova, N. 2022. "Target Russia's capability, not its intent". *Understanding War*. https://www.understandingwar.org/backgrounder/target-russia%E2%80%99s-capability-not-its-intent.

Burger, T. 1987. *Max Weber's Theory of Concept Formation*. Durham, NC: Duke University Press.

Butcher, T. 2013. "A 'synchronized attack': on Raphael Lemkin's holistic conception of genocide". *Journal of Genocide Research* 15(3), 253–71.

Campbell, I. 2017. *The Addis Ababa Massacre: Italy's National Shame*. London: Hurst.

Centre for Media Monitoring 2024. *Media Bias: Gaza 2023–24*. London: CMM.

Cesarani, D. 2002. "Britain, the Holocaust and its legacy: the theme for Holocaust Memorial Day". http://www.hmd.org.uk/files/1149797162–22.pdf.

Cesarani, D., T. Kushner & S. Milton (eds) 2009. *Place and Displacement in Jewish History and Memory: Zakor v'Makor*. London: Vallentine Mitchell.

Chalk, F. & K. Jonassohn 1990. *The History and Sociology of Genocide: Analyses and Case Studies*. New Haven, CT: Yale University Press.

Chamberlin, P. 2018. *The Cold War's Killing Fields: Rethinking the Long Peace*. New York: HarperCollins.

Chang, J. & J. Halliday 2005. *Mao: The Unknown Story*. London: Cape.

Charny, I. 1994. "Toward a generic definition of genocide". In G. Andreopoulos (ed.), *Genocide: Conceptual and Historical Dimensions*, 64–94. Philadelphia: University of Pennsylvania Press.

Charny, I. 2016. "Holocaust minimization, anti-Israel themes, and antisemitism: bias at the *Journal of Genocide Research*". *Journal for the Study of Antisemitism* 7: 1–28.

Chirot, D. & C. McCauley 2006. *Why Not Kill Them All? The Logic and Prevention of Mass Political Murder*. Princeton, NJ: Princeton University Press.

Cohen, E. 2002. "Kosovo and the new American way of war". In A. Bacevich & E. Cohen (eds), *War over Kosovo*, 38–62. New York: Columbia University Press.

Cohen, E. & P. O'Brien 2024. "How defense experts got Ukraine wrong". *The Atlantic*, 27 September. https://www.theatlantic.com/ideas/archive/2024/09/how-defense-experts-got-ukraine-wrong/680045/.

Cohen, M. 2003. *Churchill and the Jews*. Second edition. Abingdon: Cass.

Cohen, S. 2001. *States of Denial: Knowing about Atrocities and Suffering*. Cambridge: Polity.

Condos, M. 2022. "The Ajnala Massacre of 1857 and the politics of colonial violence and commemoration in contemporary India". *Journal of Genocide Research* 24(4), 568–85.

Conquest, R. 1986. *The Harvest of Sorrow: Soviet Collectivization and the Terror-Famine*. Oxford: Oxford University Press.

Coogan, T. 1997. *The Troubles: Ireland's Ordeal and the Search for Peace*. New York: Roberts Rinehart.

Cooper, J. 2008. *Raphael Lemkin and the Struggle for the Genocide Convention*. Basingstoke: Palgrave Macmillan.

Cotler, I. 2023. "Russia is in standing breach of the Genocide Convention". SWI. https://www.swissinfo.ch/eng/politics/irwin-cotler---russia-is-in-standing-breach-of-the-genocide-convention-/48228836.

Dalrymple, W. 2006. *The Last Mughal: The Fall of a Dynasty, Delhi 1857*. London: Bloomsbury.

Davis, M. 2001. *Late Victorian Holocausts: El Ñino Famines and the Making of the Third World*. London: Verso.

De Graaf, B. 2021. "Raising some flags: the problem of genocide and historical security studies". *Journal of Modern European History* 19(4), 381–5.

De Waal, A. 2025a. "How to measure famine". *London Review of Books*, 6 February. https://www.lrb.co.uk/the-paper/v47/n02/alex-de-waal/how-to-measure-famine.

De Waal, A. 2025b. "Starvation in Gaza". *London Review of Books* blog, 14 May. https://www.lrb.co.uk/blog/2025/may/starvation-in-gaza.

De Zayas, A. 1979. *Nemesis at Potsdam: The Anglo-Americans and the Expulsions of the Germans*. Second edition. London: Routledge & Kegan Paul.

Debnath, A. 2011. "British perceptions of the East Pakistan Crisis 1971: 'hideous atrocities on both sides'". *Journal of Genocide Research* 13(4), 421–50.

Defense for Children International – Palestine. 2024. *Targeting Childhood: Palestinian Children killed by Israeli forces and settlers in the occupied West Bank*. Ramallah: Defense for Children International – Palestine.

Der Derian, J. 2001. *Virtuous War: Mapping the Military-Industrial-Media-Entertainment Network*. Boulder, CO: Westview.

Dettmer, D. 2022. "Klitschko's big fight: keeping 3 million people in Kyiv over winter". *Politico*, 21 November. https://www.politico.eu/article/ukraine-russia-war-vitali-klitschko-is-ready-for-the-bout-of-his-life.

Dikötter, F. 2010. *Mao's Great Famine: The History of China's Most Devastating Catastrophe, 1958–62*. London: Bloomsbury.

Docker, J. 2012. "Instrumentalizing the Holocaust: Israel, settler-colonialism, genocide (creating a conversation between Raphaël Lemkin and Ilan Pappé)". *Holy Land Studies* 11(1), 1–23.

Drysdale, J. 1996. "How are social-scientific concepts formed? A reconstruction of Max Weber's theory of concept formation". *Sociological Theory* 14(1), 71–88.

Ebner, M. 2011. *Ordinary Violence in Mussolini's Italy*. Cambridge: Cambridge University Press.

Elhalaby, E. 2025. "Nakba denial: on the politics of history and genocide". *Parapraxis*, February. https://www.parapraxismagazine.com/articles/nakba-denial.

Elkins, C. 2005. *Imperial Reckoning: The Untold Story of Britain's Gulag in Kenya*. New York: Henry Holt.

Elkins, C. 2022. *Legacies of Violence: A History of the British Empire*. New York: Vintage.

Esparza, M., H. Huttenbach & D. Feierstein (eds) 2010. *State Violence and Genocide in Latin America: The Cold War Years*. Abingdon: Routledge.

Etkind, A. 2022. "Ukraine, Russia, and genocide of minor differences". *Journal of Genocide Research* 25(3/4), 384–402.

Evans, R. 1982. *The German Working Class, 1888–1933: The Politics of Everyday Life*. London: Croom Helm.

Evans, R. 2004. *The Coming of the Third Reich: How the Nazis Destroyed Democracy and Seized Power in Germany*. Harmondsworth: Penguin.

Evans, R. 2005. *The Third Reich in Power: How the Nazis Won Over the Hearts and Minds of a Nation*. Harmondsworth: Penguin.

Feierstein, D. 2014. *Genocide as a Social Practice: Reorganizing Society under the Nazis and Argentina's Military Juntas*. New Brunswick, NJ: Rutgers University Press.

Fein, H. 1990. "Genocide: a sociological perspective". *Current Sociology* 38(1), 1–62.

Fein, H. 1997. "Genocide by attrition 1939–1993: the Warsaw Ghetto, Cambodia, and Sudan: links between human rights, health, and mass death". *Health and Human Rights* 2(2), 10–45.

Finkelstein, N. 2000. *The Holocaust Industry*. London: Verso.

Foer, F. 2024. "The war that would not end". *The Atlantic*, 25 September. https://www.theatlantic.com/international/archive/2024/09/israel-gaza-war-biden-netanyahu-peace-negotiations/679581/.

Foot, J. 2022. *Blood and Power: The Rise and Fall of Italian Fascism*. London: Bloomsbury.

Forensic Architecture 2024. *A Cartography of Genocide: Israel's Conduct in Gaza Since October 2023*. London: Forensic Architecture.

Forensic Architecture 2025. Tweet, 11 March. https://x.com/forensicarchi/status/1899172410198303019?s=51&t=Ok8qnjMd69NmKsJq01gBOQ.

Frank, M. 2008. *Expelling the Germans: British Opinion and the Post-1945 Population Transfer in Context*. Oxford: Oxford University Press.

Freedman, L. 2022. "Putin's massive mistake" (interview). *Salon*, 21 November. https://www.salon.com/2022/11/21/putins-massive-mistake-lawrence-freedman-on-ukraine-and-the-lessons-of-history/.

Garner, I. 2022. "'We've got to kill them': responses to Bucha on Russian social media groups". *Journal of Genocide Research* 25(3/4), 418–25.

Gavin, G. 2025. *Ashes of Our Fathers: Inside the Fall of Nagorno-Karabakh*. London: Hurst.

Gerlach, C. 2010. *Extremely Violent Societies: Mass Violence in the Twentieth Century World*. Cambridge: Cambridge University Press.

Geva, M. 2016. *Law, Politics and Violence in Israel/Palestine*. London: Palgrave Macmillan.

Giddens, A. 1976. *New Rules of Sociological Method: A Positive Critique of Interpretive Sociologies*. London: Hutchinson.

Girard, P. 2007. "Caribbean genocide: racial war in Haiti, 1802–04". In A. Moses & D. Stone (eds), *Colonialism and Genocide*, 42–65. London: Routledge.

Girard, P. 2013. "French atrocities during the Haitian War of Independence". *Journal of Genocide Research* 15(2), 133–49.

Goldberg, A. 2024. "Yes, it is genocide". The Palestine Project. https://thepalestineproject.medium.com/yes-it-is-genocide-634a07ea27d4.

Goldberg, A. & D. Blatman 2025. "There's no Auschwitz in Gaza. But it's still genocide". *Haaretz*, 30 January. https://www.haaretz.com/israel-news/2025-01-30/ty-article-magazine/.highlight/theres-no-auschwitz-in-gaza-but-its-still-genocide/00000194-b8af-dee1-a5dc-fcff384b0000.

Goldberg, A. *et al.* 2016. "Israel Charny's attack on the *Journal of Genocide Research* and its authors: a response". *Genocide Studies & Prevention* 10(2), 3–22.

Goldstein, R. 1983. *Political Repression in 19th-Century Europe*. Aldershot: Croom Helm.

Gomez-Suarez, A. 2007. "Perpetrator blocs, genocidal mentalities and geographies: the destruction of the Union Patriotica in Colombia and its lessons for genocide studies". *Journal of Genocide Research* 9(4), 637–60.

Gopal, P. 2020. *Insurgent Empire: Anticolonial Resistance and British Dissent*. London: Verso.

Gordon, J. 2010. *Invisible War: The United States and the Iraq Sanctions*. Cambridge, MA: Harvard University Press.

Graf, S. 2022. "The charismatic monopoly of the genocide idea". *International Politics Reviews* 10, 7–12.

Grayling, A. 2006. *Among the Dead Cities: Is the Targeting of Civilians in War Ever Justified?* London: Bloomsbury.

Green, J., C. Henderson & T. Ruys 2022. "Russia's attack on Ukraine and the *jus ad bellum*". *Journal on the Use of Force and International Law* 9(1), 4–30.

Gritten, D. & T. Macintosh 2024. "Netanyahu warns Lebanon of 'destruction like Gaza'". *BBC News*, 8 October. https://www.bbc.co.uk/news/articles/cly3x1w0595o.

Gross, J. 2006. *Fear: Anti-Semitism in Poland after Auschwitz: An Essay in Historical Interpretation*. New York: Random House.

Guillot, M., M. Draidi, V. Cetorelli, J. Monteiro Da Silva & I. Lubbad 2025. "Life expectancy losses in the Gaza Strip during the period October, 2023, to September, 2024". *The Lancet*, 8 February. https://www.thelancet.com/journals/lancet/article/PIIS0140-6736(24)02810-1/abstract.

Gumanyuk, N. 2025. "Putin's Ukraine: the end of war and the price of Russian occupation". *Foreign Affairs*, March–April. https://www.foreignaffairs.com/russia/putin-ukraine-end-war-russian-occupation.

Gurmendi Dunkelberg, A. 2024a. "Israel does not have a sovereign claim to the West Bank: a response to IJL's legal opinion". *OpinionJuris*, 22 February. http://opiniojuris.org/2024/02/22/israel-does-not-have-a-sovereign-claim-to-the-west-bank-a-response-to-ijls-legal-opinion/.

Gurmendi Dunkelberg, A. 2024b. "Adam Kirsch's colonial revisionism should shame his publishers". *The New Arab*, 28 August. https://www.newarab.com/opinion/adam-kirschs-colonial-revisionism-should-shame-his-publishers.

Gurmendi Dunkelberg, A. 2025. "How to hide a genocide: modern/colonial international law and the construction of impunity". *Journal of Genocide Research*, 1–24. https://doi.org/10.1080/14623528.2025.2454739.

Hametz, M. 2010. "Naming Italians in the borderland, 1926–1943". *Journal of Modern Italian Studies* 15(3), 410–30.

Hamilton, R. 2011. *Fighting for Darfur: Public Action and the Struggle to Stop Genocide*. London: Palgrave Macmillan.

Hancock, I. 2001. "Responses to the Porrajmos: the Romani holocaust". In A. Rosenbaum (ed), *Is the Holocaust Unique?*, 65–95. Boulder, CO: Westview.

Haque, A. 2024. "The Amnesty International Report on Genocide in Gaza". *Just Security*, 16 December. https://www.justsecurity.org/105629/amnesty-international-gaza-genocide-report/.

Harding, L. 2022. *Invasion: Russia's Bloody War and Ukraine's Fight for Survival*. London: Guardian Faber.

Harff, B. 1986. "Genocide as state terrorism". In G. Lopez & M. Stohl (eds), *Government Violence and Repression: An Agenda for Research*, 165–87. Westport, CT: Greenwood Press.

Harff, B. & T. Gurr 1988. "Toward empirical theory of genocides and politicides: identification and measurement of cases since 1945". *International Studies Quarterly* 32(3), 359–71.

Hashemi, N. & D. Postel 2017. "Sectarianization: mapping the new politics of the Middle East". *Review of Faith and International Affairs* 15, 1–13.

Hearst, D. & I. Mulla. 2025. "David Cameron threatened to withdraw UK from ICC over Israel war crimes probe". *Middle East Eye*, 9 June. https://www.middleeasteye.net/news/david-cameron-threatened-withdraw-uk-icc-over-israel-war-crimes-probe.

Hechter, M. 1975. *Internal Colonialism: The Celtic Fringe in British National Development, 1536–1966*. Los Angeles: University of California Press.

Heerten, L. & A. Moses 2014. "The Nigeria–Biafra war: postcolonial conflict and the question of genocide". *Journal of Genocide Research* 16(2/3), 169–203.

Heller, K. 2022. "Options for prosecuting Russian aggression against Ukraine: a critical analysis". *Journal of Genocide Research* 26(1), 1–24.

Hinton, A., T. La Pointe & D. Irvin-Erickson (eds) 2014. *Hidden Genocides: Power, Knowledge, Memory*. New Brunswick, NJ: Rutgers University Press.

Hinton, J. 1989. *Protests and Visions: Peace Politics in Twentieth-Century Britain*. London: Hutchinson.

Hobsbawm, E. 1994. *The Age of Extremes: The Short Twentieth Century 1914–1991*. London: Michael Joseph.

Horowitz, I. 1976. *Genocide: State Power and Mass Murder*. London: Routledge.

House of Commons Library 2024. *Israel–Hamas Conflict: UK Response October 2023 to July 2024*. London: House of Commons Library.

Hovanissian, R. (ed.) 1987. *The Armenian Genocide in Historical Perspective*. New Brunswick, NJ: Transaction.

Howard, M. 1978. *War and the Liberal Conscience*. Oxford: Oxford University Press.

Howe, S. 2005. "Forgotten shame of empire". *The Independent*, 21 January. https://www.independent.co.uk/arts-entertainment/books/reviews/britain-s-gulag-the-brutal-end-of-empire-in-kenya-by-caroline-elkinshistories-of-the-hanged-by-david-anderson-748263.html.

Human Rights Watch 2022a. "'We had no choice': 'filtration' and the crime of forcibly transferring Ukrainian civilians to Russia". Human Rights Watch, 1 September. https://www.hrw.org/report/2022/09/01/we-had-no-choice/filtration-and-crime-forcibly-transferring-ukrainian-civilians.

Human Rights Watch 2022b. "Ukraine: Russian forces tortured Izium detainees". Human Rights Watch, 19 October. https://www.hrw.org/news/2022/10/19/ukraine-russian-forces-tortured-izium-detainees.

Human Rights Watch 2024a. "Hopeless, starving, and besieged: Israel's forced displacement of Palestinians in Gaza". Human Rights Watch, 14 November. https://

www.hrw.org/report/2024/11/14/hopeless-starving-and-besieged/israels-forced-displacement-palestinians-gaza.

Human Rights Watch 2024b. "Extermination and acts of genocide: Israel deliberately depriving Palestinians in Gaza of water". Human Rights Watch, 18 December. https://www.hrw.org/report/2024/12/19/extermination-and-acts-genocide/israel-deliberately-depriving-palestinians-gaza.

Ibrahim, A. 2018. *The Rohingyas: Inside Myanmar's Genocide*. Second edition. London: Hurst.

Ibreck, R. & A. de Waal 2021. "Introduction: situating Ethiopia in genocide debates". *Journal of Genocide Research* 24(1), 83–96.

Imseis, A. 2023. *The United Nations and the Question of Palestine*. Cambridge: Cambridge University Press.

Inbar, E. & E. Shamir 2014. "'Mowing the grass': Israel's strategy for protracted intractable conflict". *Journal of Strategic Studies* 37(1), 65–90.

International Association of Genocide Scholars. 2006. "Resolution condemning Iranian President Ahmadinejad's statements calling for the destruction of Israel and denying the historical reality of the Holocaust and calling for the prevention of Iranian development of nuclear weapons". https://genocidescholars.org/wp-content/uploads/2019/04/IAGS-Resolution-on-Iran.pdf.

International Association of Genocide Scholars 2014. "Resolution of the International Association of Genocide Scholars concerning crimes of ISIS". https://genocidescholars.org/wp-content/uploads/2019/04/IAGS-Resolution-on-ISIS-passed-18-March-2016_1.pdf.

International Court of Justice 1996. *Legality of the Threat or Use of Nuclear Weapons*. The Hague: ICJ.

International Court of Justice 2007a. *Application of the Convention on the Prevention and Punishment of the Crime of Genocide (Bosnia and Herzegovina v. Serbia and Montenegro): Judgment*. The Hague: ICJ.

International Court of Justice 2007b. *Application of the Convention on the Prevention and Punishment of the Crime of Genocide (Bosnia and Herzegovina v. Serbia and Montenegro) – Judgment: Dissenting Opinion of Vice-President Al-Khasawneh*. The Hague: ICJ.

International Court of Justice 2015. *Application of the Convention on the Prevention and Punishment of the Crime of Genocide (Croatia v. Serbia)*. The Hague: ICJ.

International Court of Justice 2020. *Application of the Convention on the Prevention and Punishment of the Crime of Genocide (The Gambia v. Myanmar)*. The Hague: ICJ.

International Court of Justice 2022. *Allegations of Genocide under the Convention on the Prevention and Punishment of the Crime of Genocide (Order)*. The Hague: ICJ.

International Court of Justice 2023. *Application Instituting Proceedings Containing a Request for Provisional Measures (South Africa v. Israel)*. The Hague: ICJ.

International Court of Justice 2024a. *Application of the Convention on the Prevention and Punishment of the Crime of Genocide in the Gaza Strip (South Africa v. Israel)*. The Hague: ICJ, 26 January.

International Court of Justice 2024b. *Application of the Convention on the Prevention and Punishment of the Crime of Genocide in the Gaza Strip (South Africa v. Israel).* The Hague: ICJ, 28 March.

International Court of Justice 2024c. *Application of the Convention on the Prevention and Punishment of the Crime of Genocide in the Gaza Strip (South Africa v. Israel).* The Hague: ICJ, 24 May.

International Court of Justice 2024d. *Legal Consequences Arising from the Policies and Practices of Israel in the Occupied Palestinian Territory, including East Jerusalem.* The Hague: ICJ.

International Criminal Court 2024a. *Statement of ICC Prosecutor Karim A.A. Khan KC: Applications for Arrest Warrants in the Situation in the State of Palestine.* The Hague: ICC.

International Criminal Court 2024b. *Situation in the State of Palestine: ICC Pre-Trial Chamber I Rejects the State of Israel's Challenges to Jurisdiction and Issues Warrants of Arrest for Benjamin Netanyahu and Yoav Gallant.* The Hague: ICC.

International Crisis Group 2008. "Kenya in Crisis". Africa Report 137, 21 February. https://www.crisisgroup.org/sites/default/files/137-kenya-in-crisis.pdf.

International Holocaust Remembrance Alliance 2016. "IHRA non-legally binding working definition of antisemitism". https://holocaustremembrance.com/wp-content/uploads/2024/01/IHRA-non-legally-binding-working-definition-of-antisemitism-1.pdf.

Irvin-Erickson, D., T. La Pointe & A. Hinton. 2014. "Introduction – hidden genocides: power, knowledge, memory". In Hinton, La Pointe & Irvin-Erickson (eds), *Hidden Genocides: Power, Knowledge, Memory*, 1–20. New Brunswick, NJ: Rutgers University Press.

Jamaluddine, Z., H. Abukmail, S. Aly, O. Campbell & F. Checchi. 2025. "Traumatic injury mortality in the Gaza Strip from Oct 7, 2023, to June 30, 2024: a capture–recapture analysis". *The Lancet*, 9 January. https://pubmed.ncbi.nlm.nih.gov/39799952/.

Jones, A. 2000. "Gendercide and genocide". *Journal of Genocide Research* 2(2), 185–211.

Jones, A. 2010. *Genocide*. London: Routledge.

Jones, A. & N. Robbins (eds) 2009. *Genocides by the Oppressed: Subaltern Genocide in Theory and Practice*. Bloomington: Indiana University Press.

Jones, O. 2024. "The BBC's civil war over Gaza". *Drop Site News*, 19 December. https://www.dropsitenews.com/p/bbc-civil-war-gaza-israel-biased-coverage.

Kalyvas, S. 2005. *The Logic of Violence in Civil War*. Cambridge: Cambridge University Press.

Khalidi, R. 2020. *The Hundred Years War on Palestine: A History of Settler Colonial Conquest and Resistance*. London: Profile.

Khalidi, R. 2024. "The neck and the sword". Interview with Tariq Ali. *New Left Review* 2(147), 5–38.

Khan, Y. 2008. *The Great Partition*. New Haven, CT: Yale University Press.

Kiernan, B. 2006. *The Pol Pot Regime: Race, Power and Genocide in Cambodia under the Khmer Rouge, 1975–79*. New Haven, CT: Yale University Press.

Kiernan, B. 2007. *Blood and Soil*. New Haven, CT: Yale University Press.

Kimmerling, B. 2006. *Politicide: Ariel Sharon's War against the Palestinians.* London: Verso.

Klein, S. 2025. "The growing rift between Holocaust scholars over Israel/Palestine". *Journal of Genocide Research*, 1–21.

Kreß, C. 2022. *The Ukraine War and the Prohibition of the Use of Force in International Law.* Brussels: Torkel Opsahl Academic EPublisher.

Krisch, N. 2024. "Speaking the law, plausibly: the International Court of Justice on Gaza". *EJIL: Talk!* Blog of the *European Journal of International Law*, 27 January. https://www.ejiltalk.org/speaking-the-law-plausibly-the-international-court-of-justice-on-gaza/.

Kuhn, T. 1962. *The Structure of Scientific Revolutions.* Chicago: University of Chicago Press.

Kumar Sen, A. 2022. *Is Russia Committing Genocide in Ukraine?* Washington, DC: United States Institute of Peace, 21 September.

Kuper, L. 1981. *Genocide: Its Political Use in the Twentieth Century.* Penguin: Harmondsworth.

Kursani, S. 2022. "Beyond Putin's analogies: the genocide debate on Ukraine and the Balkan analogy worth noting". *Journal of Genocide Research* 25 (3/4), 371–83.

Lawson, T. 2014. "Memorializing colonial genocide in Britain: the case of Tasmania". *Journal of Genocide Research* 16(4), 441–61.

Leader Maynard, J. 2022. *Ideology and Mass Killing: The Radicalized Security Politics of Genocides and Deadly Atrocities.* Oxford: Oxford University Press.

LeBor, A. 2006. *"Complicity with Evil": The United Nations in the Age of Genocide.* New Haven, CT: Yale University Press.

Lemarchand, R. 2011. *Forgotten Genocides: Oblivion, Denial, and Memory.* Philadelphia: University of Pennsylvania Press.

Lemkin, R. 1933. "Acts constituting a general (transnational) danger considered as offences against the law of nations". http://www.preventgenocide.org/lemkin/madrid1933-english.htm.

Lemkin, R. 1944. *Axis Rule in Occupied Europe: Laws of Occupation, Analysis of Government, Proposals for Redress.* New York: Carnegie Foundation for International Peace.

Lemkin, R. 1947. "Genocide as a crime under international law". *American Journal of International Law* 41(1), 145–51.

Lemkin, R. 2012. "Introduction to the study of genocide". In R. Lemkin, *Lemkin on Genocide: Introduction to the Study of Genocide and History of Genocide*, 1–50. Lanham, MD: Lexington.

Lester, A. 2022. *Deny and Disavow: Distancing the Imperial Past in the Culture Wars.* London: SunRise.

Lester, A. (ed.) 2024. *The Truth about Empire: Real Histories of British Colonialism.* London: Hurst.

Levene, M. 2005a. *Genocide in the Age of the Nation State, Volume 1: The Meaning of Genocide.* London: I. B. Tauris.

Levene, M. 2005b. *Genocide in the Age of the Nation State, Volume 2: The Rise of the West.* London: I. B. Tauris.

Levene, M. 2007. "Review of Ilan Pappé's *The Ethnic Cleansing of Palestine*". *Journal of Genocide Research* 9(4), 675–81.

Levene, M. 2014a. *Devastation: The European Rimlands 1912–1938*. Oxford: Oxford University Press.

Levene, M. 2014b. *Annihilation: The European Rimlands 1939–1953*. Oxford: Oxford University Press.

Levene-Schnur, R., T. Megiddo & Y. Berda 2025. "A theory of annexation". *Oxford Journal of Legal Studies* 20, 1–29.

Levy, Y. 2019. *Whose Life Is Worth More? Hierarchies of Risk and Death in Contemporary Wars*. Stanford, CA: Stanford University Press.

Levy, Y. 2024. "Israel has 'the most moral army,' certainly compared to the U.S.? Gaza death ratio tells another story". *Haaretz*, 22 November. https://www.haaretz.com/israel-news/2024-11-22/ty-article-magazine/.highlight/israel-has-the-most-moral-army-gaza-death-ratio-tells-another-story/00000193-5087-d58a-abdf-ddd748960000.

Lewin, M. 1975. *Russian Peasants and Soviet Power: A Study of Collectivization*. New York: Norton.

Lewis, D. 2025. *Occupation: Russian Rule in South-Eastern Ukraine*. London: Hurst.

Loeffler, J. 2017. "Becoming Cleopatra: the forgotten Zionism of Raphael Lemkin". *Journal of Genocide Research* 19(3), 340–60.

Longerich, R. 2010. *Holocaust: The Nazi Persecution and Murder of the Jews*. Oxford: Oxford University Press.

MacBride, S. *et al.* 1983. *Israel in Lebanon: The Report of the International Commission to Enquire into Reported Violations of International Law by Israel during Its Invasion of the Lebanon*. London: Institute for Palestine Studies.

MacLean, K. 2019. "The Rohingya crisis and the practices of erasure". *Journal of Genocide Research* 21(1), 83–95.

McDoom, O. 2023. "How unique is the Israel–Palestine conflict?". LSE blogs. https://blogs.lse.ac.uk/mec/2023/11/08/how-unique-is-the-israel-palestine-conflict/.

McGeever, B. 2019. "Red antisemitism: anti-Jewish violence and revolutionary politics in Ukraine, 1919". *Issues in Contemporary Jewish History* 15, 168–95.

McKernan, B. 2023. "Putin promised me he would not kill Zelensky, says former Israeli PM". *The Guardian*, 5 February. https://www.theguardian.com/world/2023/feb/05/putin-promised-me-he-would-not-kill-zelenskiy-says-former-israeli-pm-naftali-bennett.

McVeigh, R. 2008. "'The balance of cruelty': Ireland, Britain and the logic of genocide". *Journal of Genocide Research* 10(4), 541–63.

Makdisi, S. 2008. *Palestine Inside Out: An Everyday Occupation*. New York: Norton.

Malcolm, E. 2013. "A new age or just the same old cycle of extirpation? Massacre and the 1798 Irish rebellion". *Journal of Genocide Research* 15(2), 151–66.

Malyarenko, T. & B. Kormych 2023. "New wild fields: how the Russian war leads to the demodernization of Ukraine's occupied territories". *Nationalities Papers* 52(3), 1–19.

Mann, I. 2022. "Against 'genocide': towards a jurisprudence of risk". *Holocaust Studies: A Journal of Culture and History* 29(3), 317–40.

Mann, M. 1993. *The Sources of Social Power, Volume 2: The Rise of Classes and Nation-States*. Cambridge: Cambridge University Press.

Mann, M. 2005. *The Dark Side of Democracy: Explaining Ethnic Cleansing*. Cambridge: Cambridge University Press.

Marchuk, I. 2022. "Domestic accountability efforts in response to the Russia–Ukraine War: an appraisal of the first war crimes trials in Ukraine". *Journal of International Criminal Justice* 20(4), 787–803.

Marchuk, I. & A. Wanigasuriya 2022. "Beyond the false claim of genocide: preliminary reflections on Ukraine's prospects in its pursuit of justice at the ICJ". *Journal of Genocide Research* 25(3/4), 256–78.

Markusen, E. 2003. "Genocide in former Yugoslavia, 1992–1995". *Journal of Genocide Research* 5(4), 605–15.

Masalha, N. 1992. *Expulsion of the Palestinians: The Concept of "Transfer" in Zionist Political Thought, 1882–1948*. Washington, DC: Institute for Palestine Studies.

Masalha, N. 1997. *A Land without a People: Israel, Transfer and the Palestinians 1949–96*. London: Faber.

Masalha, N. 2003. *The Politics of Denial: Israel and the Palestinian Refugee Problem*. London: Pluto.

Massicot, D. 2023. "What Russia got wrong: can Moscow learn from its failures in Ukraine?". *Foreign Affairs*, February–March. https://www.foreignaffairs.com/ukraine/what-russia-got-wrong-moscow-failures-in-ukraine-dara-massicot.

Matthews, H. 2025. "Colonial desire meets TikTok in Israel's 'lingerie genre'". *The New Arab*, 31 January. https://www.newarab.com/opinion/colonial-desire-meets-tiktok-israels-lingerie-genre.

Mazower, M. 1998. *Dark Continent: Europe's Twentieth Century*. Harmondsworth: Penguin.

Mazower, M. 2009. *Hitler's Empire: Nazi Rule in Occupied Europe*. London: Allen Lane.

Mead, W. 2014. "The return of geopolitics: the revenge of the revisionist powers". *Foreign Affairs* 93(3), 69–74.

Meiches, B. 2019. *The Politics of Annihilation: A Genealogy of Genocide*. Minneapolis: University of Minnesota Press.

Melvern, L. 2000. *A People Betrayed: The Role of the West in Rwanda's Genocide*. London: Zed Books.

Merriman, J. 2014. *Massacre: The Life and Death of the Paris Commune*. New York: Basic Books.

Midlarsky, M. 2005. *The Killing Trap*. Cambridge: Cambridge University Press.

Milton-Edwards, B. & S. Farrell 2024. *Hamas: The Quest for Power*. Revised edition. Cambridge: Polity.

Morgan, W. 2025. Bluesky post, 25 April. https://bsky.app/profile/wesleymorgan.bsky.social/post/3lne6rxugnc2i.

Morris, B. 1986. *The Birth of the Palestinian Refugee Problem, 1947–1949*. Cambridge: Cambridge University Press.

Morris, B. 2001. *The Birth of the Palestinian Refugee Problem Revisited*. Cambridge: Cambridge University Press.

Morris, B. 2004. *The Birth of the Palestinian Refugee Problem Revisited*. Cambridge: Cambridge University Press.

Moses, A. 2000. "An antipodean genocide? The origins of the genocidal moment in the colonization of Australia". *Journal of Genocide Research* 2(1), 89–106.

Moses, A. (ed.) 2004a. *Genocide and Settler Society*. Oxford: Berghahn.

Moses, A. 2004b. "Genocide and settler society in Australian history". In A. Moses (ed.), *Genocide and Settler Society*, 1–48. Oxford: Berghahn.

Moses, A. 2008a. "Empire, colony, genocide: keywords and the philosophy of history". In A. Moses (ed.), *Empire, Colony, Genocide*, 3–18. Oxford: Berghahn.

Moses, A. 2008b. "Raphael Lemkin, culture, and the concept of genocide". In A. Moses (ed.), *Empire, Colony, Genocide*, 19–41. Oxford: Berghahn.

Moses, A. 2008c. "Toward a theory of critical genocide studies". SciencesPo, 18 April. https://www.sciencespo.fr/mass-violence-war-massacre-resistance/en/document/toward-theory-critical-genocide-studies.html.

Moses, A. 2010. "Raphael Lemkin, culture, and the concept of genocide". In D. Bloxham & A. Moses (eds), *The Oxford Handbook of Genocide Studies*, 19–39. Oxford: Oxford University Press.

Moses, A. 2019. "'White genocide' and the ethics of public analysis". *Journal of Genocide Research* 21(2), 201–13.

Moses, A. 2021a. *The Problems of Genocide: Permanent Security and the Language of Transgression*. Cambridge: Cambridge University Press.

Moses, A. 2021b. "Response to commentaries in *JMEH* forum on *The Problems of Genocide*". *Journal of Modern European History* 19(4), 405–10.

Moses, A. 2022. "The Ukraine genocide debate reveals the limits of international law". *Lawfare*, 16 May. https://www.lawfaremedia.org/article/ukraine-genocide-debate-reveals-limits-international-law.

Moses, A. 2023. "Genocide as a category mistake: permanent security and mass violence against civilians". In F. Jacob & K. Todzi (eds), *Genocidal Violence: Concepts, Forms, Impact*, 15–37. Berlin: De Gruyter.

Moses, A. & L. Heerten (eds) 2018. *Postcolonial Conflict and the Question of Genocide: The Nigeria–Biafra War, 1967–1970*. Abingdon: Routledge.

Moyn, S. 2021. *Humane: How the United States Abandoned Peace and Reinvented War*. New York: Farrar, Straus & Giroux.

Mudde, C. 2019. *The Far Right Today*. Cambridge: Polity.

Mykhnenko, V. 2020. "Causes and consequences of the war in eastern Ukraine: an economic geography perspective". *Europe-Asia Studies* 72(3), 528–60.

Naimark, N. 2001. *Fires of Hatred: Ethnic Cleansing in Twentieth-Century Europe*. Cambridge, MA: Harvard University Press.

Naimark, N. 2010. *Stalin's Genocides*. Princeton, NJ: Princeton University Press.

Nersessian, D. 2010. *Genocide and Political Groups*. Oxford: Oxford University Press.

New Lines Institute 2024. *Genocide in Tigray: Serious Breaches of International Law in the Tigray Conflict, Ethiopia, and Paths to Accountability*. Washington, DC: New Lines Institute.

North Herts PSC (Palestine Solidarity Campaign) 2024. X (Twitter) post, 16 November. https://x.com/nhertspsc/status/1857704629611503916..

Ó Gráda, C. 2009. *Famine: A Short History*. Princeton, NJ: Princeton University Press.

Office of the Prosecutor General, Ukraine 2022. https://warcrimes.gov.ua/en.

Oxfam International 2025. *The Cost of Inaction and Impunity: Examining Israel's Compliance with ICJ Aid Measure*. Oxford: Oxfam.

Palestinian Centre for Human Rights. 2024a. *Cultural Genocide: A Report on Israel's Intnetional Destruction of Palestinian Cultural Property during the Israeli War 2023–2024*. Gaza: Palestinian Centre for Human Rights.

Palestinian Centre for Human Rights. 2024b. *Eliminating Witnesses on Genocide and Ethnic Cleansing Crimes in the Gaza Strip*. Gaza: Palestinian Centre for Human Rights.

Palestinian Centre for Human Rights. 2025. *"We Will Leave Them Nothing": The Israeli Systematic Destruction of the Agricultural Sector and Food Production Systems in Gaza*. Gaza: Palestinian Centre for Human Rights.

Pappé, I. 2007. *The Ethnic Cleansing of Palestine*. Oxford: Oneworld.

Parsons, L. 2001. "The Druze and the birth of Israel". In E. Rogan & A. Shlaim (eds), *The War for Palestine: Rewriting the History of 1948*, 60–78. Cambridge: Cambridge University Press.

Pearlman, W. 2023. "Collective punishment in Gaza will not bring Israel security". *New Lines*, 30 October. https://newlinesmag.com/argument/collective-punishment-in-gaza-will-not-bring-israel-security/.

Penn, N. 2013. "The British and the 'Bushmen': the massacre of the Cape San, 1795 to 1828". *Journal of Genocide Research* 15(2), 183–200.

Perugini, N. 2024. "Polio and Israel's attrition genocide in Gaza". *Aljazeera*, 2 September. https://www.aljazeera.com/opinions/2024/9/2/polio-and-israels-attrition-genocide-in.

Poole, R. 2019. *Peterloo: The English Uprising*. Oxford: Oxford University Press.

Power, S. 2003. *A Problem from Hell: America and the Age of Genocide*. London: Flamingo.

Preston, P. 2012. *The Spanish Holocaust: Inquisition and Extermination in Twentieth-Century Spain*. London: Harper.

Proudfoot, P. 2024. X (Twitter) post, 17 November. https://x.com/PhilipProudfoot/status/1858234199649726659.

Prunier, G. 2009. *From Genocide to Continental War: The "Congolese" Conflict and the Crisis of Contemporary Africa*. London: Hurst.

Putin, V. 2021. "On the historical unity of Russians and Ukrainians". 12 July. http://en.kremlin.ru/events/president/news/66181 (accessed 12 December 2022).

Quénivet, N. 2022. "The conflict in Ukraine and genocide". *Journal of International Peacekeeping* 25(2), 141–54.

Rapoport, M. & O. Ziv. 2025. "'Render it unusable': Israel's mission of total urban destruction". *+972 Magazine*, 15 May. https://www.972mag.com/israel-gaza-total-urban-destruction/.

Rashed, H. & D. Short 2012. "Genocide and settler colonialism: can a Lemkin-inspired genocide perspective aid our understanding of the Palestinian situation?". *International Journal of Human Rights* 16(8), 1142–69.

Rashed, H., D. Short & J. Docker 2014. "Nakba memoricide: genocide studies and the Zionist/Israeli genocide in Palestine". *Holy Land Studies* 13(1), 1–23.

Renton, J. 2025. "Holocaust memory and the universal sovereignty of the liberal democratic state". *Journal of Genocide Research,* 1–23. https://doi.org/10.1080/14623528.2025.2517848.

Richards, E. 2000. *The Highland Clearances: People, Landlords and Rural Turmoil.* Edinburgh: Birlinn.

Robinson, P. 2002. *The CNN Effect: The Myth of News, Foreign Policy and Intervention.* London: Routledge.

Rodinson, M. 1973. *Israel: A Settler-Colonial State?* New York: Monad.

Rosenberg, S. 2012. "Genocide is a process, not an event". *Genocide Studies and Prevention* 7(1), 16–23.

Rozovsky, L. 2025. "Israel blocks UN probe into sexual crimes by Hamas on October 7 to avoid scrutiny of abuse of Palestinians". *Haaretz,* 8 January. https://www.haaretz.com/israel-news/2025-01-08/ty-article/.premium/israel-blocks-un-hamas-sexual-crimes-probe-to-avoid-inquiry-into-abuse-of-palestinians/00000194-44e0-d087-a9bd-7de1d5f20000.

Sabbagh-Khoury, A. 2023. *Colonizing Palestine: The Zionist Left and the Making of the Palestinian Nakba.* Stanford, CA: Stanford University Press.

Said, E. 1992. *The Question of Palestine.* New York: Vintage.

Sands, P. 2022. "What the inventor of the word 'genocide' might have said about Putin's war". *New York Times,* 28 April. https://www.nytimes.com/2022/04/28/opinion/biden-putin-genocide.html.

Sands, P. 2024. "War, genocide and other crimes". Imperial War Museum Institute Annual Lecture. YouTube. https://www.youtube.com/live/eBVk7nBOWHg?si=njc4MUudQA9IfzRU.

Sanghera, S. 2021. *Empireland: How Imperialism has Shaped Modern Britain.* London: Penguin.

Satia, P. 2021. "Britain's culture war: disguising imperial politics as historical debate about empire". *Journal of Genocide Research* 24(2), 308–20.

Saul, D. 2022. "Zelensky accuses Russia of genocide as allegations of civilian killings mount". *Forbes.* https://www.forbes.com/sites/dereksaul/2022/04/03/zelensky-accuses-russia-of-genocide-as-allegations-of-civilian-killings-mount/?sh=bb5e71038cd7.

Sayegh, F. 1965. *Zionist Colonialism in Palestine.* Beirut: Palestine Liberation Organization.

Schabas, W. 2000. *Genocide in International Law.* Cambridge: Cambridge University Press.

Schabas, 2022. "Genocide and Ukraine: do words mean what we choose them to mean?". *Journal of International Criminal Justice* 20(4), 843–57.

Schabas, W. 2024. "A strong case that Israel's response constitutes the crime of genocide". Interview. *Der Spiegel,* 29 November. https://www.spiegel.de/international/world/interview-with-human-rights-expert-william-schabas-a-strong-case-that-israels-response-constitutes-the-crime-of-genocide-a-da7e4524-ab3b-40e4-b409-f8fca9c081b8.

Segal. R. 2016. *Genocide in the Carpathians: War, Social Breakdown, and Mass Violence, 1914–1945.* Stanford, CA: Stanford University Press.

Segal, R. 2023a. "A textbook case of genocide". *Jewish Currents*, 13 October. https://jewishcurrents.org/a-textbook-case-of-genocide.

Segal, R. 2023b. "Statement of scholars in Holocaust and Genocide Studies on mass violence in Israel and Palestine since 7 October". *Contending Modernities*, 9 December. https://contendingmodernities.nd.edu/global-currents/statement-of-scholars-7-october.

Segal, R. & L. Daniele 2024. "Gaza as twilight of Israel exceptionalism: Holocaust and genocide studies from unprecedented crisis to unprecedented change". *Journal of Genocide Research*. https://doi.org/10.1080/14623528.2024.2325804.

Shaw, M. 1996. *Civil Society and Media in Global Crises: Representing Distant Violence*. London: Pinter.

Shaw, M. 2003. *War and Genocide*. Cambridge: Polity.

Shaw, M. 2005. *The New Western Way of War*. Cambridge: Polity.

Shaw, M. 2006. "The general hybridity of war and genocide". *Journal of Genocide Research* 9(3), 461–73.

Shaw, M. 2007/2015. *What Is Genocide?* Cambridge: Polity.

Shaw, M. 2010. "Palestine in an international historical perspective on genocide". *Holy Land Studies* 9(1), 1–25.

Shaw, M. 2011. "Britain and genocide: historical and contemporary parameters of national responsibility". *Review of International Studies* 37(5), 2417–38.

Shaw, M. 2013. *Genocide and International Relations: Changing Patterns in the Transitions of the Late Modern World*. Cambridge: Cambridge University Press.

Shaw, M. 2022a. *Political Racism: Brexit and Its Aftermath*. Newcastle upon Tyne: Agenda.

Shaw, M. 2022b. "'Genocide' and Putin's war of destruction against Ukrainian society". *Byline Times*, 14 March. https://bylinetimes.com/2022/03/14/genocide-and-putins-war-of-destruction-against-ukrainian-society/.

Shaw, M. 2023a. "Russia's genocidal war in Ukraine: radicalization and social destruction". *Journal of Genocide Research* 25(3/4), 352–70.

Shaw, M. 2023b. "Israel, Gaza and the spectre of genocide". *Byline Times*, 13 October. https://bylinetimes.com/2023/10/13/israel-gaza-and-the-spectre-of-genocide/.

Shaw, M. 2024. "Inescapably genocidal". *Journal of Genocide Research*, 1–5. https://doi.org/10.1080/14623528.2023.2300555.

Shaw, M. 2025. "Ever again: the dead end of official Holocaust memory". Substack, 28 January. https://substack.com/home/post/p-155921958.

Shaw, M. & O. Bartov 2010. "The question of genocide in Palestine, 1948: an exchange between Martin Shaw and Omer Bartov". *Journal of Genocide Research* 12(3/4) 243–59.

Shlaim, A. 2024. *Genocide in Gaza: Israel's Long War on Palestine*. Belfast: Irish Pages Press.

Simangan, D. & J. Melvin 2019. "'Destroy and kill "the Left"': Duterte on communist insurgency in the Philippines with a reflection on the case of Suharto's Indonesia". *Journal of Genocide Research* 21(2), 214–26.

Simms, B. 2001. *Unfinest Hour: Britain and the Destruction of Bosnia*. London: Allen Lane.

Smith, K. 2014. "The UK and 'genocide' in Biafra". *Journal of Genocide Research* 16(2/3), 247–62.

Smith Finley, J. 2020. "Why scholars and activists increasingly fear a Uyghur genocide in Xinjiang". *Journal of Genocide Research* 23(3), 348–70.

Snyder, T. 2010. *The Bloodlands: Europe between Hitler and Stalin*. London: Bodley Head.

Snyder, T. 2022. "Russia intends to commit genocide in Ukraine, six ways to prove it". *European Pravda*, 23 October. https://www.eurointegration.com.ua/eng/articles/2022/10/23/7149219/.

Sorek, T. 2025. "Mainstreaming a genocidal imagination in Israeli society: settler-colonialism, settler anxiety, and biblical cues". *Journal of Genocide Research*, 1–24. https://doi.org/10.1080/14623528.2025.2456321.

Stögner, K. 2025. "Critical theory of racism, antisemitism, and the demonisation of Israel: understanding their complex interrelations". *European Journal of Social Theory*. https://doi.org/10.1177/13684310251323158.

Stone, D. 2006. "Britannia waives the rules: British imperialism and Holocaust memory". In D. Stone, *History, Memory and Mass Atrocity: Essays on the Holocaust and Genocide*, 174–90. Edinburgh: Vallentine Mitchell.

Stone, D. 2007. "The historiography of the Holocaust". In D. Stone (ed.), *The Historiography of Genocide*, 373–99. Basingstoke: Palgrave Macmillan.

Straus, S. 2006. *The Order of Genocide: Race, Power and War in Rwanda*. Ithaca, NY: Cornell University Press.

Straus, S. 2007. "Second-generation comparative research on genocide". *World Politics* 59, 476–501.

Streeck, W. 2024. "A matter of state: the politics of German anti-anti-semitism". *European Journal of Social Theory*, 5 December. https://doi.org/10.1177/13684310241300838.

Sunak, R. 2023a. *Israel and Gaza. Hansard*, 16 October. London: Parliament.

Sunak, R. 2023b. *Israel and Gaza. Hansard*, 23 October. London: Parliament.

Talbot, I. 2007. "The 1947 Partition of India". In D. Stone (ed.), *The Historiography of Genocide*, 420–37. Basingstoke: Palgrave Macmillan.

Ther, P. 2014. *The Dark Side of Nation-States: Ethnic Cleansing in Modern Europe*. Oxford: Berghahn.

Thompson, E. 1965. *The Making of the English Working Class*. London: Victor Gollancz.

Thompson, E. 1975. *Whigs and Hunters: The Origin of the Black Act*. London: Allen Lane.

Thompson, E. 1980. "Notes on exterminism: the last stage of civilisation". *New Left Review* 1(121), 3–31.

Times of Israel 2025. "Biden recalls telling Netanyahu in October 2023: 'You can't be carpet-bombing these communities'". *Times of Israel*, 17 January. https://www.timesofisrael.com/liveblog_entry/biden-recalls-telling-netanyahu-in-october-2023-you-cant-be-carpet-bombing-these-communities/.

Toal, G. & C. Dahlman 2011. *Bosnia Remade: Ethnic Cleansing and Its Reversal*. Oxford: Oxford University Press.

Tooze, A. 2022. "Welcome to the world of the polycrisis". *Financial Times*, 28 October. https://www.ft.com/content/498398e7-11b1-494b-9cd3-6d669dc3de33.

Tooze, A. 2024. "On thinking in medias res: an interview with Ding Xiongfei from the *Shanghai Review of Books*". *Chartbook* 341, Substack. https://adamtooze.substack.com/p/chartbook-341-on-thinking-in-medias.

Trotsky, L. 1970 [1925]. *Where Is Britain Going?* London: Pathfinder.

Ukrainska Pravda 2022. "Ukraine war: Kyiv likens Russian 'genocidal' tactics to Soviet-era 'Holodomor' famine". 26 November. https://news.yahoo.com/russias-genocidal-war-against-ukraine-074704897.html.

United Nations 1948. Convention on the Prevention and Punishment of the Crime of Genocide. https://www.un.org/en/genocideprevention/documents/atrocity-crimes/Doc.1_Convention%20on%20the%20Prevention%20and%20Punishment%20of%20the%20Crime%20of%20Genocide.pdf

United Nations 2019. "Text of the draft articles on prevention and punishment of crimes against humanity". In *Yearbook of the International Law Commission*, 23–103. New York: United Nations.

United Nations 2022. "A/77/533: Independent International Commission of Inquiry on Ukraine – note by the Secretary-General". 18 October. https://www.ohchr.org/en/documents/reports/a77533-independent-international-commission-inquiry-ukraine-note-secretary.

United Nations 2024. *Six-Month Update Report on the Human Rights Situation in Gaza: 1 November 2023 to 30 April 2024*. 8 November. New York: United Nations.

United Nations High Commissioner for Human Rights 2010. *Report of the Mapping Exercise Documenting the Most Serious Violations of Human Rights and International Humanitarian Law Committed within the Territory of the Democratic Republic of the Congo between March 1993 and June 2003*. Geneva: UNHCR.

United Nations High Commissioner for Human Rights 2022. "Ukraine: civilian casualty update", 5 December. https://www.ohchr.org/en/updates/2022/12/ukraine-civilian-casualty-update-5-december-2022#:~:text=134%20killed%20and%20446%20injured,of%20the%20total)%3B%20and.

Valentino, B. 2005. *Final Solutions: Mass Killing and Genocide in the Twentieth Century*. Ithaca, NY: Cornell University Press.

Van Dijk, B. 2022. *Preparing for War: The Making of the Geneva Conventions*. Oxford: Oxford University Press.

Viola, L. 1999. *Peasant Rebels under Stalin: Collectivization and the Culture of Peasant Resistance*. New York: Oxford University Press.

Von Hirschhausen, U. 2021. "Western voices, monocausal explanations and taking colonial rhetoric for colonial reality". *Journal of Modern European History* 19(4), 390–4.

Waddington, L. 2024. "A very diplomatic response: the British government's reaction to the killing fields of Cambodia". *Journal of Genocide Research*, 1–22. https://doi.org/10.1080/14623528.2024.2422160.

Wakeham, P. 2021. "The slow violence of settler colonialism: genocide, attrition, and the long emergency of invasion". *Journal of Genocide Research* 24(3), 337–56. https://doi.org/10.1080/14623528.2021.1885571.

War Child UK 2024. *Needs Study: Impact of War in Gaza on Children with Vulnerabilities and Families*. London: War Child UK, 11 December.

Weber, E. 1976. *Peasants into Frenchmen: The Modernization of Rural France*. Stanford, CA: Stanford University Press.

Weber, M. 1949. "'Objectivity' in social science and social policy". In M. Weber, *The Methodology of the Social Sciences*, 49–112. New York: Free Press.

Weber, M. 1964. *The Theory of Social Economic Organization*. New York: Free Press.

Weitz, E. 2008. "From the Vienna to the Paris system: international politics and the entangled histories of human rights, forced deportations, and civilizing missions". *American Historical Review* 113, 1313–43.

Werth, N. 2007. "The crimes of the Stalin regime: outline for an inventory and classification". In D. Stone (ed.), *The Historiography of Genocide*, 400–19. Basingstoke: Palgrave Macmillan.

Wheeler, N. 2002. *Saving Strangers: Humanitarian Intervention in International Society*. Oxford: Oxford University Press.

Williams, R. 1976. *Keywords: A Vocabulary of Culture and Society*. London: Croom Helm.

Wolfe, P. 2006. "Settler colonialism and the elimination of the native". *Journal of Genocide Research* 8(4), 387–409.

Wolfe, P. 2008. "Structure and event: settler colonialism, time, and the question of genocide". In A. D. Moses (ed.), *Empire, Colony, Genocide: Conquest, Occupation, and Subaltern Resistance in World History*, 102–32. Oxford: Berghahn.

Woolfson, S. 2022. "'It's a slam dunk': Philippe Sands on the case against Putin for the crime of aggression". *The Guardian*, 31 March. https://www.theguardian.com/law/2022/mar/30/vladimir-putin-ukraine-crime-aggression-philippe-sands.

Yusuf, H. & P. Miller 2024. "RAF spy flights over Gaza risk complicity in Israeli torture". *Declassified UK*, 12 September. https://www.declassifieduk.org/raf-spy-flights-over-gaza-risk-complicity-in-israeli-torture/.

Zabrodskyi, M. *et al.* 2022. *Preliminary Lessons in Conventional Warfighting from Russia's Invasion of Ukraine: February–July 2022*. London: Royal United Services Institute.

Zimmerer, J. & J. Zeller 2008. *Genocide in German South-West Africa: The Colonial War of 1904–1908 and Its Aftermath*. London: Merlin.

Ziv, O. 2024. "The West Bank villages wiped off the map by Israeli settler violence". *+972 Magazine*, 4 December. https://www.972mag.com/west-bank-villages-israeli-settler-violence/.

INDEX